PUBLIC ANTHROPOLOGY

PUBLIC ANTHROPOLOGY

Engaging Social Issues in the Modern World

Edward J. Hedican

UNIVERSITY OF TORONTO PRESS

Library and Archives Canada Cataloguing in Publication

Hedican, Edward J., author

Public anthropology : engaging social issues in the modern world / Edward J. Hedican.

Includes bibliographical references and index.

Issued in print and electronic formats.

ISBN 978-1-4426-3589-0 (bound).—ISBN 978-1-4426-3588-3 (paperback).—ISBN 978-1-4426-3591-3 (pdf).—ISBN 978-1-4426-3590-6 (html)

1. Anthropology. 2. Social history—21st century. I. Title.

GN27.H43 2016   301   C2015-905116-9

                                                    C2015-905117-7

We welcome comments and suggestions regarding any aspect of our publications—please feel free to contact us at news@utphighereducation.com or visit our Internet site at www.utppublishing.com.

North America	UK, Ireland, and continental Europe
5201 Dufferin Street	NBN International
North York, Ontario, Canada, M3H 5T8	Estover Road, Plymouth, PL6 7PY, UK
	orders phone: 44 (0) 1752 202301
2250 Military Road	orders fax: 44 (0) 1752 202333
Tonawanda, New York, USA, 14150	orders e-mail: enquiries@nbninternational.com

orders phone: 1-800-565-9523
orders fax: 1-800-221-9985
orders e-mail: utpbooks@utpress.utoronto.ca

Every effort has been made to contact copyright holders; in the event of an error or omission, please notify the publisher.

This book is printed on paper containing 100% post-consumer fibre.

The University of Toronto Press acknowledges the financial support for its publishing activities of the Government of Canada through the Canada Book Fund.

Printed in the United States of America.

For my mother,
Margaret Mahler Hedican (1920–2011),
artist and inquiring spirit.

CONTENTS

ILLUSTRATIONS

FIGURES

BOXES

PREFACE

In a graduate course entitled "Public Issues Anthropology" at the University of Guelph, various professors and students make weekly presentations on a variety of contemporary subjects. There have been presentations on such varied issues as migration and globalization, ethnic tensions in Namibia, food security in India, Aboriginal land claims in Canada, and demographic change in modern Japan. Such topics are not necessarily unusual for anthropology classes, but what has been interesting is the diversity of topics that are covered semester by semester. What is evident, furthermore, is the range of interests in modern anthropology, especially those involving public issues.

In order to prepare for these classes, a considerable amount of time is spent searching through issues of *Current Anthropology*, *Anthropology Today*, *Practicing Anthropology*, *Anthropology News*, and the section in *American Anthropologist* on public anthropology. Topics covered in these periodicals traverse over a diversity of modern issues such as "Protest Anthropology" (Maskovsky, 2013), "Anthropology and AIDS Research" (Hardon & Moyer, 2014; Pigg, 2013), "Comparing Race and Caste" (Still, 2015), "Anthropology and the Military" (Albro, 2010), "An Anthropological Introduction to YouTube" (Scobie, 2011), "US Anti-Terrorism Laws" (M. Price, Rubinstein, & Price, 2012), "The Place of the Internet in Anthropology" (Fish, 2011), "Who Is the Enemy?" (Atran, 2012), "The Face of Global Terror" (Werbner, 2010), as well as a host of other treatises on "The Perils of Engagement" by anthropologists (Spencer, 2010). Of course, this brief purview of literature hardly does justice to the variety of subjects that interest modern anthropologists, yet one starts to get the impression by reading such periodicals that anthropology today is on a considerably different track than it was just a few decades ago.

What is also evident is that there is a need for a volume that focuses on the topic of "public issues anthropology." At present, such a volume is evidently needed to bring students and others in the discipline up-to-date with the current state of the discipline, especially in terms of how anthropologists have engaged with the modern issues of our time. Of course, it is not possible to cover all of the topics of interest in modern anthropology, while at the same time focusing on a wider overview of the theoretical and practical implications that engaging anthropology holds for the discipline as it moves forward into unchartered intellectual waters. Nonetheless, despite the selectivity of the topics chosen, it is hoped that this present volume will serve to inform the reader of the extent to which modern anthropologists are involved in understanding current public issues, and to dispel whatever lingering thoughts might remain that see anthropology as an anachronistic field of study involving so-called primitive societies. The anthropology of today has been vastly transformed in this new millennium.

This book also emanates out of my own personal experiences as an anthropologist. In the 1980s, I became involved in an Aboriginal land claims dispute in Canada's northern Subarctic region in the Thunder Bay area, in which I had previously conducted fieldwork (see Hedican, 1986a, 1986b, 2001, 2008). This whole dispute was such a confusing matter for me, and there were so many participants, each with their own varied interests. There was the Aboriginal band whose members were seeking a new home community after their original one had become flooded by a government hydro-electrical project. Other participants in the dispute included representatives from the federal government's Department of Aboriginal Affairs, a consulting firm hired by the government, local non-Aboriginal townspeople, and representatives of the provincial government of Ontario's Ministry of Natural Resources.

As an anthropologist thrust into this situation, I certainly felt that my role, whatever it was, was a non-traditional one. I searched the literature in my discipline for helpful guidelines and found little that could help me. It was definitely a "sink-or-swim" situation on my part, and as a result I have spent the better part of 30 years investigating how anthropologists might be able to play a more effective role in engaging in various social, economic, and political issues.

Hopefully, these ethnographic experiences have allowed me to become better informed about anthropology's role in modern issues than I was all those decades ago, but the literature in this area has proliferated to a startling degree. Even the very foundations of anthropology—cultural relativism, objectivity, and fieldwork—have all been brought into question as a result of the ensuing dialogue. Evidently, we need more discussion before anthropologists can begin to resolve the important issues involved in modern engagement, both practically and theoretically. Meanwhile, the world keeps spinning along.

One final note: the discussions and portrayals of various ethnographic situations in this book are meant to be polemical. An attempt is made to present various sides to a controversial subject with the intention of providing the reader with an opportunity to engage in debate over the validity of one position or another, or to help in providing that background on which an informed decision or opinion could be made. My own position is not to champion one side or another, except to say that anthropology is better served by engaging in the public issues of our time, rather than avoiding them for whatever reason.

Richard Salisbury was my PhD supervisor at McGill University and I benefited immensely from our many conversations concerning applied anthropology in Canada, as well as his research among the Cree of northern Quebec. At the University of Guelph, I wish to extend a special thanks to my long-time friend and colleague, Stan Barrett, especially for his discussions of research concerning the radical right in Canada. Beth Finnis was kind enough to comment on an earlier draft of my book proposal. Satsuki Kawano, Renee Sylvain, Belinda Leach, and Tad McIlwraith have regularly attended our graduate seminar on Public Issues Anthropology, which ultimately has been the inspiration for this book.

Chapter 1

INTRODUCTION: ENGAGING
SOCIAL ISSUES

The ultimate purpose of this book is to provide anthropology students with an opportunity to explore the discipline's current activities in the modern world. It uses the term "public anthropology" as a cover title for a wide variety of designations in the contemporary literature, such as engaged anthropology, activist anthropology, or advocacy, to name a few. While the various meanings of the term "public anthropology" are dealt with more fully in the proceeding chapter, the general focus of this book is on the manner in which "anthropologists tackle (or ignore) matters of public importance" (Eriksen, 2006, p. x) and thereby to "engage critically with the urgent crises faced by the socially vulnerable ... [which could lead anthropologists] to being politically meaningful in the here and now" (Bourgois, 2006, p. ix).

A second purpose is to examine some of the modern issues that presently concern the anthropological community with regard to specific areas of research in today's world. While a wide variety of such topics could be chosen, this task is necessarily a selective one and does not intend to cover every instance of research in the realm of public anthropology. Nonetheless, I believe that the ones discussed in the following chapters represent an interesting cross-section of modern social issues, such as race and tolerance, health and well-being, food security, rebellion and reconciliation, global terror and militarism, and media in the emerging global electronic community.

In addition, as summarized by Gomberg-Munoz's (2013) review of public anthropology, a wide range of social issues are currently being researched by anthropologists, such as immigration policies, human rights, child soldiers, AIDS prevention in Nepal, and abductions in Africa, to name a few. There is increasing evidence, therefore, that anthropologists are actively confronting a wide variety of social problems in the modern world (Hardon & Moyer, 2014; Kuper, 2013, 2014;

MacClancy, 2013; Maskovsky, 2013; Pigg, 2013; Still, 2015). As such, it is intended that students will find in these pages a wide variety of issues that presently engage the anthropological community in order that they might be better informed about such concerns.

Third, while providing background information on these contemporary issues, an additional purpose is to provide the basis by which students can find an opportunity to reflect upon and possibly debate the relevance, or pros and cons, of involvement by today's anthropologists in these controversial issues. Certainly the day of the detached (for the most part) and strictly objective participant-observer appears to be receding rapidly in the rear-view mirror of history. However, an important issue of debate concerns the philosophical underpinnings of a new brand of engaged anthropologists who would appear to have become committed to one side of an issue only on the basis, as articulated by Bourgois (2006), "under the global lie of democracy and neoliberal prosperity" (p. ix).

In other words, while this volume cannot hope to cover all of the important concerns of modern anthropology, students will be afforded an opportunity to consider what their own positions might be with regard to the issues discussed. Furthermore, they will also be challenged to reflect on the direction that modern anthropology is heading and thereby to assess where these directions might lead in terms of anthropology's enduring traditional values, such as cultural relativism and independent scholarship.

TERMS AND CONCEPTS

The term "public anthropology" cannot be understood independently from a wide variety of other designations and concepts that have emerged in the anthropological literature over the last several decades. By way of further information, it is suggested that the reader consult the book's glossary of terms (p. 208). With regard to modern terminology in anthropology, it is recognized that precise or clear-cut definitions are generally lacking in the discipline. Some terms overlap in meaning with others, some terms may cover a variety of subsidiary terms, and in a number of instances anthropologists themselves may disagree about how a particular term might be understood.

Given these various difficulties of interpretation, our intention here is not to provide a precise understanding of any particular term or concept in modern anthropology, because such a compilation of terms cannot be reasonably produced. The aim, rather, is to provide what might be commonly understood, insofar as this is possible to determine for various terms. Where it is deemed necessary, alternative meanings of particular terms will be indicated, as a way of enhancing understanding.

Applied Anthropology

We begin with the term "applied anthropology" because this is often considered a fifth field of anthropology (after socio-cultural, physical, folklore, and archaeological). *Applied anthropology* can be defined as "the practical application of anthropological theories and knowledge from all the subfields of the discipline toward identifying and solving social problems" (Sidky, 2004, p. 418). While many scholars may regard applied anthropology as a relatively new initiative, some suggest that an applied emphasis in anthropology can be traced back almost to the origins of the discipline.

Alexander Ervin (2005), for example, refers to James Mooney's (1896) study of the Ghost Dance Religion, which he notes was "remarkably advanced research" for this time period. As Ervin explains further, "As a form of advocacy, he [Mooney] sympathetically portrayed the Ghost Dance, widespread among Western tribes, as a genuinely religious expression of coping with the severe dislocation produced by the US-Indian wars and confinement to reservations" (p. 15). Similarly, throughout the ensuing decades of anthropology's history, Franz Boas's studies of racism in America, and Bronislaw Malinowski's critique of the policies of the British colonial government are just two of the more prominent examples of anthropology's interest in public issues throughout the discipline's history.

The origins of applied anthropology can therefore be found in the early work of the prominent American anthropologist Franz Boas, whose scholarly endeavours demonstrated the possible uses of anthropology for public policy. Boas applied his scientific research in an attempt to discredit notions of racial determinism, which suggested that people's behaviour can be attributed to their physical or racial characteristics. Instead, Boas argued that the behaviour of human beings was largely attributable to one's culture or sets of learned behaviour, attitudes, and beliefs, rather than to the consequences of genetic inheritance.

Practical Anthropology

An early label for the type of research conducted by Mooney and Boas emerged with British anthropologist Bronislaw Malinowski's seminal article "Practical Anthropology," published in 1929. Malinowski's concern was with the colonial pressures on Indigenous populations such as land tenure, health, and demographic change. He suggested that British colonial administrators should leave Indigenous customs intact as far as possible in order to lessen the impact of colonial rule, even allowing self-rule in tribal areas. Overall, his argument was that ethnographic information had "practical" value in understanding the internal conflict that resulted from the external intrusions of colonial administration on local social and cultural characteristics. Thus, he suggested that a separate field of *practical anthropology* could focus on the more useful aspects of ethnographic research.

Action Anthropology

Sol Tax (1907–1995), founder of the journal *Current Anthropology*, was an American anthropologist who is responsible for the use of the term "action anthropology." Tax (1958) is considered one of the founders of applied anthropology in America who, along with his colleagues at the University of Chicago, designed an applied program called the Fox Project. The Fox Project, initiated in 1948, departed from conventional fieldwork in anthropology in several ways. First, research was based on a team approach whereby a senior scholar, such as Tax, guided a number of graduate students in a field school to train future ethnographers at "the Fox," or Mesquawkie Indian reservation in Iowa. Second, rather than the conventional research approach in which the anthropologists control the course of the investigation, in the case of the Fox Project, the Fox people themselves are seen as co-investigators (see Ervin, 2005, p. 2; Hedican, 2008, p. 68).

In an apparent reversal of fieldwork roles, in the Fox Project, the anthropological investigators became students of the Fox. The Fox played a much larger role than in previous ethnographic research in determining the direction of the course of the research and in establishing research values and priorities. As such, the anthropologists and the Fox were engaged in a mutual interaction which put into action Fox priorities and objectives.

Consulting and Advocacy Roles

In another innovative aspect of the Fox Project, Tax (1958) suggested the adoption of a *consulting role* for anthropologists, which would serve the purpose of freeing "the [Fox] Indians to make changes that they wish and which would appear from our hypothesis to be in their interest" (p. 19). It is evident, then, that the traditional anthropological field role had begun to be transformed into various new roles in applied anthropology. Aside from Tax's reference to the consulting role, by the 1970s and later, reference was made in the anthropological literature to an *advocacy role* for the fieldworker (see Jacobs, 1974; Hedican 1986a; Peterson, 1974; Paine, 1985; Kirsch, 2010; Low & Merry, 2010; Johnston, 2012; MacClancy, 2013; Kuper, 2014).

Advocacy can be described as "working to assist local communities in organizing efforts, giving testimony, acting as expert witness in court, witnessing human rights violations, serving as a translator between community and government officials or corporations, and helping local groups use international principles such as human rights

BOX 1.1 Richard Salisbury (1926–1989): Advising the James Bay Cree

Richard Salisbury was born in Chelsea, England. After serving in the Royal Marines, he graduated with a doctorate in anthropology from the Australian National University in 1957. Salisbury's research during this period focused on the Saine and Tolai of New Guinea with an emphasis on economic and technological change.

In 1962, Salisbury joined the Department of Anthropology at McGill University. Later, in 1971, he became director of the Programme in the Anthropology of Development (PAD) which had earlier been founded in the 1960s as the McGill Cree Project. PAD attained a widespread reputation for training applied anthropologists, especially concerning social and economic impact studies of the Cree as part of their negotiations with the Quebec government during the James Bay Treaty negotiations of the mid-1970s. It was during this period that Salisbury initiated a pattern of client-oriented research, which was designed to provide information that would be useful to the Cree on land-use patterns and social-impact studies, among other topics, that the Aboriginal peoples could utilize to their advantage in their negotiations over treaty rights.

Salisbury suggested that anthropologists could play a practical role in the future by helping groups such as the Cree control their own development in situations where Indigenous groups could need anthropologist's specialist skills. He reviewed a number of applied anthropological studies conducted among the Cree and other Aboriginal peoples in northern Canada and noted that this previous research had laid the foundation for future impact studies because "it considered the expected deleterious effect on villages as industry and communications moved into the villages, and turned them into residences for unskilled part-time workers, who were losing their skills as hunters and being deculturated through inappropriate education" (Salisbury, 1986, p. 151).

It is evident from his description of northern research that Salisbury did not see his role as that of a detached observer; rather, his role was to document and speak out about the harmful effects that the Cree and other northern Aboriginal peoples were experiencing because of developments such as the construction of hydro-electric projects. Aboriginal peoples were not consulted about these projects, yet such forced economic change was undermining their traditional social and economic culture. These projects, because of the flooding of vast areas of northern Quebec, caused forced community resettlement to areas that the Cree were unfamiliar with, and caused a significant disruption to their traditional hunting, trapping, and fishing. Salisbury even appeared before the judicial hearings that preceded the James Bay Agreement, during which he outlined his anthropological research and the negative impacts that large scale development projects were having on Cree society.

Richard Salisbury's career as director of McGill's Programme in the Anthropology of Development, and his promotion of the Society of Applied Anthropology in Canada, did a great deal in demonstrating the practical value of anthropological research in this country. It also demonstrated to new anthropologists that it was possible for them to adopt a "public face" for their discipline through its practical applications (Hedican, 1990b).

by working to vernacularize them" (Low & Merry, 2010, p. S210). Kirsch (2002) suggests that an advocacy role is appropriate within anthropology because it is a "logical extension of the commitment to reciprocity that underlies the practice of anthropology" (p. 178). A case in point involves Barbara Johnston's advocacy role on behalf of the Marshal Islanders, in which she documents the bio-cultural effects of nuclear weapons testing in the island (Johnston, 2010). She also points out that these are "ways that emphasize the social relevance of anthropology" (p. 576).

As Peterson (1974) explained with reference to research among members of the Choctaw, an advocacy role "is that of a brief lawyer who is responsible for an analysis of possible courses of action suggested by the client and who, after the decision among alternatives is made by the client, proceeds to prepare the best possible case for his client along the lines of the alternatives chosen" (p. 312).

Mediator Role

Another possibility for new activities involved in anthropological research is the *mediator role*. This role became quite prominent during my own fieldwork among the Anishenabe, or Ojibwa, of northern Ontario (Hedican, 1986b, 2008, pp. 91–108). The fieldwork situation involved the case of an Ojibwa band called the Whitesand who lived north of Thunder Bay, on the north shore of Lake Nipigon. The Whitesand people had been flooded out of their original reserve in the 1940s and had subsequently become displaced along the Canadian National Rail line in four or five other communities.

The Whitesand people petitioned the Department of Aboriginal Affairs in Thunder Bay with a request for a new reserve so that they could all become residents of the same community again. Five different sites for a new reserve were proposed. I had previously conducted fieldwork in this area about 10 years before, and knew many of the Whitesand people, and was therefore contacted to help the Ojibwa reach a consensus on where the new reserve should be situated. Before long, divisions emerged in the Whitesand band itself about where the reserve should be situated. Conflicts also developed between the Whitesand people and the members of a consulting firm who had been hired by Aboriginal Affairs. Aboriginal Affairs personnel also became a flashpoint of resentment because they were seen to exercise too much control over the decision-making process with regard to the location of the new reserve.

My own role in this emerging conflict situation became very confused to me. I had expected to hold discussions with various band members and attempt to arrive at a consensus decision about where the new reserve might be located. Instead, I found myself attempting to *mediate* among the various conflicting parties. To tell the truth, I was not in the least prepared by my training in anthropology to adapt to the characteristics of this new role model, especially on a spur-of-the-moment basis. Before long, I also became a focus of resentment because the consultants accused me of "agitating" the band. All in all, the band did eventually chose a site for a new reserve, but after this difficult experience I became painfully aware of the potential traps that the role of the anthropologist as *mediator* can hold for those not adequately prepared.

Activist and Militant Anthropology

"Activist anthropology" is a term that refers to an involvement in political causes and struggles (Hale, 2008; Heyman, 2010; Doughty, 2011; Maskovsky, 2013). The suggestion is that anthropologists should participate in the public political process. There are anthropologists, such as David Price (2008), for example, who have been particularly critical of US military activity and suggest that anthropology should prevent its research from falling into the hands of those who promote interventionist wars, especially as this involves the selling of anthropological services and knowledge to the state.

An activist anthropology would appear to be based on Nancy Scheper-Hughes's (1995) earlier call for a *militant anthropology*. Her position is based on a common political stance in anthropology, which is solidarity with *informants* and other community members who are seen as the object of oppression by outside powers. However, it has been indicated that "fieldwork solidarity does not work well as a guideline to politics for the ethnographer when studying up" (Heyman, 2010, p. 289). In other words, anthropologists have a greater propensity to support the poor and powerless, as opposed to those in the state apparatus who wield the power over the residents of local-level communities with whom the ethnographer had traditionally conducted research. In this context, Kirsch (2010) suggests that such terms as "activist" and "advocate" "share a commitment to mobilizing anthropology for constructive interventions in politics" (p. 69).

Another variation on the activist approach is what has been referred to as *protest anthropology*. As Maskovsky (2013) explains, "Today's anthropologists who are visibly active in protest movements, revolts, and uprisings seek not just to raise their public voices in support of protestors or to repackage disciplinary knowledge to make it more useful for grass roots activists. They seek also to participate directly as activist themselves" (p. 126). It is not particularly clear, nor is it indicated in this article, the extent to which *protest anthropology* would benefit the discipline or even possibly detract from it.

Participatory Action Research (PAR)

Over the last several decades, *participatory action research* (PAR) has emerged as an alternative to conventional fieldwork in anthropology (Fletcher & Marchildon, 2014; Ryan & Robinson, 1990; Ryan & Robinson, 1996; Robinson, 2006). The idea behind PAR is similar to that espoused by Tax for *action anthropology*. PAR is different from traditional fieldwork in anthropology in that, in the PAR type of research, community members conduct most of the research and own the information that is gathered. Joan Ryan (1932–2005) was particularly well known for her PAR style of research in Canada's Northwest Territories, such as her lands claim research in Fort McPherson and Lac La Martre (Ryan 1995). Ryan also worked on PAR projects in Nicaragua and developed a research relationship with the Lubicon Cree in northern Alberta. For her innovative initiatives in developing new participatory research methods, Ryan was awarded the Weaver-Tremblay Prize for her contribution to Canadian applied anthropology.

Collaborative Anthropology

Collaborative anthropology, like PAR, can be defined as "the collaboration of researchers and subjects in the production of ethnographic text [and] offers us a powerful way to engage the public in anthropology.... The goals of collaborative ethnography (both historical and contemporary) are now powerfully converging with those of a public anthropology that pulls together academic and applied anthropology in an effort to serve humankind more directly and more immediately" (Lassiter 2005, p. 83). Similarly, "collaborative research involves shared management and direction of a research project among the scholars and the subjects of research" (Low & Merry 2010, p. S209).

A somewhat broader description of collaborative anthropology is discussed with reference to Besteman's (2010) research among the Somali Bantu, in which there is "collaboration of various media articles and research report ... [as well as] working as a mediator, advocate, and cultural translator in settings ranging from schools to health clinics" (Hepner, 2011, p. 347). Collaborative models of anthropological research have also been discussed as a form of advocacy such that anthropological research is "aimed at material, symbolic, and political benefits for the research population" (Gross & Plattner, 2002, p. 4).

Engaging Anthropology

"Engaging anthropology" is another popular term that is used today in the anthropological literature (Susser, 2010; Eriksen, 2006; Sandford & Angel-Ajani, 2006; Warren, 2006; Low & Merry, 2010; Spencer, 2010). This term appears to have its origins in Raymond Firth's influential article in the applied anthropology journal *Human Organization* entitled "Engagement and Detachment" (Firth, 1981). Firth was one of Malinowski's most prominent students, referring to his mentor as the "patron saint of applied anthropology" (Firth 1981, p. 193). Firth, however, makes a point of contrasting *commitment* and *engagement*. For example, he indicates that "My own reaction to problems of applied anthropology has not been one of detachment. But it has been one of engagement rather than commitment—a conviction of the importance of problems rather than an assurance as to the nature of the solutions or of my own role in relation to them. Probably this is partly a matter of temperament, partly a result of earlier environment" (p. 196).

Firth finally concludes that "it is increasingly clear that anthropology, like other intellectual disciplines, is being called upon more overtly to accept a notion of social responsibility. If anthropologists are to be supported from public funds they must expect to be asked for some recognizable contribution to public benefit. The intellectual climate of knowledge is changing, perhaps irreversibly, moving from the assumption that scientific enquiry can be justified as an esthetic pursuit for its own sake" (Firth, 1981, p. 200). Thus, we find in Firth's assessment that anthropologists have a public duty to engage in activities whose value extends beyond the normal theoretical contributions of the discipline.

If anthropological studies are to be of public benefit, then anthropologists need to focus their studies more on social problems and, furthermore, find ways to communicate the results of this engagement to the general public. This is also the focus of Johnston's (2012) article on "Editorial Work as Public Anthropology," which aims to expand on the possible social relevance of anthropological research and to convey this to the public at large outside of academic settings.

Firth's reference to his "earlier environment" might well be a reference to Malinowski's (1929) previous applied work with colonial administrations in which ethnographic information could be used to facilitate solutions to Indigenous problems as a form of anthropological engagement, but not necessarily in the role of a committed activist for one side or the other.

In historical perspective, this idea of an engaged anthropology extends back to some of the early beginnings of British social anthropology, as noted above. Malinowski contributed to the idea of anthropology as a form of public service as far back as 1918, at which time he presented evidence on labour conditions in the western Pacific to an Australian government inquiry. Malinowski was also an early critic of colonialism, especially in cases in which colonial administrations expropriated Indigenous people's lands and conducted forced labour practices. In *A Scientific Theory of Culture*, Malinowski (1960) explains his perspective in the following manner: "As a scientific moralist fully in sympathy with races hereto oppressed or at least underprivileged, the anthropologist would demand equal treatment for all, full cultural independence for every different group or nation" (p. 15).

This stance—of promoting engagement, but not commitment—contrasts rather sharply with Margaret Mead's own opinions on engagement, especially as stated in her book *Culture and Commitment* (Mead, 1970). As far as Mead was concerned, some degree of commitment on the part of the researcher is essential to the viability of fieldwork. In other words, Mead's stance is that simply becoming *engaged* with particular social issues does not go far enough. Rather, she argues, for anthropologists, the issue of commitment is an especially important one because it can serve to inform people about competing ideological forces, and help to inform people about which choices one can make concerning competing social ideals.

BOX 1.2 Margaret Mead (1901–1978): Culture and Commitment

Margaret Mead was perhaps the most famous publicly known American anthropologist whose work extended for over 50 years from the early 1920s to her death in 1978. She was notable for the controversial causes she took on in her professional career as well as in her public life. For example, in her fieldwork in Polynesia, her *Coming of Age in Samoa* (1928) brought a contemporary relevance to anthropology when Mead argued that the period of adolescence was a trouble-free period for teenage girls in Samoa, unlike the relatively traumatic experiences of American youth. Mead's position was that the role of culture, as opposed to biological factors, was an important determinant of behaviour. In her later career, she also became a significant international figure as she criticized the war in Vietnam and promoted the rights of women (Hedican, 2012a, pp. 74, 90).

FIGURE 1.1 Margaret Mead

It was because of her commitment to public issues that Margaret Mead became a household name during her lifetime. Her various books and public lectures established the important role of women not only in academic life but in a global perspective. We can draw from Mead's academic work in anthropology that some degree of commitment on the part of the researcher is an important factor in the success of one's ethnographic fieldwork. In her study of the so-called generation gap, in *Culture and Commitment* (1970), Mead recognized that it was becoming increasingly difficult for people to find themselves within the conflicting versions of our culture. This situation makes it difficult for people to make choices about which ideals, if any, they should commit themselves to.

During World War II, Mead and her husband, Gregory Bateson, became involved in the war effort. For example, "Bateson, as 1942 began, was using anthropology in every new way he could think of to analyse and help defeat the enemy. At Columbia University, under the auspices of the Navy and the O.S.S. [Office of Strategic Services], he was teaching a three-credit course, International Pidgin English 101C. His students were being sent by the Navy to the Pacific" (Howard, 1984, p. 231).

For her part, Mead took a special interest in studying Hitler's speeches. Many people were asking the question, What sort of people are the Nazis? Studying Hitler's speeches was part of a wider effort, as Bateson explained it, "to dissect out the relationship [between Nazis and enemies] and the whole range of phenomena—parenthood, adolescence, maturity, cleanliness, sex aggression, passivity, and death—which are embraced by the Nazi way of life" (Howard, 1984, p. 232). Mead even wrote a letter to President Roosevelt about Hitler, warning the president that Hitler was obsessed with building Europe; "This suggestion may have been the first of Mead's many efforts to pass anthropological insights on to the government" (Howard, 1984, p. 213).

Mead explained further, "It is my conviction that in addition to the world conditions that have given rise to this search for new commitment and to this possibility of no commitment at all, we also have new resources for facing our situation, new grounds for commitment" (Mead, 1970, p. xii). In this context, it is understandable that Mead was outspoken on a multiplicity of contemporary issues, such as generational conflict, nuclear disarmament, and women's roles in society.

Anthropologists such as Margaret Mead and Raymond Firth provided the foundation for the modern discourse on *engaging anthropology*. Kay Warren (2006), for example, in an article entitled "Perils and Promises of Engaged Anthropology," indicates that "today's engagement for many cultural anthropologists involves investigations that consider such issues as social justice, inequality, subaltern challenges to the status quo, globalization's impacts, and the ethical positioning of our field research in situations of violent conflict" (p. 213). However, despite this commendable list of important research initiatives in which anthropologists could become engaged if so inclined, Warren also warns that "anthropology faces a stunning paradox" (p. 217).

The paradox that Warren refers to entails the study of ethnic polarities in a "post-dichotomized global context." The dividing line between previously opposing forces—socialist rebels and rightist authoritarian dictators, for example, in Warren's Guatemalan research—has become blurred, making choices about who to become engaged with an increasingly problematic issue for the anthropologist who attempts to support one position or another. In conclusion, she offers a final warning: "For those who value engagement, it is time to come to new understandings of what makes good anthropology" (Warren, 2006, p. 222).

Finally, the meaning(s) of the term "public anthropology," which serves as the title of this book, is dealt with extensively in the following chapter. Suffice to say, after this prolonged discussion of terms and concepts, there have been a multiplicity of meanings associated with anthropological activity in the public realm. It is also important to indicate that public anthropology, however it may be conceived, has had an important impact on the conduct of anthropological research in modern settings and the types of engagement in which anthropologists become involved.

TYPES OF PUBLIC ENGAGEMENT

Malinowski was responsible for laying the foundation for an advocacy role in anthropology in the early stages of the professionalization of the discipline, while others, such as Tax, developed the idea of this sort of involvement further by putting it into practice. Malinowski suggested in particular that it was the ethnographer's responsibility to more effectively communicate studies of social change in such a way that government officials were capable of understanding. If anthropologists continued to communicate in the arcane language peculiar to their discipline, how could those in positions of power take field-workers seriously?

As the ensuing decades unfolded, other anthropologists took up Malinowski's suggestion for an advocacy role (Jacobs, 1974; Peterson, 1974; Paine, 1985; Hedican, 1986a; Low & Merry, 2010; Johnston, 2010). A number of new issues began to emerge, however, as field-workers investigated such pressing problems as inadequate housing, high unemployment rates, or lack of basic food and health care. A sort of academic tug-of-war began to develop; some began to have difficulty reconciling their fieldwork in such situations of conflict.

Private individuals' empathy toward the local people, resulting in desire on the part of the anthropologist to become more actively involved in changing these conditions, tended to conflict with professional responsibilities for maintaining an objective stance, so that the field-worker did not become involved in changing the very conditions that they had come to study in the first place. Nevertheless, the fieldwork practices of the discipline provide it with a sound foundation, since, as Orr (2009) suggests, "anthropologists have an especially meaningful position as public intellectuals and activists via their ability to tell the stories of people whom most westerners will never see" (p. 413).

The effectiveness of an advocacy role in anthropology might well become exacerbated by a well-intentioned, but possibly also ill-informed, intervention on the part of the anthropologist. As such, there are ethical and moral considerations involved in advocacy roles that need to be considered. This view is based at least partially on the idea that objectivity in the social sciences is largely an illusion, as controversial anthropologist Marvin Harris (1991, p. 355) at one time argued.

The reason underlying this point of view rests on the conviction that personal and political biases are apt to play a role in influencing an anthropologist's commitment to one particular situation or another. In fact, even to refrain from adopting an advocacy role is in itself a political act. All actions, whether taken or not, have social and political consequences. Thus, ethical dilemmas are not easily resolved. "Anthropology has a long tradition of engagement," as Kunnah (2013) summarizes, but "every form of engagement poses dilemmas" (p. 740).

One can conclude that there is some "soul-searching" on the part of anthropologists about the correct choices that one can make during their field studies. Some academics are willing to accept outright that advocacy has a legitimate role in anthropology and to leave the debating to others. As Ervin (1990) explains, "no one has the authority to say that anthropology cannot have as one of its domains a professional anthropological advocacy or that advocacy is not compatible with anthropology" (p. 26). Of course competing or alternative views on this matter are always possible and certainly anthropologists are far from reaching an agreement within the discipline on the advocacy question.

ADVOCACY ROLES IN ANTHROPOLOGY

As we review the history of anthropology from the perspective of engagement in general, and advocacy in particular, it becomes evident that one of the problems is the lack of clearly defined roles for anthropologists to play. This has led to ethnographic researchers not being sure about guidelines for what could be termed "non-traditional" roles in the discipline. Peterson (1974), for example, has suggested a type of role along the lines of a legal adviser: "My relationship with the Choct[a]w tribe is that of a brief lawyer who is responsible for an analysis of possible courses of action suggested by the client and who, after the decision among alternatives is made by the client, proceeds to prepare the best possible case" (p. 312).

A similar role has been suggested by John Cove (1987) during his fieldwork among the Tsimshian of British Columbia who "wanted to prepare for litigation and negotiation of their claim, and consequently needed a systematic analysis of precontact society" (p. 3). Among the Cree of James Bay in northern Quebec, it was noted that they were "marked by a dependency on consultants and by confrontation.... It is not surprising that one already sees some signs of a potential resentment developing among the Cree concerning the power of consultants and the difficulty of controlling them" (LaRusic, 1979, pp. 39, 51).

Another anthropologist, Richard Preston (1982), who was also working with the James Bay Cree at the time, noted a "kind of Orwellian submersion of the Crees, providing only fantasy and alien solutions to complex, overwhelming problems" (p. 38). Richard Salisbury (1986), a McGill University anthropologist, offers a less sanguine portrayal of the external influences on Cree decision-making and consultants in general when he remarks that "the Cree, after a period in which they employed a disproportionately large number of anthropologists and lawyers as advisers, have acquired the skill and the competence to employ specialists of all kinds, for jobs where Cree are currently not available" (p. 155). It is evident, therefore, that there are diverse points of view concerning appropriate roles for anthropologists engaged in public issues in the modern world. As a solution to this problem of engagement, Marvin Harris (1991) has suggested that the "only resolution to this dilemma is the one that now exists: We must search our individual consciences and act accordingly" (p. 355).

ANTI-ADVOCACY IN ANTHROPOLOGY

Adopting the soul-searching approach of Marvin Harris is evidently not good enough for a body of anthropologists. Hastrup and Elsass (1990) asked the rhetorical question, Is anthropological advocacy a contradiction in terms? (p. 301). As far as they are concerned—and apparently there are others who agree—advocacy and anthropology are incompatible with each other. "Anthropology seeks to comprehend the contexts of local interests," they explain, "while advocacy implies the pursuit of one interest.... Anthropology may provide an important background for engaging in advocacy, which in some cases may present itself as a moral imperative" (p. 301). The idea expressed by this position is that anthropologists who choose an advocacy position must do so outside the discipline because such causes are not capable of being justified in anthropological terms.

Anthropologists who reject the advocacy role think that it is best for local people to work out their own differences and thereby come to speak effectively for themselves. There is the ever-present danger that involvement by the anthropologist may even make a difficult situation worse than it already is. Another argument against advocacy, according to some, is that it is based on a patronizing position. An assumption is possibly made that the anthropologist knows what's best for the local Indigenous population, as if they are not capable of looking out for themselves. However, as time goes on, and local people become more sophisticated or competent in dealing with the outside world, they have less need for such individuals as anthropologists to plead their case or to act on their behalf.

There is no doubt then that some are skeptical about anthropologists' engagement in advocacy. Ervin (2005) argues that "they doubt that the practitioners of a science devoted to describing and analyzing all of the behaviors and ideologies of humanity can choose one cause and advocate it to the exclusion of others" (p. 142). There is also the need for anthropologists to remain objective if they are to maintain their effectiveness as credible researchers. Objectivity means keeping a certain distance, personally and intellectually, so that one can see all sides of an issue. Choosing sides, or becoming partisans for particular causes, tends to destroy the anthropologist's position as a neutral observer.

THE ANTHROPOLOGIST AS "HIRED HAND"

This problem is particularly evident when anthropologists become employees, owing allegiance to their boss, rather than the subjects of research. The issue here is that the anthropologists' traditional autonomy is apt to be compromised because the researcher is not in a situation where he or she chooses the problem to be studied, and as such loses any control of the results of the research. A classic case in point concerns Clinton's (1975) article on the "hired hand." In the situation described here, the anthropologist is pressured to produce research results which benefits the employer: "If I go down," Clinton is warned by his boss, "you go down with me" (p. 201). If the anthropologist in this case does not produce the desired (by the employer) results, there is the danger of being fired or being subject to other threats to produce compliance.

In Clinton's case, the research that he was involved in was determined by vested interests not controlled by the anthropologist; thus, the potential existed for the misuse of anthropological research. A related point of view is that articulated by Schensul and Schensul (1978) who indicate that anthropological research has tended to benefit groups who are socio-politically dominant. Advocacy in anthropology is work that serves to strengthen the representation of marginal groups and to help overcome barriers to a greater or more effective participation in society. "The underlying feature of these advocacy activities," they indicate, "is oriented toward building innovation and change on the culture resources and felt needs that exist in the community" (p. 55).

THE ISSUE OF "AVOCATIONAL TRUTH"

There are caveats involved here. In Robert Paine's (1985) work *Anthropology and Advocacy*, he warns that there is little professional training for an advocacy role. The role of the anthropologists regarding advocacy does not have very well-defined characteristics. There is also the matter of defining what he refers to as "avocational truth." In other words, whose version of "truth" does the anthropologist accept? Certain ethical dilemmas follow logically from this observation of multiple truths. If an anthropologist is unable to accept their client's point of view, is this point of view then rejected, or is it adopted nonetheless as just another version of the truth?

Do these questions provide sufficient reasons for abandoning an advocacy role in anthropology? This is an important question, because the answer might well establish anthropology's relevance in the modern world. The public issues that anthropologists might shy away from are going to exist whether anthropologists participate in a discussion of them or not. So why not become involved in the dialogue, as a means of contributing the discipline's accumulated knowledge about cultural matters? Lingering along the sidelines watching to see which groups hold sway is only going to further marginalize the anthropologist's position and knowledge base. Evidently, anthropologists need to find out more about how the knowledge of their discipline, and their skills as researchers, can contribute to the debate about public issues on a sort of "learn-as-you-go" basis.

In summary, it needs to be acknowledged that there are no rules of engagement that can be followed. Each case has its own history. In any event, the anthropologist is obligated to put their best foot forward, so to speak, and use the perspectives of their discipline to the best of their ability. Anthropologists do have special contributions to make in the transformation process of nation-building, such as adopting a holistic perspective, which is considered one of the hallmarks or special strengths of the discipline.

"It is through holistic analysis," Henriksen (1985) explains, "that we are able to provide ethnic groups with models, which they can in turn use to inform their perception of their own situation and their relations with other ethnic groups and the state" (p. 120). In other words, it is through the adoption of a holistic perspective that anthropologists can play a role in researching such issues as human rights and perspectives on cultural diversity. These are all important aspects of the realities of modern fieldwork.

THE REALITIES OF MODERN FIELDWORK

The Fox Project, my own fieldwork experiences in northern Ontario, and other previously discussed ethnographic endeavours, such as Warren's research in Guatemala, suggest that modern fieldwork has changed to a significant degree from what it had been earlier in the Boas-Malinowski era. For many decades, ethnographic research was largely in the hands of the anthropologists themselves. They chose the project, decided how it was to be conducted, and, for the most part, kept the results to themselves, except for their publications in anthropological academic books and journals, which emerged from the research.

What could be called "traditional" ethnographic research in social anthropology typically involved travel to a region of the world that was not very well known. The goal was to live in a small community for an extended period of time, usually amounting to about a year, while learning as much of the local language and customs as possible. Using such research techniques as participant observation and interviewing key informants, the anthropologist attempted to conduct what was termed "ethnography in the round." This term meant that as much of a culture as possible was described, such as religion, kinship relations, economic practices, politics, ecological relationships, and so on.

In time, after hundreds of such ethnographies were conducted, the focus of anthropological research became more specific. Not all of a local culture was described, but only those aspects that had previously gone unnoticed or been neglected by previous researchers. This period was a sort of "mopping up phase," or what Barrett (1996) has referred to as "salvage anthropology" (p. 27). As time went on, it became more difficult to find pristine cultures in their natural state, so research in anthropology focused on dying or disappearing cultures.

Eventually, the era of research typical of the periods during which Boas and Malinowski worked passed into oblivion. There were negative reactions beginning to be expressed against anthropological research. A sentiment was sometimes expressed that anthropology was the handmaiden of colonial powers (Asad, 1973; Said, 1979). Third World leaders and intellectuals sometimes regarded anthropology with a certain disdain because their societies were apparently described in the ethnographic text books as primitive or culturally backward.

Anthropologists have reacted to these challenges in several ways. Many researchers now conduct their anthropology in their home country because they no longer have as ready access to new nations as they once did during the colonial era. For those who continue to conduct research among Aboriginal or Indigenous populations, the ground rules have changed considerably. The anthropologists no longer have free rein to conduct their studies unimpeded by rules or research conventions.

The realities of modern fieldwork can be viewed in terms of three important aspects: first, the ethics of research is changing; second, the interrelationships between anthropologists and the community members who are being studied have been undergoing a transformation; and third, changing relationships among the anthropologists themselves have taken place in recent decades such that the very nature of the discipline has been altered dramatically from that of previous time periods.

The Ethics of Research

At the forefront of modern research is the idea that the people who are the subjects of research have certain rights that should be acknowledged. In other words, the ethics of research is now a prime consideration for any ethnographic study, whether the research is conducted at home or among the people of other nations. Topics such as informed consent and an avoidance of deception reflect the importance of research ethics today. In addition, most universities have constituted research ethic boards (REBs) through which all research protocols involving human subjects must pass in order to meet certain standards and guidelines.

In my own university, I have sat on such a board for several years, and have also formulated research proposals that were considered by such a committee. As such, I have had the opportunity to see both sides of the process—that of the research applicant and that of a member of the review board. The research review board typically receives proposals from many different disciplines in the social sciences. At my university, the process was started in the early 1980s when psychologists proposed to study schoolchildren, who were not able to supply the consent necessary because they were minors. Research applications by anthropologists often posed a problem for such review boards. One of the important issues involved the giving of informed consent by the subjects of research who in all probability did not understand English, or even comprehend what anthropologists were doing.

Publication of results is another concern. Should the subjects of research have prior access to ethnographic articles and books for their commentary or approval before publication? In my own case, the editor of a university press who had offered to publish my ethnography of Aboriginal people in northern Ontario required that I receive consent in writing from the leaders of the community in which the research was conducted (Hedican 1986b, 2001). This involved returning to the community for an extended period of time with the typewritten draft of the book and going through it line by line with three of the principal residents of the community. Most of the terms used in ethnographic description were not familiar to these leaders, and explaining this argot was very time consuming. Along the way, many changes were suggested, especially any descriptions of the community that could be seen in a negative light. In the end, the book was published, but in a significantly different form than was originally drafted.

On a positive note, the return to the community with a draft of the book for the subjects' approval, or at least consultation, was an opportunity to clarify and correct many issues involved in the fieldwork. For once, we were much more candid with each other about how to characterize the social, economic, and political aspects of the community. Issues were brought into the open, which were apparently at one time too sensitive to discuss, such as the path of government funding through the political hierarchy and community at large. All in all, while initially the university press's requirement to obtain community approval for the manuscript was regarded by me as a time-consuming delay, in the end, this process of community consultation resulted in a better, more accurate reflection of the fieldwork results.

AAA Statement on Ethics (2012)

The American Anthropological Association's *Statement on Ethics* (2012) is a document that contains enlightening information pertinent to the subject of public anthropology. On the topic of advocacy, for example, it is indicated that "anthropologists may choose to link their research to the promotion of well-being, social critique or advocacy." However, there is the proviso stipulated that "anthropological work must ... reflect deliberate and thoughtful consideration of potential unintended consequences and long-term impacts on individuals, communities, [and] identities." There is therefore the problem of determining what these "unintended consequences" could be, since deciding what is in the best interests of others necessarily involves value-laden points of view.

One of the main points that the AAA statement of ethics makes is that anthropology has as one of its goals "the dissemination of anthropological knowledge and its use to solve human problems." Thus, anthropology, according to this statement, is both "applied" and "public" in its orientation because it is an "irreducibly social enterprise." Yet anthropology is different from most other disciplines because it studies many aspects of the human experience in the world, and it is conducted in a wide variety of social and cultural contexts. This means that anthropology, based on its subject matter, is apt to "face myriad ethical quandaries."

The dimension of power is also an important aspect central to the realities of modern fieldwork. In Barrett's (2002, p. 71) study *Culture Meets Power*, he points to the asymmetrical dimensions of power suggesting that power is a hierarchical phenomenon. In the context of ethnography, field-workers have generally come from large, economically developed societies while the community members who are being studied are often more economically disadvantaged. The ethical issue here is that field-workers might be tempted to use the resources at their disposal to manipulate the information-gathering process.

The use of power as a manipulating tool during fieldwork, for example, has fuelled a contentious dispute outlined in Patrick Tierney's (2000) controversial book, *Darkness in El Dorado*. The claim is made by Tierney that Napoleon Chagnon's studies among the Yanomami of Venezuela were based on "hypocrisy, distortions, and humanitarian crimes committed in the name of research," as indicated on the book's jacket cover.

The AAA ethics statement clearly indicates that "anthropologists must be sensitive to the power differential, constraints, interests and expectations characteristic of all relationships. In a field of such complex rights, responsibilities, and involvements, it is inevitable that misunderstandings, conflicts, and the need to make difficult choices will arise." Nonetheless, people have various methods of getting their own way, even if it does not involve the crass use of power. One can persuade others to adopt a particular point of view or choose a course of action through arguments, moral inferences, or other less direct means than the direct use of force. Are these other methods unethical in the field? Where does one draw the line?

Asymmetries of power are therefore implicit in a range of relationships, especially in terms of the ethical obligations due to research participants in their role as collaborators. In the context of ethnographic information gathering, there are different forms of interdependencies and kinds of collaboration. Collaboration could also include other professional colleagues, students, or funding agencies, and therefore these other affected parties, aside from the research participants themselves, illustrate the sometimes conflicting or competing nature of ethical obligations in research settings. In all these cross-cutting relationships, however, some parties are more vulnerable than others, suggesting that competing ethical obligations need to be recognized and assessed in terms of the potential harm that research could cause to these various individuals and groups.

There is also the case between ethics and law, since different processes are involved in making legal decisions as opposed to ethical choices. As such, both ethics and legal matters are subject to different regulations. In this regard, as far as public anthropology is concerned, the anthropologist cannot use ethical guidelines to assess moral, legal, or political positions, because they each belong to different realms in society. Cultural variations on these matters are also an important matter of concern, since the categories used in one society may not necessarily be used or relevant in another one.

The dissemination of research results is another important ethical aspect of research that involves public anthropology. While it is generally recognized that the results of research should be made accessible to academic and public communities, there is always the possibility that the dissemination of anthropological research may expose vulnerable groups to harm. In some cases it will be entirely appropriate for the identity of individuals and groups who are research participants to be disguised using pseudonyms or other means. At times, even preventing the dissemination of research results may be the most ethical decision when significant risks are posed, in order to protect participants or their cultural heritage from harm.

This does not suggest that anthropologists can use ethical guidelines as a justification for withholding research results from the participants themselves. The collaborators of research have a right to know what is being said about them, whether this pertains to the academic realm of journals, books, or other scholarly publications, or in the public realm of newspapers, magazines, and online sources such as social media. In today's electronic information age there is the likelihood that research sharing, even in a very limited sphere, may soon become widely available. It is for this reason, as the AAA ethical code states, that anthropologists "are responsible for consulting with research participants regarding their views of generation, use and preservation of research records" so that "raw data and collected materials will not be used for unauthorized ends."

It is evident, therefore, that if anthropologists are going to engage in public issues, then there are some hard decisions to be made. Possibly the most important of these concerns the impact on various groups involved, and who the proposed solutions are meant to benefit. Anthropologists are in a privileged position. They ask for information and consent from informants, and in turn offer confidentiality and an accurate portrayal of a local situation. It is important that the rights of an individual to his or her privacy be honoured as well as the informant's identity.

Another question concerns the extent to which the various codes of ethics adopted by professional associations are merely suggested guidelines of conduct, or mandatory rules. During the Vietnam War period, for example, Cyril Belshaw thought that the code of ethics adopted by the AAA was too stringent and restricted anthropologists' field behaviour to an unwarranted degree. He discussed a case of intermarriage involving the territorial administrator of Papua New Guinea. "Much damage," Belshaw (1976) explained, "would have been done to the two individuals … by the publication of the details of my research. If any professional body had then informed me that by doing this I was unprofessionally engaged in clandestine research … I would have told them to mind their own business" (p. 284).

The issue raised by Belshaw concerns what form of compliance, if any, should restrain the field behaviour of anthropologists. Are "hard and fast" rules of behaviour appropriate for the anthropologist, and what are the supporting arguments one way or another? These are issues similarly raised by Kunnah (2013) in an article on public anthropology's ethical dilemmas. In this case, the anthropologist's research involved a Maoist insurgency in India and "the ethics of taking sides in a situation where my research participants were involved in a struggle for dignity and justice" (p. 740).

ANTHROPOLOGY AND WAR

We might also consider here the clandestine or secretive forms of anthropological research, such as has occurred during periods of war, when anthropologists could be asked by their government to work against a particular population. This is not a hypothetical issue, as anthropologists worked against the Japanese during World War II. Ruth Benedict (1887–1948), a specialist in culture and personality studies, wrote *The Chrysanthemum and the Sword* (1946), a study of the Japanese based on her wartime investigations. Her aim was quite clearly an unabashed attempt to aid the American war effort by seeking to understand Japan's militaristic aggression under Emperor Hirohito. Of course, the ultimate goal of such research was aimed at discovering Japan's possible weaknesses that could be exploited to the Americans' military advantage.

From the perspective of anthropology, Benedict's involvements in the war effort stands in particularly stark contrast to her pre-war statement in her highly influential study *Patterns of Culture* (1934), in which she indicated quite clearly a strong support for cultural relativism: "To the anthropologist," Benedict wrote, "our customs and those of a New Guinea tribe are two possible social schemes for dealing with a common problem, and in so far as he remains an anthropologist he is bound to avoid any weighing of one in favor of another" (p. 1).

Benedict's study of the Japanese in *Chrysanthemum* was an example of what became known as *national character studies*. During World War II, she worked for the Bureau of Overseas Intelligence, in the Office of War Information in Washington (Sidky, 2004, pp. 156–57). Benedict's task was to provide information on Japanese cultural values and how these values might play a role in influencing Japanese behaviour during the war. This type of anthropology also became known as the study of "cultures at a distance," since it was impossible to collect firsthand information on the basis of fieldwork because of the state of war between the two countries. Instead, she collected information using other materials, such as pamphlets, newspapers, and films.

Marvin Harris (2001) remarked that "the artful presentation of cultural differences to a wide professional and lay public by Mead and Benedict must be reckoned among the important events in the history of American intellectual thought" (p. 409). What is particularly disconcerting, though, and pertinent to this discussion of anthropologists' engagement in public issues, is the discordance between Benedict's pre-war commitment to cultural relativism, and her later war efforts, which stand as an obviously less neutral stance. If we can put this starkly, we might say that cultural relativism is the usual professional mode of thought during everyday fieldwork, but that this ideology could be jettisoned during threats to the anthropologist's home country. There are no doubt different opinions on this matter. It is obviously difficult to be objective toward someone who threatens to do you harm.

Before one begins to think that what happened 70 years ago during Benedict's time is not particularly relevant to today's anthropological issues, the reader should pay attention to the news items that stream across our computer screens. For example, at the time of writing there is a disturbing story on msn.com (6 June 2012) entitled "Muslims Sue to Stop NYPD Surveillance." The article explains that "eight Muslims filed a federal lawsuit Wednesday in New Jersey to force the New York Police Department to end its surveillance and other intelligence-gathering practices targeting Muslims in the years after the 2001 terrorist attacks."

In recent years, anthropologists have voiced their opinions on similar contemporary issues, such as on "global terror" (Werbner, 2010), "militarism in America"

(Johnson, 2005; Albro, 2010), "state security" (Goldstein, 2010; Price, 2012), and "violent extremism" (Spencer, 2012). In the context of this emergent literature in anthropology, do we need to be concerned that the events during and after 9/11 have biased people in certain ways against particular ethnic minorities, such as Muslims? In the msn.com article just cited, for example, a California-based Muslim advocacy organization suggests that "the NYPD program is founded upon a false and constitutionally impermissible premise: that Muslim religious identity is a legitimate criterion for selection of law-enforcement surveillance targets."

A Rutgers University student explained that he joined the lawsuit because "it's such an unfair thing going on: Here I am an American citizen, I was born here, I am law abiding, I volunteer in my community, I have dialogues and good relationships with Muslims and non-Muslims alike, and the NYPD here is surveilling people like me?" Another student, Abdul Kareem Muhammad, one of the plaintiffs in the case, states, "We feel that it was a violation of our constitutional and our civil and human rights.... We condemn and denounce every form of terrorism." The article also notes that because of the widespread civil rights abuses during the 1950s and 1960s, the NYPD has been limited by a court order in what intelligence it can gather on innocent people.

In summary, the AAA Statement on Ethics (2012) is an extremely important document that is informative in so many ways with regard to anthropological research in general and public anthropology in particular. While the AAA guidelines do not suggest that anthropologists should avoid research activities involving areas of social critique or advocacy, there is nonetheless a particularly strong opinion expressed about protecting research participants from harm.

Every anthropologist needs to assess the manner in which their research might cause harm that could result in a loss of dignity to participants or to their bodily and material well-being. It is recognized that this ethical obligation to avoid harm to research participants may conflict with other professional responsibilities, even to the extent that this primary obligation supersedes the goal of seeking new knowledge and the possible benefits that may result from such research.

Aboriginal Research Ethics in Canada

The *Aboriginal Research Ethics Initiative* (AREI) was launched in 2003 with the appointment of Aboriginal scholar Marlene Castellano as chairperson (Castellano & Reading, 2010). This research ethics initiative was instituted in part to combat the prevalence of Eurocentric beliefs and attitudes in Aboriginal studies (Hedican, 2014). As Taiaiake Alfred (2011) explains, "The problem we face is Euroamerican arrogance, the institutional and attitudinal expressions of the prejudicial biases inherent in European and Euroamerican cultures" (p. 3).

Eurocentrism, it is proposed by some Aboriginal scholars, "is the imaginative and institutional context that informs contemporary scholarship, opinion, and law.... It is built on a set of assumptions and beliefs that educated and usually unprejudiced Europeans and North Americans habitually accept as true, as supported by 'the facts,' or as 'reality'" (Battiste & Henderson, 2011, p. 11).These attitudes, Alfred suggests, reflect on the ethical aspects of research among Aboriginal people because of a serious imbalance of power that prevails between researchers and participants that result from the colonial settings and institutional structures in which research takes place.

It is in this context that Castellano maintains that community involvement is essential to ethical research with Aboriginal peoples. Aspects of engagement in a community may take various forms, such as seeking consent from a community's formal leadership to conduct research, or joint planning with a government agency and Aboriginal representatives. Involvement should also entail dialogue with an advisory group whose members have expertise in the customs pertaining to the knowledge that is sought during the research process. Examples of such community engagement in applying ethical guidelines have included that of Manitoulin Island in Ontario and the Mi'kmaq of Nova Scotia. In all, "the engagement of First Nations, Inuit and Metis peoples, in dialogue to devise policy on ethics of research involving humans in Canada, clearly demonstrates that they are eager to take up the challenges of knowledge creation, knowledge translation and knowledge application for the benefits of their communities and society at large" (Castellano & Reading 2010, p. 16).

The Aboriginal Research Ethics Initiative of 2003 was followed by a more recent code of ethical guidelines in 2009 by the *Tri-Council Policy Statement: Ethical Conduct for Research Involving Humans* (Panel on Research Ethics, 2009). The *Tri-Council Policy Statement* (TCPS) was originally adopted in 1998 and is a living or "evolving" document, meaning that it is updated in response to new research developments as they occur. The stated intention of the TCPS initiative is to promote high standards of ethical research, advance the protection of human research participation, and enhance accountability in research ethics.

The TCPS is a comprehensive document covering such issues as consent, fairness, and equity in research participation, privacy and confidentiality, qualitative research, and human genetic research. It also includes a very important section (Chapter 9) on research involving Aboriginal people, as indicated: "Respect for persons is expressed principally through securing the voluntary, informed consent of research participants. First Nations, Inuit and Metis concerns for their continuity of peoples with distinctive cultures and identities have increasingly led to the development of codes of research practice that address concerns arising from their world view."

It can be concluded, then, that the TCPS makes a significant contribution to social science methodology. With its emphasis on the Aboriginal community's social, historical, and cultural contexts, the TCPS initiative further develops the ethical dimensions of research as a living entity.

Anthropologists and Community Members

Modern ethnographic research is drastically different from the past, especially in terms of the relationships between researcher and community members. Today, community members typically want to know what benefits might accrue to them as a result of the research. There is a sort of trade-off, then, between the ethnographer and community residents that take place in contemporary research settings. Community residents might want help in their dealings with government officials, historical research on land claims that could bolster their position in court cases, dealings with the media, or any number of other such requests.

Today, even before ethnographic research begins, an Aboriginal band council will probably request the presence of the ethnographer to make a formal presentation to community members. Assessments will be made by political leaders as to the value of the research for the local community. In such cases, the original research might only be approved if it is drastically altered to suit local interests, or it might be rejected outright. Certainly, the day when the ethnographer had total control over the research agenda is long over.

What has occurred is that the authority of the anthropologist has been challenged. Contemporary research is now, much more than in past eras, a collaborative affair between the research and the subject such that there is more of a sharing of power taking place. The ethnographer no longer has total control over publications, the interpretation of results, or how the lives of others are to be understood. There is a demand today that the voices of the "Other" be heard—what in postmodernist anthropology has been called "dialogical" or "polyvocal"—which essentially means that the voices of the subjects of research have at least as much importance, or more, than that of the anthropologist.

Changing Relationships among Anthropologists

Finally, there are problematic relationships among anthropologists themselves that are the result of changing fieldwork conditions. One important issue concerns the charge that the interpretation of fieldwork material has suffered from an inherent male bias. It is no doubt true that social anthropology has almost from its inception been comprised of a significant number of prominent women fieldworkers, such as Margaret Mead and Ruth Benedict. However, it is also true that a male view of the world has predominated in the anthropological literature historically, and that gendered aspects of social relationships have not been given sufficient consideration (Lamphere, Rayna, & Rubin, 2007; Warren, 1988; Whittaker, 1994).

Judith Stacey (1988), for example, asks the rhetorical question, Can there be a feminist ethnography? She offers the suggestion that "most feminist researchers, committed, at a minimum, to redressing the sexist imbalance of masculine scholarship, appear to select their research projects on substantive grounds. Personal interests and skill meld, often mysteriously, with collective feminist concerns" (p. 21). Feminist anthropology, Stacey points out, is a personal matter, since most social relationships have an important gendered aspect to them, and this point influences one's research interests. There is also an implicit argument here concerning fieldwork, in that the Natives have been to the anthropologists what women have been to men, namely, "dominated, oppressed, and misrepresented," as Barrett (1996, p. 29) asserts.

Further differences among anthropologists concern individual views on whether or not anthropology should primarily be an objective, science-oriented discipline, or a subjective, relativistic, more humanistic field of study. At one extreme is the position of Nancy Scheper-Hughes' (1995) promotion of a "militant anthropology" such that anthropologists are urged to join in the oppressed Native's struggles to combat oppression. Conflicting opinions also exist among anthropologists on such topics as the role of advocacy in the discipline, participatory action research, political collaboration with informants, and several other controversial issues.

The question today is no longer whether or not anthropologists should become involved in the local affairs of their fieldwork settings; the question concerns what form this involvement ought to take. The topic of a publicly engaged anthropology, and the issues that surround it, is an extremely important point of dialogue and discussion in the discipline today. Barrett (1996) has suggested that anthropology "has been forced to attempt a revolutionary rebirth, one which has the potential of revitalizing the discipline so that it is in tune with what the pundits label the postmodern world" (p. 31).

Public anthropology is today at the forefront of this possible revitalization and rebirth, and is therefore a more than worthy focus for the topics discussed further in this book. It is therefore a central contention of this book that a focus on public anthropology will be at the centre of anthropology's future endeavours.

VISIONS OF ANTHROPOLOGY'S FUTURE

There is a saying that "today is the future we worried about yesterday." If one were to look back at the state of anthropology a half-century ago, there was certainly no lack of public issues that could be discussed in the discipline. This was a period of unprecedented student unrest on university campuses. Protests over the war in Vietnam were a daily occurrence, played out nightly on black and white televisions as narrated by such luminaries of the period as Walter Cronkite and Edward R. Murrow.

There were students being shot and killed for their activist beliefs, such as the infamous Kent State shooting of four students in May 1970 by National Guardsmen. Martin Luther King Jr. was stirring the nation with his "I Have a Dream" speech and leading marches for civil rights in Mississippi, Alabama, and elsewhere. His assassination on 4 April 1968 was a grim day for America. The Beatles were storming the airways with a message of "make love not war."

Looking back, it's hard to remember many anthropologists having much to say about these issues, at least publicly. In anthropology, Claude Levi-Strauss was a much revered personality of this period for his enigmatic pronouncements on myth and French structuralism. He also was responsible for conceptual breakthroughs in the way we viewed kinship, suggesting an approach opposed to the British models and concentrating rather on alliances and group process through marriage. However, in his much read article in *Current Anthropology*, called "Anthropology: Its Achievements and Future" (Levi-Strauss, 1966), one could have expected a visionary statement about the upcoming prospects for the discipline.

Levi-Strauss, however, did not have a crystal ball, and certainly cannot be held responsible for a failure to predict the future state of human societies, much less a somewhat obscure discipline such as anthropology, but he did make an attempt at prognostication. He used the analogy of a planet nearing earth that would never be seen again in human history. Would we not want, he asks, to devote all of our scientific efforts at examining this terrestrial phenomenon, since we will have only one chance to do so?

In this article, Levi-Strauss points to his reading of the numerous volumes of the Bureau of American Ethnology, founded in 1879, and the invaluable contributions to the store of human knowledge that such basic ethnographic descriptions contribute to the understanding of the world's vanishing cultures. He warns that "the day will come when the last primitive culture will have disappeared from the earth, compelling us to realize only too late that the fundamentals of mankind are irretrievably lost.... It is precisely because the so-called primitive peoples are becoming extinct that their study should now be given absolute priority" (1966, pp. 124–25).

Levi-Strauss died in 2009, at the age of 101. No doubt the likes of this anthropologist will not be seen again. He provided many insights into fundamental human contradictions, about the social and natural, life and death, and male and female. His brand of anthropology stressed the structural aspects of human thinking, the necessity to dichotomize (raw and cooked, gender transformations), and the peculiar nature of myths and time. There were certainly controversial aspects to his brand of explanation, which apparently contravened the conventional fundamental scientific principle that a cause must precede its effect in time; Levi-Strauss, rather, proposed that time should not be viewed in a linear fashion but should be understood as proceeding both backwards and forwards.

The point here is that, on the subject of "The Future of Anthropology," we might have expected more from one of the most innovative pillars of the discipline. Looking back, his suggestions urging anthropologists to put all of their efforts into studying what Levi-Strauss saw as the last vestiges of primitive society seems not so much short-sighted as it does out of tune with the times.

Did anthropologists follow Levi-Strauss's plea? From the perspective of a half-century later, it is apparent that the answer is a resounding *no*. Even from the vantage point of the 1960s, his plea for a widespread study of the dying, or at least vastly transformed, primitive cultures was largely outmoded. This might have been the appropriate research agenda of a generation of anthropologists who worked during Levi-Strauss's youth of the early 1900s. This was a period when the Aboriginal tribes, particularly in the American West, such as the Blackfoot, Sioux, and Comanche, were undergoing rapid cultural disintegration resulting from the slaughter of the buffalo and the unrelenting warfare of the century before.

Anthropologists of the 1960s did not take up Levi-Strauss's challenge because they were becoming far more interested in conducting research into the impact of modern society on Indigenous nations. Such topics as colonialism, economic development, and resource deterioration were beginning to dominate ethnographic interests at this time. In a sense, Levi-Strauss's vision was not forward enough; it even could be considered in a sense regressive. While not many academics, especially in North America, were willing to overtly express the thought, many thinkers probably expected more from an avowed anthropological leader of the times.

Still, it is probably not especially warranted to find Levi-Strauss culpable in not providing the discipline with a sense of direction. Part of the problem with developing a forward-looking anthropology is that there have never been a sufficient number of anthropologists capable of studying all of the interesting problems and possibilities that are presented by human societies and cultures. And it is not just a matter of numbers in the discipline; it is also a matter of academic interests shifting with the times. The so-called primitive peoples that Levi-Strauss urged anthropologists to study did not disappear, at least not entirely; they became transformed in the future decades of global capitalism, the expanding media, and other social, economic, and political forces.

Levi-Strauss, or any other anthropologist in the discipline, could hardly be blamed for a lack of insight into the future impact of these pervasive transformations. Not only are there fewer numbers of anthropologists compared to other disciplines in the social sciences—such as our sister discipline of sociology—there are also significant conceptual issues impeding progress. Anthropologists do not just restrict themselves in their research endeavours to, say, modern Western society; rather, their purview extends across the globe. It includes, in fact, every human population now and that ever existed. It also includes such associated topics as the biological aspects of human life, linguistic matters, and the vast scope of human existence in the subjects of pre-history and archaeology. It is no wonder that such a small number of researchers have difficulty coping with all the interesting questions about human life. And who would fund all of this research, when there are so many other pressing social issues in the world?

PRESSING OUTWARD, BEYOND THE ACADEMY

Three decades after Levi-Strauss's vision, James Peacock, in his presidential address to the AAA entitled "The Future of Anthropology," takes up where Levi-Strauss left off in attempts at prognostication. However, Peacock's attempt is more forward look-ing than that made by his predecessor. He asserts, for example, that "while sustaining the fundamentals, probing the deep mysteries of the human species and the human soul, we must press outward, mobilizing our work and ourselves to make a difference beyond the discipline and the academy" (Peacock, 1997, p. 9).

As far as Peacock is concerned, there are three possible scenarios for the future of anthropology. First, there is the possibility of extinction. The downsizing that has been going on in colleges and universities, and the "rationalizing" of curriculums with relatively low enrollments, could make anthropology departments a target for either outright elimination or a merger with other more powerful entities in academia. Anthropology is vulnerable because of its relatively small size compared to others in the social sciences.

Second, some perceive anthropologists hanging on in university and museum set-tings in a sort of intellectual backwater, viewed by others as a kind of quaint leftover from the halcyon days of Boas, Mead, and Malinowski. It is, after all, difficult to name one anthropologist during the last half-century who meets the widespread esteem of these international scholars. Boas took the debate about racism out of academic set-tings, and Mead spoke out against war in Southeast Asia and championed the rights of youth and women, while Malinowski was famous for his popular radio debates in which he attempted to engage the public in issues of the day, such as the war in Europe. Why is anthropology not producing such luminaries today?

A third alternative is that anthropologists attempt to reinvent their discipline, from one on the verge of possible intellectual annihilation to one that is revitalized and energetically infused with a renewed sense of mission and purpose. Anthropolo-gists could aim for a new direction of their discipline which has a more prominent position in our society; in other words, anthropology could re-establish itself, in Peacock's (1997) terms, as a discipline that is "intriguing and creatively diverse, iconoclastic and breathtaking in its sweep and perception, profound in its scholarship, but would become integral and even leading in addressing the complex challenges of a transnational, yet grounded, humanity. Society needs anthropology" (p. 9). Who would argue against such lofty goals, especially when faced with an apparent relegation to an anachronistic, out-of-touch discipline whose practitioners are more concerned with the causes of the couvade or the avunculate than with the more pressing issues of war, poverty, and racism?

CREATING INCLUSIVENESS

Even if anthropologists were to embrace the sort of research suggested by Peacock in his AAA presidential address, there is in anthropology nonetheless a certain resistance to the type of research that sees the so-called Other as somewhat "less than" the more materially rich Western nations. There is the less-than-flattering idea among some that if anthropologists are interested in studying your society, village, or culture, then you must live in an undeveloped, "primitive" condition.

There also has developed the association of anthropology with power elites and neo-colonial regimes (Asad, 1973), although Paul Farmer's *Pathologies of Power* (2003) demonstrates that at least some anthropologists are interested in human rights and the plight of the poor. Anthropology has long suffered from a perception among people colonized by Western powers that it has been the handmaiden of missionaries and colonial regimes in an earlier era, big transnational corporations today, and other oppressors of Indigenous peoples.

This long-standing perception of anthropology is not just a public relations issue. Anthropologists have done little to combat such attitudes or dispel what they would see as misconceptions of their discipline. Today, we live in the post-9/11 world of sectarian violence, gay rights, counterinsurgency, and social media. Anthropologists might well profit today by remembering what Karl Marx (1852/1978) said about history: "Men make their own history, but they do not make it just as they please; they do not make it under circumstances chosen by themselves, but under given circumstances directly encountered and inherited from the past" (p. 9).

The question is, Can anthropologists adjust to these "circumstances directly encountered," or perhaps, to use Peacock's term, "focus outward"?

To focus outward does not necessarily mean that anthropologists abandon their current research. Rather, it means that anthropologists seek ways to contribute through their research beyond the bounds of their discipline and academic settings, to society at large. One way to do this is not to retreat into a sort of intellectual seclusion in the face of budgetary cutbacks and other restrictive measures, but to connect more widely with other people and groups worldwide. Through their fieldwork, anthropologists have perhaps the widest social, cultural, and transnational connections of any discipline. There is hardly any place in the world where anthropologists have not conducted at least a cursory ethnographic survey and established a research presence. These contacts could profitably be built upon, so that anthropology could be seen as a discipline of inclusion rather than marginalization, possibly using Lassiter's (2005) suggestion for a public anthropology built upon "collaborative ethnography."

THE NEW REALITY

Whatever is happening in the world today is not something that anthropologists have created. There has been a call for some time in the discipline for anthropologists to become more socially relevant, to face up to the new reality of modern life. They also need to justify their existence in an academic environment in which accountability and results rule the show. This is not to suggest that anthropologists need to abandon their traditional interests, even though there would be many who would see in anthropology the irrelevant and arcane interests of an out-of-touch intelligentsia. How can such a perception be changed so that anthropology is viewed as a dynamic discipline in tune with today's reality and contributing in some measure to the public good?

In an interesting study called *Culture Meets Power*, Barrett (2002) suggests that "this may well be a good time to be an anthropologist, but in view of the terrorist attack on America—a poignant reminder that the mixture of power and culture sometimes produces tragedy on a grand scale—it is not such a good time to be a human being" (p. 115). Certainly, Western consciousness was forever altered by the events of 11 September 2001 when hijacked commercial jetliners crashed into the World Trade Center and the Pentagon.

This event is comparable to the consciousness-altering shifts that occurred in earlier generations with the bombing of Pearl Harbor, or the assassinations of President John F. Kennedy and Martin Luther King Jr. The world was changed in certain fundamental ways by such situations; whatever innocence we might have enjoyed up until then was taken away and replaced with a stark new reality.

This new reality is a terror-ridden place with suicide bombers, unprecedented attacks on civilian protesters, suppression by dictators, and sectarian violence on an unparalleled scale. Time will tell if anthropologists can embrace this new reality, and help the public understand its social and cultural dimensions. Or will anthropologists retreat into ever more arcane discourses and thereby view only the important issues of our time from the sidelines?

ORGANIZATION OF THE BOOK

This opening chapter has attempted to provide the reader with an introduction to the various topics and issues that are important in the field of public anthropology. There are a multitude of terms and concepts that have been used in the literature, many of which overlap one another, so that precise definitions of terminology are often difficult to make. There are also important activities that anthropologists are currently engaged in which involve various forms of advocacy and a stimulating debate about the aspects of this role playing. The ethics of research is also an important consideration and conditions many of the aspects of the realities of modern fieldwork.

In the following chapter, we will deal more specifically with the topic of "What is public anthropology?" and explore the ever increasingly large body of literature in this field of study. Here again, there are various opinions about the direction anthropology should be taking at present and in the future with regard to engaging in issues beyond the university and other academic settings. It is evident that questions about whether or not anthropologists should be more actively engaged in modern public issues have long passed. The questions are now about the form and types of engagement that are feasible and the different repercussions that will no doubt affect the discipline today and in the foreseeable future.

The topic of race and science is the topic of Chapter 3. This chapter is largely an extension of the emphasis that Franz Boas and his students placed on informing the general public where possible about the scientific facts about race, and in particular, that the idea of race itself is a questionable concept in scientific terms. There is also little basis to the idea common in previous generations of scientists that human behaviour has a racial or biological basis. Nonetheless, race, however conceived, is a significant fact of modern life to the extent that it provides a basis for social, economic, and political problems in today's society.

Chapter 4 focuses on the Pulitzer Prize–winning book by Jared Diamond, called *Guns, Germs, and Steel*, in terms of the topic of social Darwinism. In other words, in this chapter the topic of public anthropology is explored through a popular scientific study of the rise of European "civilization" and its domination over Indigenous populations. Diamond contends that favourable environmental conditions led to the domestication of various crops (wheat, barley) and animals (cows, horses, goats), and that these conditions provided the basis for the ascendency of European technological development.

On the other hand, there are those who see in Diamond's thesis an explanation based on what has been termed "environmental determinism," and suggest, alternatively, that the accumulation of wealth and power among Europeans has been the result of Europe's colonial and imperialistic policies, which have subjugated Indigenous peoples. In any event, the purpose of this chapter is to explore a popular scientific study by a well-known figure and then to examine the public issues that such a work raises for public anthropology.

Medical anthropology, in terms of the topics of health, well-being, and food security, provide the basis of discussion in Chapter 5. This discussion begins with a description of Paul Farmer, one of the most prominent public figures in modern anthropology, and his research on AIDS in Haiti. His research in medical anthropology is controversial because of Farmer's contention that it is the weaker nations, such as Haiti, having been exploited by more powerful countries, that are the source of the spread of AIDS. In other words, there is a sort of "blame the victim" mentality that sees the source of medical problems such as AIDS in the poorer countries, rather than in the wealthy nations that have exploited the people in smaller nations through such practices as sexual tourism.

Chapter 6 focuses on the field of forensic anthropology. It illustrates the manner in which scientific studies within anthropology are used in wider public settings, such as crime scene investigations. There has actually been a long history of forensic studies in anthropology, although in the past such research was not given a special label. There is much that anthropology has to offer—when murders, for example, are committed—that extends beyond the usual capabilities of police investigations.

Things that anthropologists might help determine include the biological or ethnic memberships of a victim, their sex, age, and date of death. Often, police investigation units are more concerned with recent crimes, and so anthropologists are able to contribute their expertise to offences that occurred years or decades in the past. Forensic anthropology is therefore a primary example of the manner in which anthropological knowledge is used in the public domain, beyond the usual academic settings.

The topic of rebellion and reconciliation forms the basis for discussion in Chapter 7. The aspect of public anthropology that is explored in this chapter concerns the anthropological knowledge that is used to understand the processes by which different cultural and ethnic groups attempt to find a common basis for living together in relative harmony. This chapter focuses on the rebuilding of South Africa and the attempts to rebuild in effect a new society in which there has existed a long period of segregation and political domination.

In Chapter 8, the focus is on global terror, a significant topic in our modern age. Many may not realize it, but the fact is that anthropologists have been involved in areas of militarism and counterinsurgency for quite some time, especially in terms of what has been termed the Human Terrain System (HTS). The suggestion, then, is that anthropologists' involvement in military activities is an important topic that needs to be discussed in public anthropology because of the use of anthropology in counterinsurgency measures.

The topic of media and the global village forms the basis of discussion in Chapter 9. It explores a new area of public engagement, such as anthropology and the Internet, the Arab Spring, Russian talk shows, and related areas of interest beyond anthropology's usual academic settings. It is evident that the concept of the global village has an impact in the manner in which modern anthropology is conducted. The little, isolated communities that formed the basis of anthropological research in the past have all but disappeared because of the modern media, and the Internet has posed a challenge to anthropologists to relate their research to a much wider, global context. While this book is intended to be international in scope, it is nonetheless restricted primarily to the English-language literature, meaning that many other cultural viewpoints are possible on the subject of public anthropology in addition to those presented here.

In the final chapter, the various themes that have been discussed in this book relating to public anthropology are drawn together in a discussion that looks toward anthropology's future. These themes are related to demonstrating the importance of anthropological research outside of academic settings and into the public domain as anthropology attempts to establish its relevance in the modern world.

Chapter 2

WHAT IS PUBLIC ANTHROPOLOGY?

The term "public anthropology" may appear relatively new in the literature; however, there have certainly been previous attempts in earlier decades to bring social issues to the forefront of the discipline. Malinowski (1970/1929) used the term "practical anthropology" as a broad cover term for any application of anthropological research that could have useful purposes, especially in areas of government administration and policy concerning Indigenous populations, as we have previously noted. Another designation, "applied anthropology," has been prominent in the discipline for at least a half-century, usually referring to an "anthropologist working out of a university context on a part-time basis for an outside agency" (Ervin, 2005, p. 4).

Since the 1970s, "practising anthropology" emerged as a label for the work of people trained in anthropology who apply their skills and knowledge outside of academic settings. "Public anthropology" has only entered the literature since the early 1990s, and consequently there has been a considerable discussion and debate ever since about what such a field should encompass, how it could differ from other similar designations, and how such activities may conflict with certain fundamental principles in anthropology, such as cultural relativism. The purpose of this chapter is to examine the various discussions in the anthropological literature concerning the field of "public anthropology," and to determine if possible whether or not there has emerged a consensus about what this term actually means for those who have proposed this activity as a separate field of study in the discipline.

This chapter therefore explores the wider ramifications to the discipline of anthropology when this field of study proceeds in the direction of public anthropology. While the title of this chapter asks, What is public anthropology? in effect the question has much broader consequences for anthropology as a whole. These wider consequences are explored in this chapter in terms of the topic of public anthropology serving as a forum of debate concerning the direction in which the discipline is heading.

The direction that a focus on public anthropology has for both the theory and methods of anthropology is very far reaching. For example, the culture concept, often seen as a core epistemological pillar of anthropology, has become hotly debated in the context of public anthropology. There are other consequences as well, such as the changing relationships between anthropologists and their collaborators in fieldwork.

In a wider sphere of implications, there is also the role that anthropologists might play in the arena of public policy. In this context, the question inevitably emerges whether, if anthropologists are proceeding in the direction of a more public stance in today's world, they should become more involved in the formulation of public policy issues. This question poses, as such, a need to revisit Laura Nader's long-standing proclamation that anthropologists in the public sphere are, by necessity, required to explore research among society's social, political, and economic elites by "studying up" (Nader, 1974).

This chapter also explores several case studies that have important implications for public anthropology. One of the cases discussed in this chapter is the research conducted by Nancy Scheper-Hughes in Ireland and the negative backlash that occurred as a result of discussion of the results of her research on Irish mental health in the nation's news media. The implication here is that addressing fieldwork concerns in the public arena is apt to have some negative results if the research results are not framed in an appropriate or more culturally sensitive manner.

Another case study concerns fieldwork among the Gitksan of British Columbia that had profound results for the ethnographer and the manner in which fieldwork is conducted in modern settings. In all, the various topics discussed in this chapter expand upon the topics raised in the introductory chapter by focusing on the wider implications for anthropology of an extension into the public arena. It also provides needed contextual information for a discussion of the various topics that are presented in the chapters to come in this book.

PUBLIC INTELLECTUALS, SOCIAL CRITICISM, AND HUMAN RIGHTS

Anna Tsing (2005) has made a call for "Anthropologists as Public Intellectuals" in *Anthropology News*. As Tsing explains, "For the first time in many years, scholars across the discipline are leaping into the public arena to address the general public. Gone are impenetrable language and our claims to exclusive expertise; out come new, creative and passionate forms. A new spate of public knowledge is coming into being, and anthropologists, who have thought deeply about the global situation in their research, have been prominent in these experiments" (p. 10). Her article makes specific mention of anthropological involvement in US politics, especially as it addresses the new prominence of the US military in managing global affairs.

Ironically, and as an act of anthropological clairvoyance, this article by Tsing, and the accompanying one by Chalmers Johnson (2005), concerns the Iraq war. Johnson (2005) suggests that "the Iraq war is very possibly the most serious self-inflicted wound in the history of American foreign policy" (p. 10). As this section was being written in June 2014, President Obama was pondering whether or not to again send American troops to Iraq in response to the siege of Baghdad by the Islamic State of Iraq and al-Sham (ISIS) insurgency. Time will tell if anthropologists are preparing a response to this situation of possible military intervention, and the corresponding one in Syria, as "public intellectuals."

"Anthropology has entered a new phase of advanced engagement at local, national and international levels," according to Brondo (2010, p. 208). In a review article for the year 2009, it is pointed out that practicing anthropologists have made significant contributions in such areas as race relations, civil rights and policy reforms, human rights, and war and peace issues in this "time of crisis." It is also noted (Clarke, 2010) that recent anthropology has become much more "critically engaged" and that the "politics of activism" has become prominent in the discipline as anthropologists take on the role of social critic with a special concern for issues of power. In another recent review of anthropological trends for the year 2010, Mullins (2011) points to "a rapidly growing body of public scholars [who have] continued to conduct engaged research that involved various forms of collaboration, advocacy, and activism" (p. 235).

As these reviews of the discipline would appear to indicate, there is a growing body of scholars who contend that if public anthropology is to mean anything, or have any meaningful or legitimate role to play in society, at the heart of this endeavour should be the idea that anthropology be more fully engaged in social criticism. Many anthropologists conduct research among marginalized populations whose members suffer from poverty, economic exploitation, and political manipulation.

In this context of ethnographic research involving local-level communities suffering from the effects of various forms of oppression, the anthropologist is in a position to witness these adverse effects and become engaged in finding solutions to these problems. As an example, in her article "The Anthropologist as Social Critic," Ida Susser (2010) discusses her HIV/AIDS research in southern Africa. Most of the people that she worked with were women who were poor and homeless. Treatment for their disease was nonexistent, so that protection was apparently the only route possible as a means of asserting their rights to safe sex.

Susser (2010) explains that her research on HIV/AIDS was guided by several crucial questions that "were always framed in terms of an activist approach to ethnography" (p. S227). This activist stance is based on the idea that anthropologists should be engaged in efforts at social transformation because "we are all global citizens"

FIGURE 2.1 Ida Susser (top)
Source: Reprinted by permission of Dr. Richard Lee

(p. S232). She also suggests that participation in efforts at social transformation can be documented in much the same manner as with other forms of participant observation. In this way, contributions can be made to both the field of anthropological theory and work for social justice.

Barbara Johnston (2010) also argues that, as public citizens, anthropologists have a social responsibility to become more engaged in the various issues of our time. As she explains, "To work in the public interest is an honor, a duty, at times an intensely problematic burden that demands explicit attention to the social terms and potential ramifications of engagement" (p. S235). As is the case with Susser, Johnston also sees anthropologists as "global citizens" whose research has historically focused on the world's vulnerable people. This research then imposes on anthropology certain disciplinary obligations to speak out in some manner when, for example, "the states in which we live or work are engaged in actions that result in gross violations of human rights" (Johnston, 2010, p. S44).

THE AAA HUMAN RIGHTS DECLARATION

The American Anthropological Association voted in 1999 to adopt a Human Rights Declaration, which is situated in the broader body of human rights law (http://www.aaanet.org/about/Policies/statements/Declaration-on-Anthropology-and-Human-Rights.cfm). AAA members, in adopting this declaration, acknowledge that they have a responsibility and an obligation to uphold international human rights, through their research and other scholarly activities. In addition, anthropologists are similarly obligated to respect the terms of other human rights covenants, such as the United Nations General Assembly's adoption of the Indigenous Rights Declaration.

As early as 1947, the Executive Board of the AAA submitted its Statement on Human Rights to the United Nations (Engle, 2001). However, there has been concern and some degree of controversy within anthropology ever since, because some have seen this statement as limiting tolerance. The problem stems from the idea that culture and human rights can be seen as antithetical to each other. For example, if one were to accept the universality of human rights, then this could entail a possible opposition to cultural practices that might conflict with one's interpretation of human rights' norms. As Engle (2001) therefore posits, "To support an acceptance of conflicting cultural practices would be to oppose human rights" (p. 536).

The 1999 AAA Declaration on Human Rights attempted to clarify this disjunctive separation of basic principles. This is an important issue for public anthropology in particular because the AAA Declaration is generally considered to embody the Boasian concept of cultural relativism. The pro-rights anthropologists of today continue to struggle with the same issues as the 1947 AAA board confronted regarding the limits of tolerance. "In particular," Engle (2001) summarizes, "the question of how one might be a cultural relativist and still make overt political judgements guides today's Human Rights Committee in much the same way it guided the 1947 Board" (p. 537).

In an attempt to clarify its position on culture and tolerance, the 1999 AAA Declaration has produced the following statement: "People and groups have a generic right to realize their capacity for culture, and to produce and change the conditions and forms of their physical, personal and social existence, so long as such activities do not diminish the same capacities of others. Anthropology as an academic discipline studies the bases and the forms of human diversity and unity; anthropology as a practice seeks to apply this knowledge to the solution of human problems" (AAA, 1999, n.p.).

HUMAN RIGHTS AND CULTURAL TOLERANCE

The AAA Declaration therefore goes a long way toward establishing anthropology's position concerning the relationship between cultural tolerance and human rights: if certain cultural practices violate a person's human rights, then these practices are clearly not acceptable. In other words, universal principles of human rights override specific anthropological principles, such as cultural relativism, no matter how ensconced such principles are within the discipline's epistemology.

These various human rights declarations can therefore become problematic for anthropologists who are conducting research in nations in which an obligation to abide by these international codes or treaties does not exist. In such cases, anthropologists are apt to find themselves in an ambiguous or untenable situation when the rules, laws, or other norms of the states in which they are conducting research conflict in some manner with international obligation or the professional codes of ethical conduct in their own discipline.

Central to the AAA Statement on Ethics (2012), for example, is "a primary ethical obligation shared by anthropologists to do no harm." Under conditions where anthropologists work in the service of governments or corporations whose actions produce societal harm, there is obviously a conflict of interest concerning ethical research behaviour that needs to be addressed or resolved in some satisfactory manner. In fact, the AAA Statement on Ethics (2012) does refer to the "myriad ethical quandaries" faced by anthropologists due to the contexts in which they work and the kinds of issues they address.

THE POLITICAL CONTEXT OF PUBLIC ANTHROPOLOGY

Anthropologists, who see themselves as global citizens imbued with a sense of social responsibility, must therefore acknowledge the political nature of their research. If the aim of their research is to document certain social conditions with the objective of exposing and addressing the abuse that they might witness during the course of this work, then the anthropologist might well generate a wide array of personal, professional, and societal risks (Johnston, 2010, p. S245). In turn, under such ethnographic conditions there are apt to be unintended consequences of anthropological research.

The political ramifications of an engaged anthropology have been considered by Paul Mullins (2011). He asserts that "nearly every scholar has become politicized in the past decade or so, and it is now common place to find researchers in almost any discipline and beyond university walls invoking their commitment to applied scholarship, civil engagement, and a variety of other overtly politicized positions" (p. 235). As such, it is hardly a debating point anymore about the political nature of engaged scholarship, as it appears here to stay. If there is a question to discuss, though, it has to do with the nature of this scholarly politicization and the various ramifications that it holds for a discipline such as anthropology.

The problem for public anthropology as a political activity is that becoming political almost always involves choosing sides, or at least making hard choices about which groups anthropologists would support, and those they would not. If the matter is always one in which the anthropologist sides with the least powerful or more economically disadvantaged sectors of a society, there is also the corresponding possibility of alienating those in the upper echelons, such as the political elites. Adversarial politics has its costs as well as its opportunities, but one fact is clear: it is very difficult to stay in the middle and antagonize no one.

STUDENT TRAINING IN THE PUBLIC SPHERE

Training students to become practicing anthropologists is another facet of the politicization of engaged anthropology. In an article on "Re-Functioning Ethnographic Pedagogies," Lassiter and Campbell (2010) assert that contemporary fieldwork can no longer be conceptualized as a place free from scholars' everyday lives. As such, they encourage training students for collective activism that is based on collaborative programs between students and community members. As an example of one such area of study in the area of public issues, in the case of urban revitalization in Detroit, Wayne State University offers a program designed to "train students to become globally aware and locally engaged citizens" (Briller & Sankar, 2013, p. 157).

Training programs in the context of practicing anthropology can involve different facets, such as classroom instruction, individual mentoring and advising, as well as various pedagogical programs that encourage forms of engagement (Low & Merry 2010, p. S208). At my own university (University of Guelph, Ontario) anthropologists in the combined department of Sociology and Anthropology have initiated a master's graduate program in "Public Issues Anthropology" as a means of encouraging scholarly activity and meeting students' interest in a central focus of research in socio-cultural anthropology (http://www.uoguelph.ca/socioanthro/masters-program-public-issues-anthropology).

A central core of this program is a weekly seminar course in which different anthropologists make presentations on their current research in public anthropology. Faculty ethnographic areas are quite diverse and include Sub-Saharan Africa, Asia, the Caribbean, Europe, Latin America, and North America. Graduate students have conducted research in a variety of cultural settings including Botswana, Canada, Honduras, Jamaica, Kenya, Nepal, and Paraguay. A main focus of the program is on "the interface between anthropological knowledge and issues crucial to governance, public discourse, livelihoods, civil society and contemporary public issues" (from the program website). The program draws on the faculty expertise of anthropologists who have conducted research on a wide range of topics, such as migration, globalization, human rights, Aboriginal issues, dietary practices, families and aging, social inequalities, and the anthropology of development.

STUDENT MENTORING IN PUBLIC ANTHROPOLOGY

In another program in public anthropology, Susser (2010) describes ethnographic training on AIDS in the context of Namibia and South Africa. In Norway, Howell (2010) discusses the role of anthropologists in the country's public debate on such topics as immigration and Indigenous rights. In this context, one can see that teaching can take place in such varied areas as the public media and popular writing, in addition to specific training programs in the discipline. Similarly, Norma Gonzalez (2010), in her article "Advocacy Anthropology and Education," discusses the importance of anthropological involvement in schools so that teaching provides insights into racial inequality through engaged practices.

Wayman (2009) discusses the Sumatra-Andaman earthquake of December 2004, in which an anthropologist, Simron Jit Singh, adopted the role of an adviser to help the Nicobarese Islanders make more informed decisions about their future. Thus, working with local informants in an adviser role also served in a teaching and training capacity, so that community members could make more informed decisions when confronted by aid offerings from the Indian government and other non-governmental relief organizations. In another educational context, Chrisman (2008) provides advice to graduate students concerning the 2008 AAA meetings that took place in San Francisco under the theme "Inclusion, Collaboration & Engagement."

As an "engaged activity," teaching can therefore have many forms, including "class room teaching, community outreach, training, workshops, and numerous other pedagogical and didactic forms, including serving as a public intellectual" (Low & Merry, 2010, p. S208). In an educational context, topics germane to public anthropology can also offer a wide range of opportunities for students, their advisers, and community members to participate in the process of using anthropological knowledge to help solve human problems in a collaborative manner.

PUBLIC ANTHROPOLOGY: A SHIFTING FORUM OF DEBATE

As with many labels in anthropology, the term "public anthropology" has had a tendency to mean different things to different individuals. Trevor Purcell (2000), for example, suggests that the term "public anthropology" is "an idea searching for a reality" (p. 30). His definition of the term, however, is somewhat convoluted: "I use the term *public anthropology* here to mean a type of anthropology, which, in its formal (i.e., within the academy) and its 'informal' (outside the academy) activities, is practiced with a view toward directly and indirectly contributing to the general public good—not just to the academic or career good" (p. 30).

Unfortunately, such a definition is broad enough to include just about anything within the varied activities that engage anthropologists, whether these activities are theoretical, practical, and political, or just about anything else that one could imagine. Possibly, though, this lack of definitional precision is merely a reflection of the uncharted territory in which contemporary anthropologists find themselves, and there is the further possibility that greater clarity will emerge in the future. In the meantime, anthropologists are becoming increasingly engaged in many activities hardly imagined just a few decades ago.

The spectrum of undertakings that such a label as public anthropology entails is therefore very broad. Anthropologists today are interested in research on war and counterinsurgency, the Internet and social media, AIDS, genital mutilation, humanitarian advocacy, and a variety of other topics. It hardly seems possible, then, that one should expect a clear-cut definition that includes all of these sorts of interests. Nonetheless, with many terms that are difficult to verbalize, we have some idea of what is commonly meant by them.

Several presuppositions are implied by the term, namely, that anthropologists are willing to engage in some variety of public discourse, that they see their behaviour as ultimately "contributing to the general public good" (to use Purcell's phrase), and that the lives of anthropologists become imbued with a certain commitment to participation in social and political affairs.

WHOSE "PUBLIC" IS PUBLIC ANTHROPOLOGY?

One is led to wonder, though, about whose social and political affairs this could refer to—that of the anthropologist, or their "Other"? What are the ethical dimensions of participating *across* cultural boundaries (which in some manner we do anyway in the normal course of most research in social and cultural anthropology, but probably not always in a proactive way)?

After all, we built our careers on research involving people in other cultures, which some no doubt could regard as a form of exploitation in itself, and now we push to become politically engaged as well in the lives of the people we study. It is for this reason that Purcell refers to "an ontological discontinuity" between the lives of the people studied in anthropology and the lives of the academic researcher.

What does this say, then, about whether or not the lives of the people who are the objects of anthropological study are in reality a constituent part of *our* public? Is a *native* anthropologist also an outsider or part of what we see as *our* public? Obviously, then, perspective matters in terms of how we view the term "public."

Perspective also matters in terms of how we see "objective" detachment in a conventional sense in anthropology in the context of the time-honoured view of cultural relativism, and how a sense of disciplinary detachment has provided the fundamental basis for the very need for a public-oriented anthropology. Certainly, in a very real sense, we are all part of a universal global society today, and therefore also participants in the same *public*.

THE CULTURE CONCEPT AND PUBLIC ANTHROPOLOGY

Not to be overlooked in all of these reflections is the fact of a certain hierarchical ascendency in which anthropology has historically participated. Edward Said (1979),

Lila Abu-Lughod (1990, 1991), and Arjun Appadurai (1991), for example, have all been important participants in the debate about the use of knowledge as power in anthropology. As Barrett (2002) explains, "Culture is a conceptual tool, a discourse that has generated and sustained the unequal relationship between the West and the non-West. Cultural stereotypes, homogenizes, and essentializes 'the Other,' while ignoring change, conflict, and individual agency" (p. 5).

Similarly, Abu-Lughod (1991) writes that "culture is the essential tool for making other. As a professional discourse that elaborates on the meaning of culture in order to account for, explain, and understand cultural difference, anthropology also helps construct, produce and maintain it. Anthropological discourse gives cultural difference (and the separation among groups of people it implies) the air of the self-evident" (p. 143).

These issues are raised because of the distinct possibility that the goals of Western and non-Western anthropologists are at odds with each other. This could further mean then that anthropologists in each of these camps would not necessarily see themselves as belonging to the same *public*, or, for that matter, see themselves as participating in the same agenda. Even more troubling, from a disciplinary perspective, is that certain fundamental concepts in the discipline, such as *culture* itself, while so essential in the view of many, could have always been flawed from the beginnings of the anthropological enterprise.

Certainly there are troubling aspects of this concept, and of course with "culture relativism" itself, which tends to predispose anthropology in an unfavourable light from the perspective of non-Western academics. There are certain assumptions threaded through the history of anthropology that have tended to presuppose a view of culture characterized by stability and to some degree of uniformity of a "bounded" homogenous population, whether this is the case or not.

THE CHALLENGE OF "ORIENTALISM"

In all this discussion of public anthropology, and who is in this *public* as well as who is not in it, it is evidently important that Said's emphasis on knowledge as power in *Orientalism* (1979) be kept in the forefront of the discourse concerning the nature of public anthropology. For Said, there can be no knowledge that is separated from power. The ruling class in society tends also to have the dominant ideas, and therefore the foremost intellectual strength. It is also evident from Said's argument equating knowledge with power that academic discourse can be effectively directed against ruling elites and their privileged position in society, and, as such, knowledge is an effective tool of resistance, rather than a mechanism which legitimates the ruling classes' position (Barrett, 2002, pp. 68–70).

The manner in which we view "culture" is also changing in a way that demands a discussion concerning the nature of what is meant by public anthropology. A definition of culture today requires that anthropologists take into consideration the fact that views of non-Western perspectives are at least as legitimate in an epistemological sense as those of the dominant, centralized positions in the discipline. This centralized intellectual force is shifting, becoming more malleable, and more susceptible to less rigid conceptions. In other words, the concept of culture is becoming transformed into a more phenomenological force, away from the more inflexible stringencies of science.

There are those who would furthermore argue that the culture concept has been an instrument in sustaining the inequities of the relationship between Western and non-Western modes of thinking in anthropology. The culture concept, Whittaker (1992) suggests, "is the very epitome of othering. It depends for its existence on the subjective ordering of a world full of Others" (p. 113). Roger Keesing (1994) states this argument perhaps even more forcefully, suggesting that the so-called Other is such an essential or fundamental basis of anthropological understanding that if "radical alterity did not exist, it would be anthropology's project to invent it" (p. 301). Even the idea of relativism can be seen as culpable in the subjugation of "Others" in the sense that by promoting the notion of equality across what are perceived to be distinct cultural boundaries, the unequal power relationships between them become obscured in the process.

One of the possible ironies about the discourse of public anthropology, then, is that the culture concept, and its associated conceptual apparatus of relativism, may actually become associated with the very thing it is trying to replace. Abu-Lughod (1991), for example, suggests that "the culture concept retains some of the tendencies to freeze difference possessed by concepts like race" (p. 144). Kamala Visweswaran (1998), similarly, refers to "cultural racism" and suggests that the passing of the modern concept of culture should not be a cause for regret (pp. 65, 79).

The argument here is that even though the concept of culture was originally meant to replace racial attitudes about differences in human societies, it nonetheless—in the opinions of some, such as Michaels (1992)—has turned out to be a means by which racial thought is sustained rather than repudiated. One result of this contemporary discourse about culture is that "the landscapes of group identity—the ethnoscapes— around the world are no longer familiar anthropological objects, insofar as groups are no longer tightly territorialized, spatially bounded, historically unselfconscious, or culturally homogenous" (Appadurai, 1991, p. 191). It is obvious also that whatever anthropologists may mean by the term "public anthropology," such a term must contend with a shifting forum of debate within the discipline about its basis and perhaps not so veritable concepts of culture and relativism.

THE PUBLIC ANTHROPOLOGIST AS A ROLE MODEL

Anthropologists keep creating dichotomies. There are those who would contrast the-oretical anthropology with its applied or practical applications. There are also dis-tinctions made between what goes on in the academic setting versus the activities of anthropologists in the public sphere. The problem is that creating such distinctions also creates walls of thought, and these walls of thought prevent one from traversing conceptual areas that would be useful for the types of work anthropologists could or should be doing.

Take for example the issue concerning the advocacy role, which is such an impor-tant dimension of modern anthropology. Often anthropologists conduct their field-work among people who have pressing social and economic problems. In such cases, anthropologists would like to help with these problems in some way but lack guide-lines for conducting such work. On the other hand, anthropologists receive abundant training in fieldwork methods, such as participant observation, conducting surveys and interviews, and similar data-gathering techniques.

What is lacking in the anthropological training manual are any sort of suggestions that could be used in a more "proactive" anthropology. Certainly, even though there are anthropologists who are interested in helping out in some manner with practical matters during the course of their fieldwork, which could aid the people who are the subjects of a field investigation, the details and problems that are involved in this sort of involvement have not been worked out in the discipline in any sort of systematic or rigorous manner.

When anthropologists wish to aid the local population in some fashion during their fieldwork, such incidents pose a professional as well as personal difficulty. Even though the anthropologist may wish to become engaged with certain issues, there is always the possibility that such involvement could have unintended results that may actually harm local people. In other words, there are serious ethical problems that could entail noncon-ventional involvement in local issues. The ethical and moral issues have to be taken seri-ously; much thought has to be given beforehand because of the very real possibility that, even though one is prepared to help, such aid might actually exacerbate a social problem by well-intentioned but ill-informed involvement on the researcher's part.

As one might expect, there are various opinions expressed by anthropologists con-cerning an advocacy role. There are those who would accept outright the legitimacy of anthropologists to become involved in local issues. Such involvement could actually aid in the gathering of more information than could be obtained otherwise, so there are academic considerations here as well.

If we accept this position, then there is also the need for a training process that would involve a study of the various accounts that other anthropologists have been involved in so that one might weigh the pros and cons of certain forms of activities as to whether or not they were successful in achieving their intended results. At present, the literature in anthropology has not dealt with involvement in troubling situations in any methodical manner, except for various articles published here and there on a wide variety of related topics.

In sum, anthropologists must be aware that they might possibly cause more harm than good when they jump into a controversial local problem. Their intentions may be good, but harm may come to local people nonetheless. The problem for the discipline has to do with the nature and extent of their participation in local affairs and the unexplored avenues that their actions could take.

Bronislaw Malinowski, for example, was one of the first to recognize this problem of involvement. He had familiarity with colonial administrations in the Western Pacific and Africa. On the basis of this experience, he wrote a paper in 1929 entitled "Practical Anthropology," in which he referred to nonconventional involvement in the field as an "anthropological no-man's land" (1929/1970, p. 13). However, he did suggest that anthropologists could be advisers to colonial administrators when the local Indigenous populations were undergoing disastrous or devastating changes as a result of contact with the outside world.

When anthropologists venture out of their professional academic settings and adopt new roles that they are likely to enact as a result, this can also lead them into the midst of controversy among the local population. For instance, there could be competing factions in the local community and the anthropologist might be forced to choose sides. Sjoberg and Nett (1968) warned that "the social scientist may wield considerable power and authority, but in the negotiation process the combatants often try to co-opt him, each side seeking through a variety of means, overt and covert, to gain his support" (p. 90). Worse yet, such involvement may lead researchers into a situation where they become "the focus of hostility on the part of one or both factions" (p. 90).

Similarly, Rosalie Wax (1971), during a study of a Japanese-American relocation camp during World War II, found that "when groups are forced into confrontation each takes what it needs from the confrontation and does not perceive it in the same way even when both are moving toward a satisfactory rapprochement" (p. 52). In other words, there are numerous pitfalls that await the unwary anthropologists who are not prepared to take very seriously the possibility of becoming embroiled in local disputes that could ruin their original research program.

SOCIAL RESPONSIBILITY AND PUBLIC ANTHROPOLOGY

The issue for anthropology pertains to a notion of social responsibility. The enactment of new roles for anthropologists might make matters worse for local people because of their involvement. The field anthropologist may advise the local people to adopt a certain strategy but this may lead to antagonism with other nearby communities, or even with government officials who may regard the well-meaning anthropologist as a troublemaker who is usurping local control. What this means is that any type of advocacy work in anthropology could also involve a certain degree of conflict management.

Marx's (1981) research on Bedouin land expropriations in the Middle East examines the role of anthropologists as mediators. The idea here is that the role of the mediator, or ombudsman, occupies more neutral ground than the advocate. Without taking sides, which is implied in the advocate position, there is the possibility that the anthropologists could bring conflicting parties together, and thus benefit both participants in a dispute. The logic, then, behind the mediator role is that one attempts not to choose sides in inter-group conflicts.

The problem with taking sides in local disputes is that, as far as the anthropologist is concerned, some participants then become cast in the role of allies and others as adversaries. Thus, the anthropologist can become more of a problem creator than a problem solver. Divisions within the discipline are thus created in this manner. There are anthropologists who are strongly supportive of the advocacy role, believing that it is about time that they jumped off the conceptual fence and started taking a stance on certain moral and ethical issues. In modern anthropology, then, there is an ongoing process of discussion among anthropologists themselves concerning the direction that public anthropology should be taking, but whether or not a consensus is emerging around this topic is another matter altogether. However, even though there are debates among anthropologists themselves about their professional roles in the modern world, they are nevertheless bound by basic principles of social responsibility.

PUBLIC ANTHROPOLOGY DEBATED AMONG COLLEAGUES

To illustrate the divisions within the discipline on matters of involvement, Purcell (2000) discusses a panel dialogue on public anthropology that took place at the AAA annual meeting in Chicago in 1999. When questions were directed by students at the members of the panel, "what soon became evident was that the students were asking questions that indicated a strong desire to make anthropology relevant in ways that appeared to disturb the professional-'scientific' sensibilities of a few panelists" (Purcell, 2000, p. 31).

The implication of this comment is that there was an evident rift between the anthropology students and the more senior members of the panel on the matter of engagement by anthropologists. According to Purcell (2000), the reason that certain senior anthropologists were uncomfortable with a more engaged anthropology was because "anthropologists, especially the prominent ones, are too invested in their careers and their institutional values to assume a truly critical participatory stance" (p. 31).

In all fairness to the senior panel discussants, it is possible that their discomfort was a result of experiences in fieldwork in which anthropologists reacted to local situations without taking due consideration of the consequences of their actions. Marvin Harris, for example, was a member of this same panel and has counselled on exercising caution, echoing one of the old maxims that "fools jump in where wise men fear to tread." In Harris's case, he points out that "no consensus exists among anthropologists about how to resolve these different views of the proper relationship between knowledge and the achievement of controversial practical goals. Perhaps the only resolution of this dilemma is the one that now exists: We must search our individual consciences and act accordingly" (Harris, 1991, p. 355).

It would appear that "searching our individual consciences" does not provide a very strong disciplinary guideline that could be used to instruct anthropologists on their new roles as public anthropologists. Surely what is needed are a set of policies that are similar to the ethical statements released by such organizations as the American Anthropological Association or the Canadian Anthropology Society. Lacking such guidelines, it would be advisable that certain publications in anthropology, such as *Current Anthropology* with its discussion sections, produce special issues with a stated goal of examining appropriate public roles for contemporary anthropologists.

At present, there are certainly many articles on the subject of "non-conventional" role-playing by anthropologists going back to at least the 1970s, but this literature is scattered over many publications and topics. It is beyond the scope of this chapter to review this literature further in any systematic manner; however, such a project would certainly be a useful addition to anthropology's body of knowledge. As it now stands, each anthropologist goes about their business in the area of public anthropology on a more or less ad hoc basis using common sense and "individual consciences," to use Harris's term. The result is a discipline pretty much in disarray when it comes to modern role playing which is relatively isolated from other anthropologists conducting their affairs in somewhat the same fashion.

ANTI-PUBLIC ANTHROPOLOGY

Another member of the discussion panel mentioned above is Robert Borofsky, who is considered a leading figure in the public anthropology discourse. He has expressed concern that anthropologists are building a wall around themselves in recent years. As Borofsky (1996) explains, "Anthropologists have tended to turn in on themselves, to direct their conversations primarily toward other anthropologists. They now rarely engage in extended discussions, as public intellectuals, with those beyond the walls of academia" (p. 6). It is also pointed out by Borofsky that anthropologists do exhort their peers to reach out to others beyond their disciplinary boundaries, but there would appear to be some resistance in doing this.

There could conceivably be any number of valid reasons that would underlay an opposition to an engagement in public anthropology. In general terms, these reasons fall into two broad categories: conceptual and practical. Conceptual reasons would be those that are seen by some anthropologists as contradicting the basic fundamental principles of anthropological research and theory. For example, some anthropologists may suggest that public anthropology runs counter to the principles of objectivity, based on the concept of cultural relativism. Practical reasons could mean that engagement in public anthropology involves too many pitfalls, such as advocates choosing sides in various disputes, and as such alienating those on the other side.

The objections voiced by Merrill Singer (2000) in his article entitled "Why I am not a Public Anthropologist," fall into this latter, practical category of objections. According to Singer (2000), at least half of all new anthropology PhDs, and almost all MAs, find permanent employment outside the academic areas of universities and colleges. He then suggests that applied anthropologists are becoming "an underclass of laboring grunts who sell their labor on the open market for immediate application" (p. 6).

Public anthropology, Singer (2000) suggests, has become a label for what some academic anthropologists do as a part-time activity. Therefore, "given that many applied anthropologists already do the kinds of things that are now being described as PA, it is hard to understand why a new label is needed, except as a device for distancing public anthropologists from applied anthropology" (p. 6). He suggests further that this perceived schism in the anthropological ranks is responsible for Borofsky's comment that "anthropology has turned in on itself" (Borofsky, 1999, p. 9).

This portrayal of contemporary anthropology may be an accurate description of some sectors of academia, but does it "even remotely describe the work of the growing number of applied/practicing anthropologists who earn their keep outside the academy?" (Singer, 2000, p. 6). The basic argument, then, is that while some anthropologists brand public anthropology as something entirely new to the discipline, and therefore presumably divorced in some manner from the decades of other applied activities that came before, there is a danger of the creation of a "two-tier" system. In the upper "tier" are the mostly academic intellectuals who foray into applied anthropology on a sporadic manner when they perceive that to do so would benefit their careers. In the lower "tier" are those applied anthropologists who are mostly employed outside academic settings, who are not given the same recognition and are largely outside of the media spotlight.

Some of this resistance also stems from uncertainty about whether or not anthropologists should engage in the role of public intellectuals generally. There is also concern specifically about the role of anthropologists performing in the capacity of advocates for various political and social causes, all of which has generated a degree of discussion in the literature. The desire to "help out in some way" may stem from humanitarian impulses or even from moral compulsion. Advocacy, however, implies the pursuit of only one interest and is therefore at odds with an objective or neutral free pursuit of knowledge.

Members of the Society of Applied Anthropology in Canada (SAAC) considered the anti-advocacy position in its newsletter, *Proactive*. Commenting on the position of Hastrup and Elsass (1990) who hold to the anti-advocacy position, Ervin (1990) suggests that "their conclusions seem equally patronizing [and] I find their points of view basically irrelevant to applied anthropology. First of all they didn't indicate whether they actually participated in the advocacy exercise or not, although one would be led to believe that they did not" (p. 24). Ervin comments further that he finds their view of applied anthropology "very superficial," probably because they apparently lack previous experience in this field or in dealing with the practical issues that they so negatively commented on.

BASIC VERSUS APPLIED ANTHROPOLOGY

What is laid bare in this debate is an apparent rift that has developed in anthropology between what one might term "basic" anthropology and its "applied" counterpart. This whole issue about the so-called basic versus applied aspects of anthropology is in need of clarification. One position could be that applied anthropology is not really even part of social or cultural anthropology at all because it is too goal oriented, whereas basic or "traditional" research does not pursue goals other than academic or intellectual ones.

The position of many applied anthropologists is that it is long overdue that the discipline should become more accountable for the research dollars that are spent on what some would regard as esoteric or even frivolous intellectual goals. The problem, as Ervin (1990) explains, is that the result of traditional anthropology "lies gathering dust in libraries and is too arcanely constructed and inadequately framed, theoretically and methodologically, to deal with public policy issues" (p. 25).

Further antagonism between the two apparent divisions in anthropology could result from the perception among applied anthropologists that the "traditionalists" could be accused of meddling in issues that they do not understand. There is also the possible perception that those engaged in basic anthropology lack any sort of commitment to applied research, and as a result should refrain from acting as if they are expert enough to counsel others on whether or not advocacy or other forms of public anthropology are an appropriate role model. However, "a public anthropology, based as it should be on the interplay of theory and practice, questions the dichotomy between the applied and the theoretical, and it does this not only on philosophical but also on moral grounds" (Purcell, 2000, p. 32). What is posed, then, is a question about the moral justification for a discipline, such as anthropology, whose activities are restricted only to academic settings.

However this debate should be resolved, it is hoped of course that the long-standing merits of social/cultural anthropology will remain intact. For example, a holistic perspective has served the discipline in a favourable manner for most of its history. When anthropologists are studying matters of human rights or cultural diversity in a broad sense, the ability to examine topics from a diversity of points of view remains an ongoing strength. As one anthropologist noted when commenting on the usefulness of anthropology, "It is through holistic analysis that we are able to provide ethnic groups with models, which they can in turn use to inform their perception of their own situation and their relations with other ethnic groups and the state" (Henriksen, 1985, p. 120). In other words, whichever path anthropology is to take in the future, it should do so by building on the merits and strengths that have served it so well for most of its long history.

IRISH ANTHROPOLOGY AND THE PUBLIC ARENA: A CASE STUDY

The discussion thus far in this chapter about public anthropology and the concerns about different roles for anthropologists has been framed in a fairly general manner. In the following focus on Irish anthropology, we can see how the views of an anthropologist can result in discord during fieldwork. In the case now discussed, the Irish people who were the objects of ethnography took exception to the manner in which they were portrayed in publications emanating from the fieldwork. As such, this case illustrates possible conflicts between anthropologists and informants as to the manner of the latter's portrayal, especially when the results of the field study emerge into the public arena.

There could be any number of reasons for this present debate in anthropology about public anthropology and the possible effects on local people. It could be that anthropologists are unclear about what sort of role they could play, and therefore are hesitant to proceed into what would seem like uncharted territory in which the unintended consequences of their activities remains unclear. As mentioned previously, there is furthermore a certain degree of uncertainty about how anthropologists might effectively speak to broader audiences. According to Borofsky (1999), a central questions remains:

"Are anthropologists willing to move out of their present comfort zones of compla-
cency to actively engage the very publics they continually feel should engage them?"
(p. 6).

This is no doubt a good question, and one that would profit from more discussion when pursuing new activities, but there could also be uncertainty about
whether their advice would be valued or acknowledged outside of university settings. There are also dangers and unexpected pitfalls as research in rural Ireland has
so amply illustrated in the following case study. This is an exemplary case in which
an anthropologist was highly criticized for views that were brought into the public
realm.

THE CONTROVERSY

This case involves that of Nancy Scheper-Hughes (2001) and her research on mental
illness in rural Ireland. Wilson and Donnan (2006, pp. 46–47, 171–72) provide an
extended discussion of this issue in their overview of *The Anthropology of Ireland*. As
they explain, Scheper-Hughes "returned to the site of her original Irish fieldwork, to
meet, perhaps even confront ... her former hosts, some of whom felt betrayed and sad-
dened by her portrait of them" (p. 34).

In her original research in County Kerry, Scheper-Hughes suggests that mental illness in rural Ireland is exacerbated by sexual norms associated with high incidences
of celibacy and late marriage. This characterization brought on a heated debate in the
Irish national press and an outcry of discontent from the local Irish residents themselves. Apparently, Scheper-Hughes (1987, p. 73) was surprised by this outcry. From
the Irish perspective, local residents resented the intimate portrayal of the sexual
norms of people in rural Ireland. Furthermore, this research into family life in County
Kerry "revealed a lovelessness and lack of warmth in personal relationships and
an ambivalence towards intimacy composed of both longing and fear" (Wilson &
Donnan, 2006, p. 47).

As far as the wider picture in anthropology is concerned, such imbroglios pose a
difficulty for anthropologists who are tempted to embrace controversial subjects in
the public arena. In the Irish case, there were issues raised about ethical propriety.
This anthropological study was the source of a long-standing debate in both academic and media spheres over anthropological portrayals of community residents
in which their privacy was apparently invaded. A reviewer of *Saints, Scholars, and
Schizophrenics*, Sidney Callahan, suggested that Scheper-Hughes showed a callous
disregard for the concerns of her local informants and only protected her own self-
interests, and in the end "plowed on and probably got her doctorate out of it and was

FIGURE 2.2 "Ballybran," where Scheper-Hughes completed her study, is a small, rural community in Ireland
Source: Photo by Terry Ballard. Licensed under the terms of CC-BY 2.0

awarded a new research grant" (as cited in Wilson & Donnan, 2006, p. 170). Callahan also wryly concludes that "after the English there's still the problem of the invading social scientist."

ATTEMPTS AT RECONCILIATION

In 1999, Scheper-Hughes returned to the site of her original doctoral research in southwest Ireland, 20 years after the publication of her original ethnography. Her goal apparently was to attempt reconciliation with village members, and to resolve some of her perceived responsibilities, as a scholar on the one hand and as a community guest on the other.

As far as the local residents of Ballybran (a pseudonym) were concerned, they took exception to the central argument of Scheper-Hughes's book, in which the rural Irish are portrayed, in the words of reviewer Graham McFarlane, as "a self-denying, nearly puritanical, ascetic strain of Irish Catholicism [which] was creating mutual hostility between the sexes, repressing sexuality, and subverting warm maternal behaviour" (as cited in Wilson & Donnan, 2006, p. 170). The villagers' response to Scheper-Hughes's overture of reconciliation was not that she might have hoped for, because she was all but shunned and expelled from Ballybran.

LESSONS FOR PUBLIC ANTHROPOLOGY

There are lessons here for anthropologists wishing to engage in controversial public issues. First, in the Scheper-Hughes case, the villagers' response was probably predictable given the sensitivity in Ireland concerning issues relating to mental health, supposed suppressed sexuality, and what could be perceived as attacks on the Catholic Church. Such a situation could, in turn, be perceived as an attack on the very basis of Irish culture and society.

Second, any attempt to speak "the truth about Irish society" could also not be favourably received when such an assessment is delivered by scholars outside the country. "Yet most of these topics [folk Catholicism, sexual repression, or impression management meant to fulfill the expectations of tourists]," according to John Messenger (1989), another anthropologist who has experience in such matters, "among others equally controversial, have graced the plots of novels, plays, and short stories by Irish writers" (p. 124).

In other words, it is not the perceived criticism itself that is the point of concern, but its source. The wider lesson, then, is that it is acceptable for anthropologists to engage in controversial topics, but a great deal of sensitivity should be exercised in the manner in which such topics are published in the literature. Every community has its problems, but generally people do not wish to have these widely advertised or discussed. The Irish response to Scheper-Hughes "reflects the manner in which the research results were received as negative images by the people in the communities that offered their hospitality to these ethnographers so many years ago" (Wilson & Donnan 2006, pp. 171–72).

In sum, this case study of Irish ethnography, and the negative results as perceived by the local population, suggests that a much greater interaction between the ethnographer and the informants in the study would have led to more favourable results. Hindsight at times can be wonderfully constructive, and in this case it is evident that a greater collaboration between the ethnographer and the local people could have resulted in a portrayal of the Irish population that was acceptable to both the anthropologists and the village residents. Anthropologists often encounter significant difficulty in reconciling the need for honest reporting of their fieldwork perceptions while maintaining respect for the local people who share their lives, secrets, and inner thoughts.

COLLABORATIVE ETHNOGRAPHY
AND PUBLIC ANTHROPOLOGY

All of the difficulties discussed so far suggest that anthropologists could profit from building some bridges, both with the subjects of their research and the public at large. The designation of the "Other," which has tended to marginalize non-Western peoples, and the antagonistic portrayals of local peoples, are hardly strategies conducive to engendering support for the discipline.

In order to counteract some of the divisive effects occurring in contemporary anthropology, Luke Lassiter (2005) has suggested that "collaborative ethnography— the collaboration of researchers and subjects in the production of ethnographic texts—offers us a powerful way to engage the public with anthropology" (p. 83). Seen in a larger historical context, Lassiter's suggestion builds on a renewed emphasis to direct anthropological efforts toward increasing anthropology's relevance to wider publics. It also builds on previous efforts that call for a redirection or reinvention of the discipline along the lines suggested previously by such hallmark studies in anthropology as Sanday's (1976) *Anthropology and the Public Interest*, Hymes's (1969) *Reinventing Anthropology*, or the previously mentioned call by Peacock (1997) to "change our priorities and hence our work" (p. 9).

Dell Hymes's (1969) suggestion, even though it was written in the 1960s, sounds particularly modern: "The issue is ... between a bureaucratic general anthropology, whose latent function is the protection of academic comfort and privilege, and a personal general anthropology, whose function is the advancement of knowledge and the welfare of mankind" (p. 47). It is evident, then, that even as far back as the 1960s anthropologists have struggled with redirecting the discipline along one vision or another, or in reconciling its various applied, public, and academic components.

In addition, there has historically developed a rift between the type of anthropology practiced in colleges and universities, and that which is practiced outside of these settings. Reconciliation of these diverse trends would seem to be a practical necessity of survival, given anthropology's small university component compared to other allied disciplines such as sociology, history, or economics. If resources in the form of research grants or publication subventions are apt to flow to the more powerful interests, then further fragmentation of anthropology, which is a discipline that has long been divided along cultural, physical, linguistic, or archaeological lines in any event, would appear to further reduce prospects for survival in these challenging economic times of rationality and accountability.

Any attempt that would serve to pull together some of these divergent tendencies should therefore be worthy of discussion and further consideration. The task ahead is not an easy one, given the trends pulling apart the discipline in different directions. As Lassiter (2005) explains, "The larger problem remains the integration of theory and practice, research and training, the joining of academic and applied anthropologists, uninhibited by hegemony, in a common project, and the engagement of anthropologists with wider publics within and outside of academia" (p. 84).

Surely this large-scale integration project poses a daunting task for anthropologists. How can Lassiter's call for "collaborative ethnography" ever hope to resolve such a myriad of issues on such an immense scale? The starting point for such a discussion could be the recognition that collaborative efforts are at the centre of what anthropologists do in social and cultural settings. This could be the more conventional role of a single anthropologist as a field-worker gathering information through the use of participant observation or various other interviewing techniques. Alternatively, a group of anthropologists could join together in pooling their efforts and tasks, as described by Stull and Schensul (1987) or Salzman (1986), which demonstrates that the team approach to fieldwork has a lengthy history in the discipline. However, collaborative research with research subjects is a more recent phenomenon.

FIELDWORK RELATIONSHIPS UNDER STRESS: THE GITKSAN CASE

What could be called "traditional role performance" in anthropological research has changed dramatically over the last several decades. Long gone are the days when ethnographers called all the shots in research, and published whatever they felt like. The subjects of research now demand a much greater say in how research is conducted. They may even ask for a share of royalties in book revenues, and almost certainly will want to scrutinize any publications before they actually appear in print. The issue of who—anthropologists or local residents—controls the research agenda adds a political dimension to the already uncertain economic and social ones. Where this is all going in the future is a matter of some uncertainty. However, what can be said with a degree of confidence is that new relationships during the course of fieldwork are evolving on a continuing basis even as they are placed under stress by the changing environments of research.

What is different today from previous eras in anthropology, then, is that local residents are expressing a desire to become much more actively involved in what is said about them in professional books and journals. They are particularly concerned about the images that are portrayed, as the Irish case aptly illustrates, and the possible benefits that anthropological research might bring to their community. In other words, local residents are looking at ways to enhance and promote their own interests. Who can blame them? Their time and knowledge are commodities that must be worth something, otherwise the anthropologists would not be interested in them, one would presume.

In today's world, it is expected that an anthropologist wishing to conduct a study in a particular community will approach the local leadership body with a research agenda that outlines such possible areas as the information that will be requested of local residents and how this data might be used. Local leaders will also be interested in the possible benefits of this research to their community. A partnership is therefore formed and the research discussed at length so that each party has a concrete expectation of what is involved.

Some anthropologists may be wary of these new relationships that are evolving in the field, concerned that they are losing their traditional position of ascendency. Nonetheless, there are advantages as well to loosening up the reins of control and allowing local residents more influence in how research is conducted. One of the most obvious benefits is that community members could feel more involved, and not just like bystanders as they used to be, in the progress of anthropological fieldwork. Under the new research circumstances, it is possible that local people may wish to participate to a greater degree than before, although such a change may encroach on the autonomy that the researcher previously enjoyed.

Shattered Images

All of these issues of research in new environments of participation are particularly illustrated in John Cove's (1987) book *Shattered Images*. His research among the Gitksan, a branch of the Tsimshian of British Columbia, illustrates how anthropologists can profitably engage in collaborative efforts during fieldwork. Cove was originally interested in conducting research into traditional Northwest Coast salmon fishing in order to test several hypotheses he entertained about the ecological influences on the potlatch. This research was supported by a grant from the National Museum of Man, now the Canadian Museum of Civilization. However, the Gitksan-Tsimshian Tribal Council did not allow Cove permission to conduct this research. "The grounds" for this refusal, he explained, "were the irrelevancy of my topic to the needs of the people, and questions of insufficient native control over data and reporting" (p. 3).

The leaders of the tribal council suggested that Cove could be allowed to conduct research in their community if he would agree to a number of conditions. One of these conditions was that the focus of the research be changed so that local land claims, a prominent political issue of concern to the tribal council, become a major point of the investigation. The tribal council also suggested that he relinquish his museum grant, thus severing possible influences on the research by the curators of this institution. Alternatively, it was indicated, the community itself would support his newly conceived research by providing housing, subsistence, and information.

In all, Cove's research among the Gitksan-Tsimshian continued for another eight years, much more than the usual 12 months or less of conventional fieldwork. He expressed concern initially with the personal commitment that such an extended research project on land claims demanded, yet it nonetheless served to "strip away layers of rationalization [such that] much of my ambivalence about being relevant began to make sense" (1987, p. 4).

The value of anthropological research in the case of the Gitksan-Tsimshian land claim was furthermore the subject of an article in the *Vancouver Sun*, where it was noted that "historians usually deal with dusty documents and dead people. They seldom have the opportunity to eat, talk and joke with the warm, sweaty, fallible but always wonderful human beings who are the anthropologists' subjects. It's a dangerous practice, getting close to people—one that could cloud your judgement" (*Vancouver Sun*, 22 March 1991, cited in Hume, 1991, p. 31).

MUTUALLY BENEFICIAL RELATIONSHIPS

In the case of Cove's land claims research among the First Nations of British Columbia, a mutually beneficial relationship was therefore developed. While, as we have indicated, some in the discipline may feel that scientific objectivity may be compromised, anthropology needs to adapt to these new realities of collaborative research, or become extinct, as Peacock warned. Attempts to cling to the previous asymmetrical relationships between anthropologists and their informant hosts only serve to retard the development of the discipline into a more credible area of study. This previous relationship may have benefited the anthropologist to an immeasurable degree in the past, especially in terms of career advancement, but little was returned to the local community in exchange.

Collaborative ethnography is therefore a possible way to engage anthropology with informants in the field and also with the public at large. As Lassiter (2005) concludes, "Engaging the publics with which we work in our ethnographic research and writing necessarily cast ethnography as a public act" (p. 96). The most beneficial aspect of the integration of ethnographic approaches with collaboration is that the research process could possibly result in a broader commitment in the relationship between the people who are the subjects of research and the investigators. This sort of situation is illustrated by Cove's experience among the Gitksan-Tsimshian. A greater sense of collaboration engenders among the people with whom the anthropologist works feelings that the results of a research project also belongs to them and could possibly benefit or improve their lives in some manner. In the Gitksan-Tsimshian case, a successful land claims result in the British Columbia courts, aided in large measure by the collaborative efforts involved in Cove's ethno-historical research, ultimately benefited the local community by securing title to a large tract of property that was previously not in the First Nations' control. In other words, collaborative ethnographic research in the Tsimshian case illustrates the convergence of applied anthropology with an engaged, public focus.

ANTHROPOLOGY AND PUBLIC POLICY

There is little doubt that many of the issues that anthropologists are concerned with during the course of their fieldwork are also issues of importance in the area of public policy. As Wedel, Shore, Feldman, and Lathrop (2005) indicate, "Anthropologists have been long engaged in research that implicitly deals with public policy, for issues that pertain directly to policy lie at the heart of anthropology" (p. 30). These issues, as Shore and Wright (1997) further indicate, include such areas of investigation as institutions and power, the politics of culture, ethnicity and identity, and interactions between global processes and local communities. Public policies emanate from a variety of sources, such as a multiplicity of governmental levels (municipal, provincial, national, and so on), business organizations, nongovernmental organizations (NGOs), private individuals, or various combinations of these.

Public policy plays a crucial role in the shaping of society because it connects available resources with the participants in the complex relationships of power and decision making. Many anthropologists may not realize how central these public policy processes are to their own research, and therefore may miss an opportunity to engage in public debates concerning their ethnographic interests. For example, Basch and the other contributors to *Transforming Academia: Challenges and Opportunities for an Engaged Anthropology* (1999) refer "to the anticipation of changes that will affect anthropology and to developing strategies to deal with them proactively and intentionally, rather than waiting to react" (p. 291).

This suggestion of acting proactively and developing strategies in the arena of public policy is fine if there are suggestions as to the manner in which such goals could be accomplished. Yet, as T. Weaver (1985) indicated years ago, "Anthropologists appear to be confused about the use of anthropology in public policy" (p. 97). Similarly, Hinshaw (1980) concludes that "anthropologists have not had significant, visible impact on policy formation in any major domestic or international policy area" (p. 516). In addition, Cyril Belshaw, in his seminal study *The Sorcerer's Apprentice: An Anthropology of Public Policy* (1976), offers the suggestion that anthropological relevance could be enhanced if colonial processes would be a focus of study because the discipline developed along with colonialism, at least among British social anthropologists. Anthropologists, because of their local-level research, are in an advantageous position to study how social identities are constructed, and how nationalistic processes are developed from the ground up.

Many anthropologists, however, feel inhibited about extending their fieldwork into the public domain because of a sort of academic self-consciousness. As such, the very idea of "policy" in anthropology is problematic for some because of the possibility that Western-derived values and biases could be transferred, even unwittingly, to solutions posed by the problems in other societies or countries. A fundamental commitment in the discipline to cultural relativism is also an inhibiting factor because it encourages an approach which is non-directive and non-judgmental in perspective.

FIELDWORK AND PUBLIC POLICY

Anthropologists are in an advantageous position to comment on wider policy issues that affect local communities because of their fieldwork involving participant observation, which serves to provide information concerning the problems experienced by the residents of local communities on a firsthand basis. Thus, on the one hand, anthropology has a fundamental philosophical basis, which tends to possibly deter a wider involvement beyond the local level, but on the other hand, the discipline also has a corresponding commitment to wider cross-cultural comparisons, which places its members in an expedient position to comment on policy issues.

It could be suggested, then, that this emphasis on cultural comparisons, which promotes more far-reaching perspectives as opposed to the more circumscribed or introspective viewpoint of participant observation, is an avenue or a way out of the current anthropological malaise concerning public policy. In order to engage in these more far-reaching perspectives, anthropologists need to curtail their self-consciousness about speaking out, about being noticed in the crowd, which includes administrators, development economists, political scientists, and government personnel. The members of other disciplines are far less inhibited about commenting on social and political issues, but anthropologists have the right to speak out as well.

Erve Chambers (1985) once suggested a way to achieve a philosophical shift in the discipline so that the idea of policy becomes more palatable. "The word *policy*," he explains, "is a lot like the word *culture*. It can mean almost anything, practically nothing, or it can be operationalized to mean something very particular. [Generally], the policy idea represents those intentions which can be associated with deliberate action in any sphere of human activity" (p. 38). Thus, if we can begin to see policy in much the same context as culture, then this resituates the somewhat enigmatic aspects of policy back onto more familiar turf for the anthropologist. By following this conceptual route, we can imagine policy as a concept that is analogous to other areas of social organization that are familiar aspects of ethnography, such as marriage, kinship, or politics.

The starting point for an anthropological understanding of policy could therefore begin with a loosening up of our perspectives on conventional concepts so that they could accommodate a wider range of culturally derived content. Through such a process of conceptual "shape-shifting" a concept such as policy, then, could become a more conventional one to examine and scrutinize in the discipline in much the same manner that a whole host of other concepts are handled. The starting point is the realization that any action has its consequences, affecting many people or just a few of them, and in this manner we might begin to anticipate the eventual outcome of this action. Chambers (1985) referred to something along similar lines of thought as "the intentionality of human activity" (p. 38), suggesting as such that notions of intent are what eventually becomes policy.

From an anthropological perspective the idea of policy then becomes a study of human intentions and outcomes and the specific social and cultural characteristics in which they are situated. It matters little in the long run whether these intentions seem to proceed along a coherent line of thought and action, or whether they are precisely formulated or vague; what matters is that a start is made to study policy *as a process*, as interconnected patterns of human behaviour. This is the very sort of research that anthropologists are particularly qualified to handle. When we consider policy in the context of forms of human interaction, it also means that it can be viewed as a matter of human competition such that debate takes place over alternative courses of action and competing points of view.

In summary, anthropologists can therefore play a role in attempting to make intelligible these various points of view about public policy, and then translating them to a wider audience or a wider stream of change. This process of translation is contingent upon anthropological skills at understanding local idioms through fieldwork, and therefore serving to understand the discourse taking place in local communities concerning the characteristics of particular policies. It would not be unusual for traditional societies to participate in intense debates over policy matters, especially when such societies are undergoing rapid social change. Anthropologists situated "on the ground" are in a position to study such policy debates and to assess the outcomes of particular points of view as a matter of conflicting human intentions and consensus formation.

POWER ELITES AND PUBLIC ANTHROPOLOGY

This focus of studying the processes of policy formation at the local level can then be combined with Laura Nader's (1974) well-known suggestion that anthropologists would benefit from "studying up." Nader's proposal is that anthropologists should analyze powerful institutions and elites in complex societies, a focus which would act as a counterbalance to the traditional approach in anthropology of studying people in poor, marginalized societies. As she suggests, "A reinvented anthropology should study powerful institutions and bureaucratic organizations in the United States, for such institutions and their network systems affect our lives and also affect the lives of people that anthropologists have traditionally studied all around the world" (1974, pp. 292–93).

This proposal is therefore a compelling argument for "reinventing" anthropology from studying the destitute and downtrodden to focusing anthropological research on the power centres of society. There are however important reasons why anthropologists have had difficulty in studying power elites in the past. For one thing, those inhabiting centres of power in a society are much better able to shield themselves from public scrutiny than the poorer members of a society whose lives are often more accessible to the sorts of inquiries that anthropologists typically conduct. Despite Nader's (1974) argument that "There is certain urgency to the kind of anthropology that is concerned with power (p. 292)," it is necessary that anthropologists find new avenues of accessibility into the positions inhabited by power elites if public anthropology is to become more relevant than it presently is to the study of modern social issues.

Aside from issues of accessibility, there are practical financial or economic issues to consider as well. Typically the funding for research grants in anthropology emanates from the very centres of power in society—government agencies, or private corporations—that Nader urges anthropologists to investigate. Presumably these centres of power are willing to fund social scientific research because some value adheres to this type of activity.

Why, then, would those in the power elites want to have their own lives scrutinized using their own money? Surely the grants they provide are issued so that information could be gathered which is of use to government administrators or corporate executives for their own purposes. This is not to suggest that securing research grants is all a matter of manipulation and control, but certainly the more that is known about a particular group in society, the more these people are placed in vulnerable positions. In this sense of anthropological research serving to isolate certain sectors of society for special attention, Wedel et al. (2005) observe that "empirical and ethnographic methods can show how policies actively create new categories of individuals to be governed" (p. 30).

ETHICS IN THE PUBLIC DOMAIN

As far as anthropological research into the public domain is concerned, there are certainly also important ethical issues that need to be addressed. Anthropologists have certain responsibilities toward the subjects of their research, so that they are not placed in vulnerable positions of manipulation as a result of research activities.

It is entirely possible, for example, that conflicts of interest exist between the subjects of a study and the institutions, groups, or organizations that provide the funding for such research. Of course anthropologists can hardly be held responsible for all the possible uses of their information collected during field studies, yet they nonetheless cannot also be oblivious to this issue. Conflicts of interest could emerge when the sponsors of research feel that they should be in a position to decide on how the results of studies should be used because they are the ones paying for the expenses of collecting the data in the first place.

There is much more that could be discussed in this chapter on the topic of research in public anthropology. Many anthropologists today are studying contemporary global processes, militarism and national security, climate change, industrial disasters, human rights, and public health issues. The pronouncement is that anthropology is on "the threshold of a new era," and "we are on the brink of a new anthropology," as Checker (2009, pp. 167–68) optimistically asserts. We will need to await future assessments of anthropology's contemporary engagement in public issues before we can judge the validity of such confident pronouncements.

CONCLUSION

It is not possible unfortunately to provide a clear, entirely unambiguous definition of "public anthropology." Most definitions are of a fairly general nature, such as Vine's (2011) characterization of anthropologists "attempting to engage with and serve the needs of public audiences outside academia" (p. 336). Despite attempts by a number of scholars, the term remains somewhat obscure as to its meaning and applications. About the best that could be said is that public anthropology refers to the application of anthropological knowledge, techniques, and epistemology beyond university and college settings to the public domain. The deficiency in this definition is that it includes the very terms that it seeks to define. We are left, therefore, with a somewhat vague reference point, but no one has ever claimed anthropology is or should be an exact science.

Anthropologists cannot be held responsible for having only an imprecise definition of public anthropology, in the same way that one might define an electron, or entropy, because the field is an evolving one. There just has not been enough discussion in the discipline yet to come to some general agreement about what public anthropology is or is not. There again, if we can have several different hundred possible definitions of culture, then some variability in defining public anthropology should not bother anyone. Arguably, this is the very point of this chapter—that what we might refer to as public anthropology is a contested ground, possibly emerging more clearly in its own time and space in the future.

Despite these various caveats there would appear to be some consensus in the discipline that public anthropology is a variety of applied anthropology aimed at addressing issues outside the academic setting or outside what could be termed "traditional" or "conventional" anthropological research. The aim is to use the various concepts, techniques, and epistemologies developed in anthropology to examine or possibly solve human social issues in the public domain.

In this case, the term "social" would have a wide interpretation to include the cultural, economic, political, or other characteristics of human societies that anthropologists would deal with through the course of their research. In this sense, it is not so much what public anthropology is that counts, but what anthropologists do that matters. In other words, this is a term that can be best defined by the research activities that occur under its rubric, as opposed to some objective criteria.

Chapter 3

RACE, SCIENCE, AND THE
PUBLIC FORUM

IN THE NEWS

In the news, the Associated Press (11 August 2014) reported that a candlelight vigil for a young unarmed black man who was fatally shot by a suburban St. Louis police officer was followed by the looting and burning of stores, vandalized vehicles, and confrontations with police officers who tried to block access to parts of the city. Nearly three dozen people were arrested after tensions erupted following the vigil for 18-year-old Michael Brown, who had been shot multiple times the day before in a scuffle with a police officer.

The press had also reported previously (18 July 2013) that Trayvon Martin's parents were shocked by the acquittal of George Zimmerman in the 2012 shooting death of their son at the Sandford, Florida, housing complex where the teenager was visiting his father. Martin's parents made several appearances on network morning news shows after a jury found Neighborhood Watch volunteer Zimmerman not guilty of second-degree murder. "I think if Trayvon had been white, this would never have happened," said Tracy Martin, father of the slain black teen.

In Canadian news (29 July 2014), the CBC reported that a fertility clinic in Calgary, Alberta, had apparently prohibited women from using sperm donors from a different race. No reason was given for this policy, if true, yet miscegenation attitudes about the adverse effects of the mixing of racial groups have a long history.

RACE AND PUBLIC ANTHROPOLOGY

Throughout the history of anthropology there has probably never been such an important topic of research and discussion for public anthropology as race. It is no doubt true that Franz Boas was a vociferous critic of race discrimination and intolerant attitudes toward minorities. Yet, historian Hamilton Cravens asks, "What's new in science and race since the 1930s?"(Cravens, 2010).

Such a rhetorical question is not meant to suggest that there has been a lack of progress in understanding the scientific dimensions of racism over the last 80 years or so. What Craven proposes is that science, race, and public policy have not been interconnected phenomena. Since the Civil Rights revolution of the 1960s, racial segregation in many areas of American life has diminished. In November 2008, voters elected the first ever African-American President of the United States, overturning an American political tradition. What Craven argues is that despite the outlawing of racial segregation, "This has not, however, led to extensive racial integration outside of public institutions. But government has been a prime mover of this new feature of American life" (2010, p. 299).

Today most people, at least in the scientific or academic sectors of society, would place little credence in the idea of racial determinism. It is stated, for example, that racial determinism is "obviously a flawed concept without a shred of scientific standing." In fact, as far as anthropology is concerned, the rejection of racial determinism within the discipline could be seen as an extremely pivotal point because "it very well may be that this was their greatest and most important contribution to their science" (Craven, 2010, p. 304).

The news stories reported at the beginning of this chapter are not necessarily pivotal points in America's history; the point is that the events described could have occurred in any recent day, month, or year because they provide such common evidence of a society fractured along racial lines. These situations are therefore immensely important for the emergence of public anthropology. While Boas and his colleagues initiated the attack on racial and cultural intolerant attitudes in their day, today's society appears as riddled with racial strife as it ever was.

Despite nearly a century of scientific research on the topic of race by anthropologists, the general public does not seem to be getting the message that we all belong to a single species of Homo sapiens and not to various sub-species or "races." As far as all scientific evidence is concerned, there is only one human race, which is now beyond doubt with the discovery of DNA and the subsequent mapping of the human genome which points to the emergence of modern people out of Africa some 50,000 years ago. So, if public anthropology is going to have any relevance in today's world, the scientific facts about "race" need to be more forcefully brought to the attention of people in contemporary society. Only in this manner might tolerance of those different from ourselves have a change of prevailing in the future.

ANYTHING NEW IN SCIENCE AND RACE?

To return to Cravens's question about what's new in science and race since the 1930s, one could point to the continuing interest in this subject in academic circles, such as

Farber and Cravens's edited collection entitled *Race and Science: Scientific Challenges to Racism in Modern America* (2009). This edited volume comprises contributions by a wide variety of scientists, including anthropologists, suggesting that anthropologists are indeed engaging with their colleagues about such an important topic in today's society.

There is also a certain measure of intellectual self-reflection expressed by several authors, even angst if one wishes to characterize such assessments in this manner. For example, Bair (2011), in a review suggests that "implicit in these essays are underlying questions of the moral authority of social science, its claims to rationality and empiricism, and the culpability, bias, and influence—for ill or good—of its practitioners" (p. 744). In fact, Farber and Cravens (2009) go so far as to argue that "science and its misuse had indeed been a large part of the problem of scientific racism by providing a strong intellectual foundation to legitimate racism" (p. 131). In other words, a grave matter of concern for academia is the evidence provided by such studies that chronicle the perpetuation of racism in the intellectual history of the social sciences (Marks 2012, pp. 46–47).

The purpose of this chapter is to explore the topic of race and science in historical perspective, and then to examine some of the means by which public anthropology could be used in attempts to inform the general public about anthropology's contributions to the study of human similarities and difference. In this manner, ideas that are taken for granted inside the walls of academia could be more widely shared beyond university settings into the public domain. Such an attempt at engaging in public anthropology could serve to diminish the mistrust of academia by those in the general public who would see intellectual debates as not serving any useful purpose to society.

THE REJECTION OF RACIAL DETERMINISM

The term "racial determinism" has been in wide circulation in anthropology since at least the 1960s (see Stocking, 1968, pp. 64–65, 251–52; Harris, 1968, pp. 80–107). Alternatively, the term "racial essentialism" is also found in the literature of other disciplines, with the meaning that "a person's character and conduct rests entirely on his or her racial identity" (Cravens, 2010, p. 299). It has been recognized outside the discipline that "what the anthropologists did was absolutely fundamental to the scientific basis for rejecting racial essentialism. The changes in public and governmental policy would have been unimaginable without such scientific validation" (Cravens, 2010, p. 301).

Anthropology has never been a stranger to issues of race. The eventual rejection of racial determinist ideas began to take place during its early history in the nineteenth century as a result of the evolutionists' proposals that cultural progress from primitive to civilized societies was based on biological characteristics.

Later, Franz Boas (1948) attempted to dissociate race from culture, arguing that these were separate entities, and that cultural innovations were not related to racial background.

Boas's attack on racial determinism was then also based on a fundamental criticism of the underpinnings of evolutionist ideologies. In addition, it is important to take note of the political and social climate of America during this period which was "the era of the passage of Jim Crow laws, racial segregation, and anti-black and anti-foreigner agitation" (Lewis, 2010, p. 453). However, Boas and his colleagues did help to "coax popular consciousness and public policy toward ideas of diversity, difference, and social construction that countered insidious arguments by antimiscegenationists and eugenicists" (Bair, 2011, p. 745).

BOX 3.1   Franz Boas (1858–1942): The First Public Anthropologist

If one is willing to accept a definition of public anthropology in which anthropologists use their scholarly research to contribute to the public good and make an attempt to influence modern public issues outside of academia, then a strong argument could be made that Boas was anthropology's first public anthropologist, at least in America. Certainly he was one of the first social scientists to directly challenge existing racist attitudes in America and to issue a plea for cultural tolerance.

One of the hallmarks of Boas's anthropology is a deeply felt commitment to an understanding of various social issues. In his many books and scientific papers, such as *Anthropology and Modern Life* (1928) and *Race, Language, and Culture* (1948), for example, Boas demonstrates his particular concern with issues of racial equality, tolerance of others, and human rights. He also wanted to prove his theories scientifically, rather than simply appealing to people's emotions or sense of social justice. It was this very striving for scientific accuracy that tended to separate the anthropology of Boas from that of his predecessors and provided the foundation for a new approach in anthropology in which conclusions were supported by concrete, firsthand observations and measurement, rather than ingrained social and racial prejudices. Thus, Boas "tapped his scholarly credentials to fight for good causes, such as civil rights and civil liberties.... His contributions to the discipline of anthropology were as towering as anyone has ever made" (Whitfield, 2010, p. 430).

FIGURE 3.1 Franz Boas
Source: National Anthropological Archives,
Smithsonian Institution, NEG MNH 8300

Boas's attack on racially intolerant attitudes was based in part on his aversion to classifying or pigeonholing people into different categories. Boas was against categorizing people into different racial groups because this made certain disadvantaged people a ready target for discrimination and prejudice. In this regard, Boas was a fervent believer in equal opportunity and equal rights for all people regardless of their physical characteristics. Boas used his anthropological research to demonstrate that the concept of race, as a stable set of physical characteristics, was not supported by scientific facts. He stated his attitude of individual and cultural tolerance quite early in his career: "The general theory of valuation of human activities, as developed by anthropological research, teaches us a higher tolerance than the one which we now profess" (Boas, 1911/1988, pp. 208–09).

Tolerance, though, has its limits, especially when confronted with the concept and practice of human rights. Although the emergence of Nazism occurred when Boas was in his mid-seventies and close to retirement (he retired from Columbia University in 1936 at age 78), he nonetheless felt obligated to engage in what he regarded as the rising menace of the Third Reich. Boas had spent a lifetime engaged in resistance to racism so he felt obligated to undertake a fight for democratic and liberal values. "I am ashamed to be a German," he proclaimed (as cited in Whitfield, 2010, p. 436). In 1936, *Time* put Boas on its cover—a testament to his public presence and intellectual statue in America.

Later in anthropology's history, Ashley Montagu (1942, 1963) referred to race as a "fallacy," and called it "man's most dangerous myth." As Barrett (1987) points out, "Attempts to define and rank the perceived racial types in terms of such physical criteria are both obsolete and meaningless" (p. 328). However, even if the concept of race makes little biological sense because people's conceptions are based on such a limited range of observable physical criteria (phenotypes) as skin colour, stature, or hair type, the concept nonetheless has validity as a social construct because people behave according to what they see and believe to be true, and not necessarily on what the scientific community believes to be the facts of the matter.

It would not be incorrect to say, then, that anthropology and conceptions of race have had intertwined histories, or even that anthropologists have had a complicit role in misrepresenting the concept of race in certain ways that are not scientifically valid. As Eugenia Shanklin (2000) makes clear, "We anthropologists have a lot of work to do to repair and strengthen our image—as critics of race and racism.... There are not enough accurate representations of anthropology and its practitioners to counter some of the bad press that we have attracted" (p. 102). This chapter, then, is a discussion of representations of race and racism in modern anthropology which is one of the discipline's core public issues.

REPRESENTATIONS OF RACE AND RACISM IN ANTHROPOLOGY

"The modern consensus concerning the relationship between race and culture," Harris (1968) asserts, "is that the rate and direction of culture change among the various infra-species groupings of Homo sapiens are not at present significantly affected by genetic specialities" (p. 131). Little has changed in the last 50 or so years in anthropology to seriously affect this pronouncement. The old debate concerning "nature versus culture," however, still continues in the form of socio-biological and culturally determinist views of human behaviour, neither side achieving a clear victory. Nonetheless, "The basic assumption in socio-cultural anthropology," as is generally understood today by members of the discipline, "is that the range of variation in human belief and behaviour cannot be explained or reduced to biology" (Barrett, 1996, p. 10).

CHALLENGES TO SOCIAL DARWINISM

This is not to suggest that what has been termed "biological determinism" or "social Darwinism" has been completely expunged from the anthropological record. It has been pointed out that "Social Darwinism was highly compatible with right wing politics and offered a convenient theory to justify capitalism and free enterprise and the rational for attacking government intercession, socialism and communism" (Sidky, 2004, p. 115). Since social Darwinism is a dogma that justifies all sorts of social agendas, such as white supremacy, slavery, colonialism, and genocide, it is therefore incompatible with most liberal philosophies. Yet, this philosophy is still adhered to by some, both within and without academic life, who harbour misanthropic beliefs used as a rational for discrimination and exploitation.

As far as the biology and culture issue is concerned, Boas played a leading role in attempting to purge anthropology of biological deterministic beliefs. He attacked biological determinism by marshalling a large body of ethnographic literature that demonstrated the degree to which the earlier evolutionists distorted Indigenous people's social and cultural accomplishments. It was these distortions, based on "armchair" data collection, that supported the belief in the superiority of Europeans and the ascendancy of their "civilized" culture.

Even the racial categories, in which the evolutionists assigned different human groups, were, in Boas's opinion, a further distortion of scientific reality. The racial category "contains so many individuals of different hereditary make-up that the average differences between races freed of elements determined by history cannot readily be ascertained, but appear as insignificant" (Boas, 1940, p. 248). Thus, because of Boas's extrication of culture from biological factors, there was only one explanation or causal determinant for human thought and behaviour left, and that was culture itself. Unfortunately, from a research perspective, this means that for "Boasian anthropology ... culture is beyond the domain of nature and not amenable to scientific analysis" (Sidky, 2004, p. 122).

CULTURE AND BIOLOGY

For much of anthropology's early history, then, there has been a furious battle between culture and biology. Victory has apparently gone to culture, celebrated from the Boasian period onward. As such, this victory has "been celebrated ever since as the hallmark of human existence," according to Barrett (1984): "We applaud the victory and rejoice in the flexibility of human social organization while reaffirming the basic mental identity of the world's variegated population, the realization that there are no superior societies, and the principles that the fundamental nature and capacity of the human brain is everywhere the same. But along the way we have failed to appreciate the degree to which racism continues to shape relationships among people" (p. 223).

As we happily applaud anthropology's role in ostensibly disentangling culture from its biological determinants, we are nonetheless left with a poignant modern issue— racism did not evaporate with culture's *apparent* victory over biology. Furthermore, it is difficult to point to truly significant works by anthropologists on racism in the post–World War II period, although the publications of Ashley Montagu (1942, 1963, 1980) could arguably fall into such a category. This situation contrasts with the vigorous dialogue on the subject of racism in the prewar period.

ASHLEY MONTAGU (1905–1999)

Ashley Montagu, a physical anthropologist by training, mounted a vociferous attack on the prevailing scientific views of race and the presumed biological determinants of human culture and behaviour. Montagu (1963) observed that race, up to the midpoint of the twentieth century, was the physical anthropologist's key concept. The primary reason for Montagu's intense dissatisfaction with the so-called scientific view of race (i.e., the "fallacy" and "dangerous myth" references) was that physical anthropologists, in his opinion, were misplacing their efforts by focusing on humans' observable biological characteristics (phenotypes) rather than on the more meaningful genes and chromosomes (genotypes). His argument was that if we focus on the genotypic characteristics of human beings, there is actually very little chromosomal variation from one human population to another, thus reducing the scientific importance of the concept of race.

Montagu's (1964) conclusion was a rather blunt condemnation of his discipline: "Race is, to a large extent, the special creation of the anthropologists" (p. 63). He further suggested that race is an entirely meaningless scientific concept which supported "a thoroughly exploitive period in the development of Western man" (1963, p. 3). While the emphasis in the study of human biology began to shift from phenotype to genotype, and to genetic drift and mutation, there were those in the scientific community, such as Brace (1964), who suggested that race was not even a significant biological concept in the genetic sense.

THE "DUAL-INHERITANCE" THEORY

Ashley Montagu can be credited with moving the discourse on race in anthropology away from the historical particularistic interpretations of the Boasians toward what has come to be known as the "dual-evolution" theory. Also known as the "dual-inheritance" theory, the argument underlying the dual-evolution approach is that a unified theory of human evolution required both biological and cultural approaches.

When racial determinist theories began to lose credibility after World War II, some anthropologists, such as Montagu, sought allies among the evolutionary biologists and human geneticists. From the 1960s onwards, several anthropologists and biologists moved to fuse their research into a multi-disciplinary effort in an attempt to develop evolutionary perspectives combining cultural and biological aspects. As an example of this new alliance, Theodosius Dobzhansky, a geneticist, and Montagu published a seminal paper in the prestigious journal *Science* (1947). The main suggestion of this article was that humans were the result of two processes of evolution: one biological, and the other cultural.

A combination of biology and anthropology served to undermine, to some extent at least, the particularistic and mentalist schools of anthropology, such as the culture and personality theorists that emerged after Boas, and bring evolution back into focus in the discipline. A revival of nomothetic approaches began to take place outside of biological perspectives as well. One example was George Murdock and his cross-cultural comparisons, which allowed for the study of cultural evolution, under the guise of "human development," and the suggestion that certain "laws" guided changes in many different societies.

RACE AND SOCIO-BIOLOGY

Biological approaches continued to gain strength in later decades as attempts to provide biological explanations for cultural phenomena emerged with the theoretical orientation of socio-biology (i.e., Wilson, 1978) which Barrett (1987), correctly or not, has referred to as one of "the latest fads in scientific racism" (p. 329). Scientific racism utilizes what are regarded (by some) as scientific "facts" in an attempt to demonstrate that certain human populations are essentially inferior to others because of such characteristics as low intelligence, exemplified by eugenicist Arthur Jensen's (1969) claim that whites are an advanced, intellectually superior race. White supremacists and anti-Semites valorize such work because it demonstrates in their minds the scientific foundation or validity of their misanthropic beliefs.

Socio-biology can therefore be seen as a godsend to the far right, validating their claims that the low IQ scores of blacks on intelligence tests are due to genetics, not environment. As Fromm and Varey (1983) suggest, "In sociobiology, conservatives have an extraordinary blueprint and assurance. It points to a national policy that seeks to stem Third World immigration and protect the ethnic balance; that promotes a property-owning, free enterprise economy; that reduces regulations and curbs institutions, like human rights commissions, that restrict the use of private property; that abolishes artificial programmes to enforce equality, such as affirmative action schemes; and that protects the family unit" (as cited in Barrett, 1987, p. 201).

A conservative platform has traditionally used these measures as supportive planks, and socio-biology serves to strengthen these planks by lending them academic validity and justification, which are reputedly based on sound social scientific principles.

These sorts of principles are also the planks of "scientific racism," which is to say, the justification of racist beliefs on the basis of academic research. Racists believe that there is a high correlation between intellectual achievement, biological background, and cultural development. The linking together of these three factors therefore justifies the belief that whites rank higher than other human populations on these scales. In turn, socio-biology provides the scientific justification for these assumptions.

Anthropology has figured prominently in the right-wing and white supremacist literature. Any suggestion in the anthropological literature of ethnic conflict is seen to justify the belief that racial strains provide evidence for the opinion that racial harmony is not possible and that members of different races cannot live together. Canada's Western Guard, for example, referred to anthropology in one of its documents as "the queen of the sciences," adding further that "for a few thousand years now the most important science of mankind has been its anthropology" (Barrett, 1987, p. 329).

Members of the Western Guard, in particular, are fond of quoting passages from the work of anthropologist Carlton Coon's (1962) book *The Origins of Races*, pulling passages out of context in an attempt to prove that peaceful racial coexistence is not possible. In sum, it is not possible to dismiss racists as uneducated crazies because many, at least, would appear to be versed in the scientific literature on race, of which anthropology plays a central role.

INSTITUTIONAL RACISM

Stokely Carmichael, a Black American political activist from the 1960s, is usually credited with initiating the term "institutional racism." As Carmichael explains, "Institutional racism ... is less overt, far more subtle, [and is] less identifiable in terms of *specific* individuals committing the acts. But it is no less destructive of human life. [It] originates in the operation of established and respected forces of society, and thus receives far less public condemnation" (Carmichael & Hamilton, 1967, p. 112; emphasis in original).

The key terms in this quotation about institutional racism point to the *established* and *respected* forces of society. Gillborn (2008, pp. 27–28), in a study of *Racism and Higher Education*, concurs with this assessment, indicating that an understanding of the dynamics of institutional racism requires the adoption of a critical perspective focusing on the nature of the general characteristics of politics and society.

FIGURE 3.2 Protesters Demand Justice for Freddie Gray
Source: Wikimedia user Veggies. Licensed under the terms of CC-BY-SA 3.0

Institutional racism has also been defined as "those patterns, procedures, practices, and policies that operate within social institutions so as to consistently penalize,
disadvantage, and exploit individuals who are members of non-white racial/ethnic
groups" (Better, 2008, p. 19). Many different social institutions are involved in perpet-
uating this form of racism, from the criminal justice system, newspapers, schools, and
businesses. Thus, certain ideologies and practices are used to support and justify the
domination that historically exploits those in the minority population. The domination that perpetuates institutional racism is often caused by the persons who produce
these inequalities.

Institutional racism is sometimes also referred to as *systemic* racism, meaning that
discriminatory practices tend to pervade the sociocultural system as a whole (Feagin,
2006, 2010). In turn, these practices place certain groups at a disadvantage when such
valued assets as political positions or economic resources are distributed within the
system. For example, in a reference to Canada, often seen as one of the most equi-
table and least socially repressive countries in the world, Bolaria and Li (1988) note,
"Many Canadians have little idea of what constitutes race and racism, let alone what
constitutes racial antagonism. Many misconceptions of race appear in Canadian society, ranging from outright bigotry to racial idealism. These misconceptions permeate
many aspects of Canadian society in Canada; they cannot be dismissed as the isolated ideas of misinformed individuals. Like other dominant ideas, the roots of racist

ideology are grounded in the daily experiences, and in the practice of social institutions" (p. 13).

An oft-cited source of institutional racism in Canada concerns the entrenched policies toward Aboriginal peoples, which serve to continually keep the Indigenous population in a disadvantaged position. The Indian Act, for example, is frequently seen as a means by which federal legislation maintains the Aboriginal population in a state of marginality and dependency. It is noted by James Frideres (1976) that this legislation is a prime example of the relationship between institutional structures and economic deprivation: "The Indian Act continues to regulate every aspect of lives of Native people.... The effects of the Act were and are devastating for personal autonomy and group morale, as well as traditional native political and social organization" (Frideres, 1988, p. 76).

RACE AND EDUCATION

Educational institutions have also been implicated in this form of racism (Law, Phillips, & Turney, 2004; Chesler, Lewis, & Crowfoot, 2005). Gillborn (2008), for example, suggests that members of educational departments have a tendency to equate discussions of racism with questions of semantics, "as if racism were merely a *word* rather than a structured, recurrent and deeply embedded *reality*" (p. 127; emphasis in original). He notes that educators frequently use the "language of race" but often fail to adopt a critical perspective on the concept "that seeks relentlessly to get beneath the rhetoric of legal and public policy debates to expose the material racist equalities that are created and sustained behind an inclusive and progressive façade" (p. 28). In other words, under the guise of a liberal education, the subject of racial injustice may be discussed in the classroom. However, it is another matter to engage in a determined and consistent critique of the very social institutions responsible for the inequalities that are the subject of these classroom criticisms.

Chesler, Lewis, and Crowfoot (2005), commenting on the topic of institutional racism in higher education, suggest that "the legacy of racism in higher education organizations ... pervades the curriculum, pedagogy, structure of departments and disciplines, formal and informal relationships among participants, and decision making about hiring, promotion, and retention" (p. 19). The suggestion, then, is that there are very few aspects of higher education that are not tainted by institutional racism. It is for this reason that Law, Phillips, and Turney (2004) offer an "antiracist tool kit" for dealing with institutional racism in higher education. This tool kit offers suggestions on antiracist actions, such as race equality and employment, and research on ethnicity and racism.

In another study of institutional racism, Shirley Better (2008) describes it as a "2000-pound elephant." "As we explore the ramifications of institutional racism," she explains, "we will discover that it is analogous to a 2000-pound elephant residing in one's living room. Everyone in the house is disgusted with the elephant taking over the living room.... Nonetheless, everyone in the household continues to act as if the elephant is not there. Why is this? ... No one in the house has the political will to force the elephant to leave. And it never will leave until someone in the house develops the courage to acknowledge the beast's existence and create an action plan to rid the house of it" (pp. xv–xvi). This analogy of the elephant residing in one's house is particularly appropriate because institutional racism is so embedded in the social, political, and economic institutions of society—is apparently such an embedded phenomenon—that many individuals hardly notice it at all.

RACE AND HISTORY

One of the problems with eradicating institutional racism has to do with what one might term historical momentum, reinforced by the attitudes of people holding positions of power in society. For example, Better (2008) further elaborates "It is exceedingly difficult for us to control our institutions which, being products of their history, cannot but perpetuate practices which advantage the typical white and handicap the typical minority person" (p. 13).

The problem is that social institutions are firmly embedded in the very mechanisms of society itself, in the operation and acting out of our daily lives, and in the cultural mores and values passed down from generation to generation. It is analogous in some ways to an attempt to escape from the very skin that protects us. We depend on our skin to shield us from the harmful effects of the external world in the same manner that we depend on cultural mechanisms to guide and protect us through the perils of life.

Similarly, Rangasamy (2004) explains that "institutional racism is rooted in history. It is a symptom of fundamental maladjustments in the interactions of culturally and ethnically different beings" (p. 27). As such, this is a problem that deserves appropriate academic analysis and should be informed by social research. Yet, "only then," Rangasamy suggests, "can the wealth of good work and good intentions be founded on an understanding which effectively addresses the cultural problems that underlie institutional racism" (p. 27).

So, if the conclusion is that the problem of institutional racism is essentially a cultural one, why is it that anthropologists have played such a minimal role in focusing on this issue and contributing to its understanding through ethnographic research? Is it, as Better suggests, such an embedded phenomenon that it has become invisible to us? Or perhaps, from an anthropological perspective, not exotic enough to spark our interest in comparison to other cultural phenomena that are seen as mysterious, arcane, or otherwise more worthy of our intellectual curiosity?

FIGURE 3.3 A member of the National Guard stands at the ready as protesters demonstrate in front of the Baltimore Police Department in early 2015.
Source: Courtesy of the National Guard

REPRESENTATIONS OF RACE IN ANTHROPOLOGY

It is evident from the foregoing discussion on racism that there is no lack of research on the subject. Granted, anthropologists throughout the history of the discipline have made contributions in some areas, but this has not been a major thrust of anthropological research. Perhaps the problem lies in the very characteristics of anthropologists themselves. Mary Huber (1998), in a study of college faculty and their attitudes, noted that American anthropology remains one of the country's least integrated and "whitest" professions. It is for this reason—because the anthropological community lacks internal ethnic diversity—that Shanklin (2000) suggests that anthropologists have failed to arrive at a consensus on what race means in American society and how to deal with the effects of racism.

As Shanklin (2000) explains further, "Among the consequences of this failure are that American anthropologists deliver inchoate messages about anthropological understandings of race and racism, especially in introductory text books, and [yet] they do not participate in public discussions of race and racism" (p. 99). This is not to suggest that the profession of anthropology is virtually "color-blind," to use Shanklin's (1998) term. There are, for example, introductory texts in (physical and cultural) anthropology with at least an adequate discussion of race and racism.

Out of 15 introductory anthropology texts examined by Shanklin (2000), only 5 of these contain what she would regard as "good discussions of race and racism" (p. 99).

Shanklin is particularly impressed by Harris's (1991) attempt to refute racist claims and explanations for poverty or inequality based on unequal abilities or physical characteristics, such as skin colour. Harris (1991) comments with regard to the "New Racism" of the 1980s that "the fact that Ronald Regan's administrations devalued civil rights, encouraged resentment against affirmative action, and fostered racial polarization by cutting back of critical social programs," coincided with a "marked deterioration in the economic prospects of the white majority" (p. 373).

Other anthropology texts mentioned are given less than favourable reviews. One text mentioned "gave pointless or confusing examples," while "other books gave old-fashioned or faulty definitions of race" (Shanklin, 2000, p. 100). Another text "never mentioned race as a contemporary problem," while another is faulted for having "no discussion of race as a sociocultural concept or of racism in contemporary societies in the sociocultural anthropology sections" (p. 100). A further text offers the opinion that "belief in 'race' is presented as a universal mistake, but there was no suggestion that steps might be taken to understand or correct" this problem (p. 100). The reader no doubt by now gets the point of the discussion—at the very least, "it is clear that there is no anthropological consensus about how or whether to present anthropological ideas about race and racism" (p. 101).

Shanklin (2000) suggests that more interest was shown in topics of race and racism in the 1970s and 1980s than is the case today. A possible reason is the general abandonment of the four-field approach taught to earlier generations of anthropology students, which gave them greater exposure to treatments of race from the perspective of physical anthropology. Considering today's texts, "if the point is that 'race' is really just 'ethnicity,' then I doubt that we are doing our students any favour by telling them just that and then dropping the subject" (Shanklin, 2000, p. 101).

As a general summary then, today's anthropology texts, in their treatment of race and racism, "make our profession look ignorant, backward, deluded, or uncaring. Worse, the profession of ignorance is taking place at a time when the rest of American society, as well as the rest of the world, *is* concerned about these matters.... It seems to me a shame that anthropologists are opting out of an important, perhaps critical dialogue" (Shanklin, 2000, p. 101). This statement placed in historical perspective suggests that, although Franz Boas spent many decades combatting racism and was followed by several of his students into the 1960s, today's anthropologists "seem to be ignoring Boas's example of participating in ongoing intellectual debates on the nature of race and racism" (p. 101).

ANTHROPOLOGICAL COMPLICITY?

Shanklin's assessment of anthropology's role in the study of race and racism—there was Boas and several of his students, then little else—is an oversimplification. There is no doubt that the social scientific literature on racism, and anthropology's role therein, is a complex matter, and that a multiplicity of points of view is prevalent (Mulling, 2005; Carter & Virdee, 2008). One anthropologist, for example, has put forth the view that humankind has a "natural" predisposition toward racism (Kallen, 1982, p. 22), while others, such as Banton (1977) and Stepan (1982), hold to the view that the idea of race has not been a universal phenomenon in history, going so far as to suggest that the early Greeks and Romans were not prejudiced on the basis of colour. However, Isaac (2006) disagrees, suggesting that the term "proto-racism" is a more apt characterization.

The charge that anthropologists have been complicit in promoting racist attitudes, especially with reference to "scientific racism," has been made by several authors, such as Dewbury (2007), Gravlee and Sweet (2008), Gustav (2009), and Mevorach (2007). The general charge against anthropology is that it has participated in an academic complicity that provided a source of racist mythology. In the past, anthropology, it is claimed, provided the intellectual schema for the rationalization that people in certain cultures were "savages" and thus inferior to those in "civilized" societies.

Possibly the suggestion could be made that anthropologists did not promote overt racist attitudes, but that their academic complicity was more implicit in that they promoted outmoded racist concepts. Mevorach (2007) explains that "perhaps the most insidious aspects to the shameful legacy of the science of race ... is that the concept of 'race' continues to underwrite the biologization of difference within the academic community from undergraduate classrooms to biogenetic research laboratories and think tanks" (p. 239). In this manner of thinking, the concept of race can be seen as a social construct, as a way of managing cultural and physical difference, or as a metaphor. However, the charge by Merorach that anthropologists have actively participated in a "shameful legacy" is different than Shanklin's (2000) position that anthropological complicity is more one of benign neglect or of an abrogation of intellectual responsibility than a willful participation in promoting racist attitudes.

The term "biologization of difference" has also been used by other scholars, such as Azoulay (2006), to suggest that race is essentially a bogus academic concept. Furthermore, as Paul Gilroy (2001) argues, "Whether it is articulated in the more specialized tongues of biological science and pseudo-science, or in the vernacular idiom of culture and common sense, the term 'race' conjures up a peculiarly resistant variety of natural difference" (p. 29). In other words, despite whatever earlier conceptions academics may have held about race, Smedley and Smedley (2005) suggest that race as a social problem is a very real one, even though many in the scientific community may regard race as a dubious biological entity, or as largely a "fiction," or "myth" following Montagu.

UNDERSTANDING RACISM IN ANTHROPOLOGY

In Gravlee's (2009) study "How Race Becomes Biology," the idea is presented that physical characteristics have been reified in various ways in order to justify the isolation of certain groups. This isolating process then places certain groups in a vulnerable position and makes them more likely to become targets of discriminatory practices. Similarly, in Jane Helleiner's (2000) ethnographic study of Irish Travellers (tinkers or gypsies), she uses the term "same race racism" to suggest that race does not necessarily have a biological foundation. In the Irish case, the Travellers who are the subject of discriminatory practices are the same "race" as those perpetrating these practices.

From Helleiner's (2000) perspective, her Irish study of anti-Traveller discourse demonstrates that the dialogue that places the Travellers as targets of longstanding discriminatory behaviour by the Irish majority is linked to other social processes of inequality such as gender and class. Traveller collective identity and culture then, at least in part, is shaped by the oppressive forces of racism which illuminates the manner in which "Irish racism [points] to its articulation with other forms of social inequality" (p. 9). The discriminatory practices at work in Ireland that act to disadvantage the Traveller population also play a role in the state's institutional framework, serving as a basis for unfair employment practices or a basis for restrictive immigration policies, as Lentin (2007) suggests.

Similar arguments are advanced for other areas of Europe, such as those made by Goodey (2007), and Gorodzeisky and Semyonov (2009), who refer to "terms of exclusion" that restricts the "admission and allocation of rights of immigrants." Because of this wider European perspective, Helleiner (2000) suggests that her ethnography of Irish Travellers needs to be understood "within local, national, and increasingly globalized arenas structured by unequal power relations" (p. 241). The suggestion, then, is that "race relations are essentially group power contests" (Baker, 1978, p. 316).

Other anthropologists have also used the concept of power as an explanatory tool in understanding discriminatory practices. Similarly, Barrett (1987) in his ethnographic study of racist attitudes of members of right-wing organizations in Canada, notes that "racism has been fostered by a range of factors such as the individual's need for scapegoats, the propensity for ethnocentrism, the search for security, stability, and simplicity; in the latter regard, racism acts as a classificatory tool, carving up, categorizing, and thus simplifying the social universe" (p. 342). The exercise of power was also an important part of Ruth Benedict's (1960) explanation: "racism remains ... merely another instance of the persecution of minorities for the advantage of those in power" (p. 148).

Several other anthropologists, such as Hughes and Kallen (1974) in their study *The Anatomy of Racism*, echo similar sentiments when they suggest that "racism, in the context of majority-minority relations, is a political tool, wielded by the dominant ethnic group to justify the status quo and rationalize the disability to which the minority group is subject" (p. 105). It is evident, therefore, that explanations of racism may involve a diversity of disparate factors, but the dimension of power appears particularly significant, especially pertaining to the highly controversial subject of racial profiling (Glover, 2009; Gumbhir, 2007; Tanovich, 2006).

RACIAL PROFILING AND "THE COLOUR OF SUSPICION"

Gumbhir (2007), using the term "the color of suspicion," defines racial profiling as "any police initiated action that relies on race, ethnicity, or national origin rather than the behavior of an individual or information that leads the police to a particular individual who has been identified as being, or having been, engaged in criminal activity" (pp. 16–17).

It is for this reason—that members of minority groups tend to be overrepresented when it comes to police scrutiny—that Glover (2009) suggests such racial profiling is an aspect of "systemic racism [which] is also appropriate as a theoretical guide because of its emphasis on the separating, distancing, and alienating relations that emerge under racial systems.... Clearly, racial profiling processes emerge from these radicalized ideas, stereotypes, and inclinations at social control via the legal system" (p. 66).

The idea that racism is essentially linked to the exercise of power, and that it is an institutionalized or systemic aspect of the wider society, is also an important aspect of anthropologists Carol Tator and Frances Henry's (2006) study of *Racial Profiling in Canada*. In this monograph, the authors link together the institutions of power in society, such as the criminal justice system and policing, with the oppression of racial and ethnic minorities. At the centre of this work is the proposition that "the first crucial element in racial profiling is its links to the practices of racialization—practices that can be seen to operate in virtually every sector of society. Racialization is part of the broader process that inferiorizes and excludes groups in the population.... The discourses around criminal acts by particular minority groups depends on essentialized and stereotypical thinking" (Tator & Henry, 2006, pp. 8–9).

In Tator and Henry's (2006) study the argument is made that Aboriginals and people of colour are seen by the police as "problem people," or to use their term, "a few bad apples." This designation means that they are people who are frequently the subject of special scrutiny by the criminal justice system. The expectation on the part of law enforcement officers is that such people are trouble-makers. Aboriginals and people of colour are also overrepresented in prisons, lending credence to the suggestion that such people tend to be charged with offences to a greater extent than other citizens. In turn, these greater overall incarceration rates can be seen as a further justification for special scrutiny, leading to additional detentions and arrests.

THE AMERICAN ANTHROPOLOGICAL ASSOCATION'S STATEMENT ON "RACE"

The discussion thus far in this chapter details the long and sometimes convoluted dialogue in anthropology about what the discipline's viewpoint should be on the topic of race and human difference. What has emerged from this dialogue is a public education initiative put forward by the AAA, the largest body representing anthropologists in America, although members from other countries are also participants.

In 1998, the Executive Board of the AAA released a statement on race, which is believed to represent "generally the contemporary thinking and scholarly positions of a majority of anthropologists" (www.aaanet.org/stmts/racepp.htm). However, it also recognized that such a statement does not reflect a consensus of all members of the AAA, "as individuals vary in the approaches to the study of 'race'" (AAA, 1998, n.p.).

The statement begins by presenting scientific knowledge about race, such as the fact that all of humankind is thought to be a single species because of the continued sharing of genetic material that has resulted from different groups coming into contact with each other. The result of this contact has been an interbreeding of different peoples in neighbouring populations so that the result is much overlapping of genes and their phenotypic (physical) expressions.

A second point made in the statement is that physical variations of any given human trait, such as skin colour or hair type, tend to occur gradually rather than abruptly over geographic areas. In addition, each of these traits also tends to vary independently from the others, so that hair texture, for example, is not related to nose shape. In this context, physical traits are inherited independently of one another, making "any attempt to establish lines of division among biological populations both arbitrary and subjective" (AAA, 1998, n.p.).

A third point, which follows from those above, is that "physical variations in human species have no meaning except the social ones humans put on them" (AAA, 1998, n.p.). In historical terms, "race" can therefore be regarded as a social mechanism invented during the eighteenth century that referred to the various populations, such as slaves from Africa, conquered Indigenous populations, or European settlers, brought together during the colonial era. What emerged from this classification system was a "growing ideology of inequality" which was devised as a mechanism used to rationalize European attitudes and treatment of the enslaved or conquered peoples. Such an ideology was also used to justify the retention of slavery and to aid in the establishment of a rigid hierarchy of social and economic exclusiveness.

A fourth point refers to the concept of culture. The statement indicates that human cultural behaviour is learned; no human is born with built-in linguistic or cultural skills. Beginning at birth, infants are conditioned to behave in certain ways, although this conditioning is always subject to modification as the child grows into an adult. The main point made is that "regardless of genetic propensities … it is a basic tenet of anthropological knowledge that all normal human beings have the capacity to learn any cultural behavior" (AAA, 1998, n.p.).

PUBLIC EDUCATION ABOUT RACE: ARE WE SO DIFFERENT?

The AAA statement on race was designed to address public misconceptions about race and intelligence. As an attempt to further this initiative and as a result of the public's continued confusion about the meaning of "race," in 2014, the AAA developed an online project called "Race: Are We So Different?" (www.aaanet.org/resources/RACE-Are-We-So-Different). From the Carnegie Museum of Natural History website (http://carnegiemnh.org/exhibitions/event.aspx?id=21884/), it is explained that this "is the first nationally travelling exhibition to tell the story of race from biological, cultural, and historic points of view. These diverse perspectives merge into an unprecedented examination of race and racism in the United States."

"Race: Are We So Different?" involves a series of exhibitions, principally held at various museums, that focuses on an "exploration of the experience of living with race in America. The exhibition weaves together personal stories of living with race along with expert discussions of the history of race as a concept, the role that science has played in that history, and emerging research that challenges the foundations of what we perceive as race" (AAA, 2014, n.p.).

The exhibition was created with funding from the National Science Foundation and the Ford Foundation, along with various local organizations. As Damon Dozier, AAA director of public affairs explains, "The unique value of the RACE exhibit among others that address this topic is the wide range of questions it both answers and raises by integrating the lenses of science, history and everyday experience." It is also pointed out that "race is about culture, not biology." Dozier adds, "The RACE exhibit is one big 'ah-ha' moment" (AAA, 2014, n.p.).

CURRENT ANTHROPOLOGY: THE BIOLOGICAL
ANTHROPOLOGY OF LIVING HUMAN POPULATIONS

The journal *Current Anthropology* is the official publication of the Wenner-Gren Foundation for Anthropological Research and is published by the University of Chicago Press. *Current Anthropology* was founded in 1959 by Sol Tax (1907–1995) and is one of the few journals that publish research across all sub-disciplines of anthropology. As such, the journal provides a forum of communication across the subfields of social, cultural, and physical anthropology, as well as such fields as archaeology, linguistics, and folklore.

In 2012, *Current Anthropology* published a series of articles on the topic of "The Biological Anthropology of Living Human Populations" (Aiello, 2012). The purpose of these articles is the result of what is thought to be biological anthropologists' general embarrassment "by the history of their discipline and [who therefore] rarely have an interest in delving into it" (Aiello, 2012, p. S1). As Michael Little explains, "I never talked about the history of my field, because I was embarrassed by it" (as cited in Lindee & Santos, 2012, p. S3). This embarrassment stems, at least partly, from biological anthropology's history concerning ideas about race difference which produced an emotional state that silenced or negated certain questions (Lindee & Santos, 2012, p. S3).

Dealing with the topic of race in the history of biological anthropology is a source of embarrassment. It is stated, for example, that "the word 'race' is highly charged in ways that make it difficult to use without sounding as though one is engaged in an accusation, and much of the historical literature does sound a bit like exorcism" (Lindee & Santos, 2012, p. S5). Perhaps because of this situation in which "the word 'race' can only be used to condemn racism" (Lindee & Santos, 2012, p. S5), the word itself has become scientifically suspect, and is now replaced in some circles with terms such as "ethnicity" or "population."

One would expect that this special issue of *Current Anthropology* would provide a sort of cutting-edge scientific view of the concept of "race" from the position of biological or physical anthropology. It is disappointing to find that this is not the case, and that the series of articles seem to suggest that the biological side of anthropology is now moving away from such an important contemporary dialogue on race and racism because their practitioners find the topic "too embarrassing" to even discuss.

CONCLUSION

The AAA statement on race is a powerful and straightforward condemnation of racism in America. It clearly points out that "race" is an arbitrary categorization of people used in a "growing ideology of inequality," that has very little biological meaning. The subsequent "Race: Are We So Different?" exhibit is an attempt to bring this scientific knowledge to the point of public awareness as it reaches out to people in schools, museums, and other public forums.

There are certainly those who would applaud the AAA for their various initiatives at bringing the scientific aspects of "race" to the public's awareness. However, the race riots in Ferguson, Missouri, and Baltimore, Maryland, demonstrate the volatile nature of peoples' reactions to threats to their security and well-being. Television news portrays the American army lobbing tear gas into violent crowds bent on destroying public property, with President Obama himself indicating that the trouble seems to be caused by "outside agitators and anarchists" intent on exploiting this situation for their own political ends.

In this context of modern, everyday history, one wonders about the relevance of the AAA statement on race and whether or not the scientific community has missed the point somehow in their public education endeavours. In other words, perhaps the riots are not about race at all, and it might matter little whether or not "race" has any scientific validity. What matters is the manner in which race is used to exploit social injustice and to keep certain sectors of the American population in a socially, politically, and economically disadvantaged position.

As is noted previously in this chapter, as far as the educational realm is concerned, Eugenia Shanklin's (1998, 2000) studies of the representation of race in anthropology textbooks suggests that there is a diminishing interest by anthropologists in comparison to the earlier work of Franz Boas and his students on the subject. In this chapter, we do not wish to argue with her conclusions pertaining to American textbooks; however, the wider implications of this charge, which is to say that anthropology is a "profession of ignorance" and that anthropologists "seem to be ignoring Boas's example of participating in ongoing intellectual debates on the nature of race and racism" (Shanklin, 2000, p. 101), deserves attention. If correct, then this is a serious condemnation of the discipline and suggests that race and science become once again a serious focus of research in the reorientation of public issues anthropology.

The review of anthropological and other social scientific studies of race and racism presented here is not meant to be inclusive, since there is hardly room for such a study in this brief chapter. However, the topics reviewed in the present discussion in the decade after Shanklin's conclusions lead to the deduction that there has indeed been a lively debate among anthropologists about race in recent years. Relatively recent research includes Isaac (2006) on proto-racism in the ancient world; several authors on the scientific racism in anthropology (Dewbury, 2007; Gravlee & Sweet, 2008; Gustav, 2009; Mevorach, 2007); Helleiner (2000) on same-race racism in Ireland; Barrett (1987) on racist beliefs by the radical right; and Tator and Henry (2006), as well as various other authors, on the subject of racial profiling.

As mentioned previously, this brief review is not meant to be exhaustive, yet it does indicate a fairly active engagement by anthropologists and others in related disciplines to further an understanding of race and racism through their research. The conclusion is that, on the basis of this review of literature, anthropologists have not been ignoring this important aspect of contemporary life over the last decade, and, contrary to Shanklin's assumptions, have been participating in a lively exploration of the topic of race.

Nonetheless, aside from the debates about race and racism within the discipline (i.e., among anthropologists and their other colleagues in the social sciences), the question remains: How have these largely intellectual debates impacted or otherwise informed the public's perception of these issues? Furthermore, have anthropologists embraced the apparent need to bring their research results to the public forum of debate about discrimination in society at large?

The news items brought to the reader's attention at the beginning of this chapter on various contemporary issues, such as the trial of George Zimmerman for the killing of Trayvon Martin and the dismissal of the murder charges against him, are widely known situations that could be discussed by anthropologists outside of academic settings. Anthropologists could bring their expertise and research to the public's attention through the news media, through newspaper articles, television and radio interviews, and presentations in community settings as an attempt to further an understanding of society's ills and promote a dialogue about the repressive practices in today's society. Attempts at engaging in public anthropology about race and racism in contemporary society would serve to make anthropology more "practical," to use Malinowski's term, and bring anthropological knowledge about discriminatory social processes out of the sheltered halls of academia and into the public realm where the real lives of people are lived.

Chapter 4

JARED DIAMOND: SOCIAL DARWINISM REVISITED

Jared Diamond, professor of geography at the University of California, has written a very popular book called *Guns, Germs, and Steel*. In fact, his book is so popular that it won a Pulitzer Prize for non-fiction, and was made into a documentary produced by the National Geographic Society, broadcast by PBS in 2005. So, why should such a book be of concern to public anthropology?

To answer this question, one needs to examine Diamond's basic assumptions about how societies change. In *Guns, Germs, and Steel*, Diamond attempts to explain

FIGURE 4.1 Jared Diamond
Source: AAP Image/Lloyd Jones. Reprinted by permission of the Australian Associated Press

why Europeans have been so successful in conquering other societies. European domination over Indigenous populations, Diamond argues, is the result of their technological advantages and resistance to endemic diseases that have originated because of certain environmental advantages. Favourable environmental conditions concerning soil and climate allowed for the comparatively early rise of agriculture, and subsequent food surpluses based on such protein-rich crops as wheat and barley. Early Europeans also had access to animals easily domesticated, such as cows, goats, and horses, which were used for food and transportation. Thus, the ascendency of Europeans, Diamond explains, is largely the result of the influence of geography on societies and culture.

SOCIAL DARWINISM REVISITED

From the perspective of public anthropology, the popularization of Diamond's work extends out into the public domain certain current issues for contemporary anthropology. These issues concern the manner in which the public perceives and understands the relationship between culture and environment. There is also a contradiction between Diamond's thesis on the causes of cultural development as generally understood through most of the history of anthropology and almost a century of research on the relationship between cultural adaption and ecological settings. From the perspective of anthropology, the salient critique of Diamond's popular book concerns the re-emergence of social Darwinist thought in explaining such important topics as the role of the environment in cultural development, the basis of human diversity, and the reasons for the spread of Europeans around the globe.

Social Darwinism as a mode of thought and explanation can be traced back in history to the ideas expressed by Hebert Spencer (1820–1903), who is considered one of the founders of sociology. Spencer believed that society evolved from relatively simple forms to more complex ones through the process of adaptation and progress. As far as Spencer was concerned, there were close parallels between social and biological evolution. In fact, Spencer is generally credited with coining the phrase "the survival of the fittest"—used by him in 1852 in an article on population theory—which is often mistakenly attributed to Charles Darwin (see Claeys 2000, p. 227). Thus, from Spencer's perspective, the same natural laws that guided the non-human world were also responsible for directing the development of human society.

Anthropologists over at least the last century have argued against such evolutionary schemes. This is not to suggest that societies do not change; the problem is that societies tend to change at different rates, along different paths, or in some cases hardly at all. The point that anthropologists have attempted to stress is that changes in human societies do not follow "natural" laws as may be the case in other realms.

The characteristics of human societies are also not determined by their environmental settings, as anthropologists have been arguing as far back as Franz Boas. The trouble with Spencerian modes of thought, as Barrett (1996) suggests, is that "in many respects Spencer's writings bear a remarkable resemblance to the tracts of contemporary right wingers. His evolutionary perspectives became an apology for capitalism, private property, and free enterprise, and an onslaught against government intercession, socialism, and communism. In Spencer's view, capitalism and free enterprise were consistent with the laws of nature" (p. 52).

Claeys (2000) has attempted to explain the Spencerian point of view in terms of the history of ideas: "The distinctiveness of much of Social Darwinism, then, resulted not from the popularization of the metaphor of the 'survival of the fittest' or of human 'fitness' to the end of a common goal.... Instead, the *specificity* of Social Darwinism lay in ... the mapping of a quasi-ontological racial discourse onto a redefinition of 'fitness' and 'intelligence' and an identification of 'intelligence' with the 'white' races.... Its use in justifying the Holocaust finally debased the language so far as to nearly remove it from common currency" (p. 420).

So what does all of this have to do with Diamond? Well, for starters, from a social Darwinist viewpoint, biological evolution and cultural evolution were seen to be fused together, which is an ideology known as *biological determinism*. It therefore follows from this point of view that "the reason Euro-Americans occupied the top of the evolutionary ladder of progress, while other groups were at the lower levels of the evolutionary scale, was because Euro-Americans were biologically superior to other peoples" (Sidky, 2004, p. 115). Social Darwinism is also a dogma that could be used to justify slavery, colonialism, and the political domination of Indigenous people.

In a similar fashion, Diamond in *Guns, Germs, and Steel* would appear to suggest that European ascendency, and the hegemonic power they wield over Indigenous populations, is somehow a phenomenon following natural laws. For example, he notes that "peoples of Eurasian origin ... dominate the modern world of wealth and power" (p. 15). Other peoples who have thrown off the yoke of colonial domination, nonetheless, still lag behind in power and wealth. For some, there is something particularly enticing about the idea that people of European origin have a natural propensity for ending up on top of the social and economic heap of humanity. It seems "natural" for them that Europeans occupy the top rung of the world's civilization.

DOES ENVIRONMENT DETERMINE CULTURE?

Anthropologists, and indeed most social scientists, would hardly disagree with Diamond's thesis that culture and behaviour is not determined by race, genes, or biology. However, it is the suggestion that environment precipitates social change or in some manner determines its outcome that is likely to cause concern among academics. Granted, Diamond attempts to fend off charges of environmental determinism, but it is too early to judge how successful he will be in countering this indictment. For many social scientists, the central issue is not so much pitting environment against biology as it is the view that environment is an apparent determinant of history. Rather, the issue concerns the relationship between culture and geography: does environment determine culture?

Phrased this way, the biology-environment dichotomy can be seen as somewhat of a red herring that diverts the reader's focus away from a problematic issue (environment versus culture) toward one that is no longer contentious (culture versus biology). Diamond's thesis hinges on a certain number of assumptions that are hidden in a somewhat common-sense sequence of historical transformations. For example, the so-called Fertile Crescent of Southwest Asia, now comprising much of present-day Iran and Iraq, is seen to have some unique ecological opportunities for humans not existing anywhere else on earth. The most important of these opportunities are the locally available resources that allowed for the domestication of a special combination of plants (mainly wheat and barley), and domesticated animals (sheep, goats, and later cows) 10,000 years ago. Later, by 4000 BC, horse pastoralism developed, which combined with the invention of the wheel, allowed for the spread of the Indo-Europeans living in this region to most parts of the world.

A very tempting comparison can be made by a more recent study of Indo-Europeans, titled *The Horse, the Wheel, and Language: How Bronze-Age Riders from the Eurasian Steppes Shaped the Modern World*, by archaeologist and linguist David Anthony (2007). Whereas Diamond, as a geography professor, appears to gloss over many of the intricacies of culture change, Anthony's research spans several decades of concentrated research in the very geographical area that was the focus of Diamond's attention.

It is apparent that Anthony's conclusions are at odds with those postulated by Diamond. "Jared Diamond, in *Guns, Germs, and Steel*," according to Anthony (2007), "suggested that the cultures of Eurasia enjoyed an environmental advantage over those of Africa or the Americas partly because the Eurasian continent is oriented in an east-west direction, making it easier for innovations like farming, herding, and wheeled vehicles to spread rapidly between environments that were basically similar because they were on the same latitude. But persistent cultural borders like the Ural frontier delayed the transmission of those innovations by thousands of years even within the single ecological zone of the steppes" (pp. 662–63). In other words, both studies provide a unique opportunity to compare the approaches of three different, but associated disciples (anthropology, geography, and archaeology), where environment is stressed on one side, and culture on the other.

THE ORIGINS OF "CIVILIZATION"

The word "civilization" is placed in quotation marks here because it is a value-laden term, especially in anthropology. Its use harkens back to over a century ago when anthropologists believed that societies evolved through a series of stages, from savagery, to barbarism, to civilization. The conceptual scheme became known as the unilinear evolutionary approach because it was thought that societies changed, or "progressed" (another problematic term), through these various stages on their way to a higher, possibly more enlightened state of being. Of course, this scheme is now seen as ethnocentric and does not today have any general acceptance in anthropology; however it has survived, albeit in a much more disguised fashion.

Diamond doesn't bother much with these sorts of polemics and discredited terminology. However, he does attempt to address a central issue in differential societal change in his prologue, entitled "'Yali's Question,' or 'The Regionally Differing Courses of History'" (1999, pp. 13–32). We learn, for example, that "historical inequalities have cast long shadows on the modern world, because the literate societies with metal tools have conquered or exterminated the other societies. While those differences constitute the most basic fact of world history, the reasons for them remain uncertain and controversial" (p. 13). Yes, indeed—very controversial.

The controversy stems, in part, not from the use of guns and steel to defeat other societies, but from Diamond's apparent claim that it is inevitable that some societies will dominate some others, and certainly there is ample evidence for this. Yet a more fundamental question concerns what German philosopher Friedrich Nietzsche (1968) called "The Will to Power." According to Nietzsche, the main driving force (*der wille zur macht*) behind human achievement is ambition, or a seemingly universal human striving to reach the highest pinnacle or status in life.

In *Culture Meets Power* (2002), Barrett explains that the differential use of power is a key social scientific concept because "*Power is an aphrodisiac. Who needs Viagra when power is available?*" (p. 74; emphasis in original). He does point out though, following Etzioni (1993), that there is an important distinction that should be made between the capacity to exercise power, on the one hand, and its actual exercise, on the other. More to the point, one may possess significant resources (such as guns and steel) but lack the skill or will to use them to their advantage over others. But does power always bring change?

The interrelationship between the differential use of power and its role in social change is an extremely important aspect of Diamond's thesis. For Diamond, the use of force seems inevitable, but is it? Or, put another way, does the exercise of power always bring about change? Certainly one would expect that the use of power involves decisions that are goal-oriented, or driven by ambition, in Nietzsche's sense of some form of an innate psychological force which lies behind the need for human achievement. There is also what Barrett (2002) has referred to as "degrees of ambition," in that "some people seem to suffer from a deficit of ambition, others from an excess" (p. 30).

One would also think that any discussion of human achievement would by necessity entertain in some fashion the ideas of Karl Marx. In Diamond's discussion, there is scant mention of Marx, as he enters into the discussion on only one line pertaining to the question, "For any ranked society, whether a chiefdom or a state, one thus has to ask: why do the commoners tolerate the transfer of the fruits of their hard labor to kleptocrats?" (Diamond, 1999, p. 276). Kleptocracies in this instance refers to societies in which there is a transfer of "net wealth from commoners to upper classes.... The difference between a kleptocrat and a wise statesman, between a robber baron and a public benefactor, is merely one of degree: a matter of just how large a percentage of the tribute extracted from producers is retained by the elite" (p. 276).

This statement by Diamond is too much of an oversimplification of the universal characteristics of political economy. Surely a much more involved discussion of Marx's concept of historical materialism is worth more than a mere one-word mention of his name in a book encompassing the scope of human history staked out by Diamond. It is hard to imagine any social theorist who has had a greater impact on the social sciences than Karl Marx. When Marx (1859/1904) explained, for example, in the preface to his *Contribution to the Critique of Political Economy*, that "the mode of production in material life determines the general character of the social, political, and spiritual processes of life [and that] it is not the consciousness of men that determines their existence, but, on the contrary, their social existence determines their consciousness" (pp. 10–11), we have a direct answer to "Yali's Question" as to why there are such inequalities in the world.

Granted, there is a certain similarity between Diamond's explanations for social inequality—elites steal from the common person who produces the wealth in society—and that of Marx—who lays the blame on capitalists exploiting the proletariat; yet Marx's explanation has more depth and texture. For example, Marx's theory of historical materialism draws an important distinction between an economy's *mode of production* (the manner in which the techno-economic factors are organized) and its *mode of reproduction* (technologies that affect population size). Thus, a significant aspect that Marx illuminates is the conflicts of competing interest groups and how these conflicts are responsible for the underlying force of social change. It is the divergent interests, therefore, between wage-earners and the owners of the means of production that, from Marx's perspective, are the dynamic or mechanism that drives social change. Such a distinction also ultimately became a crucial cornerstone of later cultural materialist perspectives in American anthropology, especially those associated with Marvin Harris (1991) and others in the cultural ecology school.

When anthropologists rejected the far too simplistic, and ultimately inaccurate, evolutionary school postulating a unilinear transition from primitive to civilized societies, they didn't throw the baby out with the conceptual bathwater. Instead, they remodelled the scheme in the form of what has been termed "neo-evolutionism." This new format is nonetheless inspired by Marx. The neo-evolutionary school sees two main forms of social change: what has been termed "specific" or "multilineal" evolution (Sahlins, 1960; Steward, 1955), which deals with more local level changes, and the larger, pan-human variety called "universal evolution" (White, 1949). This historical aspect of anthropological theory is mentioned, not to enlighten anthropology students who are no doubt already familiar with such terminology from the introductory level and beyond, but to suggest that Diamond needs to reach deeper into the social scientific knowledge base to provide a more convincing argument.

The intent here is not to criticize in a gratuitous manner a Pulitzer Prize–winning book; however, Diamond himself put his theory on the social scientific chopping block, as it were, because of his direct criticism of anthropology's interpretation of human social evolution. By the way, the subject of anthropology is not even noted in his book's index, although many arcane facts are listed there. We note with some dismay, therefore, Diamond's dismissal of anthropologists' attempts to deal with the perplexing problem of human diversity.

Diamond (1999) engages in a disparaging critique of anthropology's attempts to deal with the palpable epistemological problem of cultural comparisons and human social diversity. He claims, for example, that "cultural anthropologists attempting to describe the diversity of human societies often divide them into as many as a half a dozen categories. Any such attempt to define stages or any evolutionary or developmental continuum ... is doubly doomed to imperfection" (p. 267). Actually, most cultural anthropologists would not necessarily disagree with Diamond's dictum, since defining categories of cultural characteristics has been a perdurable practical problem almost since the beginning of the discipline of anthropology. We note, for example, the work of George Murdock and his colleagues at the University of Pittsburgh to develop the World Ethnographic Atlas and the Human Relations Area Files (Murdock, 1949, 1963, 1967).

As Murdock (1937) found out early on, the attempt to develop statistical correlations across cultural boundaries is a process fraught with difficulties. One of the most important of these difficulties is the problem of isolating certain cultural or social aspects, in an attempt to provide discrete units for purposes of comparison. Another tactic was developed by cultural anthropologist Morton Fried in *The Evolution of Political Society* (1967). In Fried's case, he proposed the now very familiar categorization of band, tribe, chiefdom, and state; however, it should be stated that he was very cautious about implying any evolutionary transition between these various categories. Maybe we should state this somewhat differently: given that, at one time, all human societies existed at the band level, other categories by necessity must have transitioned from this incipient level. So what Fried was cautious about was specifying the links that would be seen as responsible for any transition from bands, for example, into tribes, chiefdoms, or states.

What is perhaps surprising, then, given Diamond's prediction of anthropology's apparent failure to describe human societies by dividing them up into a number of identifiable categories, is that he uses these very categories postulated by Fried (see, for example, Diamond's use of the band, tribe chiefdom, and state categories in his tables on pp. 268–69 and then throughout the remainder of Chapter 14). The reader would therefore be excused for being perplexed at such usage of anthropological concepts when they are deemed to be "doubly doomed" to failure.

WHY ARGUE ABOUT ENVIRONMENT AND CULTURE?

The hope is that readers will not find the preceding response to Diamond's book too reactionary; nonetheless, there are important issues that need to be discussed. These issues are not just interdisciplinary feuds of an arcane academic nature. Some of these issues, such as an understanding of the relationship between culture and environment, are crucially important to our understanding of the sustainability of human life on this planet. It is for this reason that anthropologists are particularly interested in issues of human ecology—because they are matters of our very survival. Academics argue about the relationship between environment and society because these arguments have a lot to do with such matters as public policy, about how the environment is treated, and, ultimately, about our ability to live long-term in our earthly world.

Environmental determinism as an explanatory basis of socio-cultural evolution has a particularly long history, going back at least to the Enlightenment period. As Harris (1968) explains, "The most sustained Enlightenment elaboration of geographical determinism was the contribution of Montesquieu. Northern peoples tend to be brave, vigorous, insensitive to pain, weakly sexed, intelligent and drunkards; southern peoples are the opposite" (p. 42). Various permutations of these sorts of ideas emerged later in history, such as theories that promoted an ecological explanation for racial differences.

One of these is "Bergmann's Rule," suggested in 1847, which stated that human body size is determined by geographical location. The Inuit, for example, need to conserve body heat because they live in a cold arctic environment. Such people therefore have a relatively short, stocky body with smaller skin area, while in Africa a long, lanky body, characteristic of the Zulus or Masai, helps to dissipate it (Coon, 1962). Examples contrary to this theory, such as Pygmy peoples of the equator, or the Norseman of Scandinavia, are obviously not explained by this theory.

There is no need here to lay out the whole history of anthropology's concern with the environment, for this would take many volumes. Suffice to say that the emergence of modern anthropology begins with Franz Boas's rejection of geographical determinism. In the latter part of the nineteenth century, Boas was part of a research team sent to Baffin Island, which formed the basis for his groundbreaking ethnographic study *The Central Eskimo* (1888). On the basis of this research, Boas (1940) was to write later that "environmental conditions may stimulate existing cultural activities, but they have no creative force ... the same environment will influence culture in diverse ways.... Thus it is fruitless to explain culture in geographical terms" (p. 266).

Boas's view of environmental relationships as they influence culture became later known as "possibilism." His student Alfred Kroeber, in *Cultural and Natural Areas of Native North America* (1939), explained the concept in the following manner: "While it is true that cultures are rooted in nature, and can therefore never be completely understood except with reference to that piece of nature in which they occur ... the immediate cause of cultural phenomenon are other cultural phenomenon" (p. 1). In the perspective known as possibilism, "the environment sets limits upon what is possible but does not determine sociocultural phenomena" (Sidky, 2004, p. 435).

Kroeber also introduced the notion of the "culture area concept." This concept stresses the adaptive responses that people in different cultures will make to environmental conditions. In an area with similar environmental conditions, such as the Great Plains, the Arctic, or the Pacific West Coast regions, adaptation to these conditions leads to cultural similarities. Thus, in the Great Plains area, there emerged a convergence of such cultural practices as horse pastoralism, buffalo hunting, skin teepees, sweat lodges, and the Sun Dance ceremony, even though the origins of the various Plains cultures were often quite different. Some groups, such as the Comanche, were originally Algonquian hunters and gatherers from the Great Lakes area, while others, such as the Mandan, were horticulturalists who lived a marginal Plains life before they acquired horses. The Sioux were originally from the Carolinas where they split from their Iroquoian relatives.

The point that Kroeber makes with the culture area concept is that an environmental area with attractive natural resources will draw into this region a diversity of cultural groups. Over time, as the members of these different groups begin to adapt to these new conditions, and borrow subsistence techniques from other nearby groups, similarities in cultural characteristics begin to emerge. The environment itself does not determine these similarities in cultural form; it is the interaction of environment and culture through the adaptive process that is responsible for the emerging cultural resemblances (Hedican, 2012a, pp. 80–81).

Kroeber's concept was a definite advance over Boas's possibilism. The culture area concept provides an explanation for culture change beyond the mere "possibilities" of what might emerge. However, there are certain defects in Kroeber's approach that

FIGURE 4.2 Alfred Kroeber (centre)
Source: Reprinted by permission of the Phoebe A.
Hearst Museum of Anthropology

later anthropologists began to work on in the 1950s. For example, it is evident that Kroeber's approach probably goes too far in stressing the cultural similarities affected by the ecological adaptation process. There is a lingering question: Are all aspects of a culture affected in the same manner by the adaptation to environmental conditions? The answer is "evidently not." Some cultural aspects, such as tools and technology, substance patterns, or economic systems of exchange, have a direct relationship to ecological resources. Other cultural patterns, such as kinship systems, religious beliefs, or world views, are far more removed from the environmental substrate.

This idea, then, that not all aspects of a culture are affected equally by the adaptive process to environmental conditions, lead anthropologists such as Julian Steward (1955), in his *Theory of Culture Change*, to suggest that the adaptive process should be viewed in terms of two significant parts. One part is termed the *core*, or the techno-economic aspects of a culture, and the other the *superstructure*, comprising ideology, religion, folklore, or politics. In other words, the *core* is more directly tied to and influenced by the local ecological conditions, while the *superstructure* of a culture is far less affected because it is less directly impacted by changing environmental factors.

Steward's approach has come to be termed "cultural ecology," by which is meant "an anthropological approach that focuses on the environmental effects of cultural behaviour in such areas as labour patterns, exchange systems, and socio-political organization" (Hedican, 2012a, p. 266). Steward's approach builds on that of Kroeber's culture area concept stressing adaptation, in which the environment is understood in ecological terms as "the total web of life wherein all plants and animal species interact with one another and with physical features in a particular unit of territory" (Steward, 1955, p. 30). Steward differs from Kroeber in the specification of particular cultural aspects that are either directly or less directly influenced by environmental factors.

The anthropological approach to the interaction of culture and environment was further refined by the idea of "habitat," as in Daryll Forde's (1963) *Habitat, Economy and Society.* "His main contribution," Harris (1968) explains, "is to warn geographers that they could not hope to understand cultures as mere reflexes of environment" (p. 664). In Forde's (1963) terms, "the habitat at one and the same time circumscribes and affords scope for cultural environment in relation to the pre-existing equipment and tendency of a particular society, and to any new concepts and equipment that may reach it from without ... physical conditions enter intimately into every cultural development and pattern.... They enter not as determinants, however, but as one category of the raw material of cultural elaboration" (p. 464).

Later work in cultural anthropology, such as Marvin Harris's (1991) "cultural materialism" approach, focused on assigning a causal priority to the material conditions of social life. Harris's underlying assumption is that such aspects as philosophy or poetry (or the awarding of prestigious literary prizes, for that matter) can only be developed after people first provide for their basic material needs, such as the provision of food and shelter. Thus, human activity is organized around the satisfaction of the material conditions of life based on the level of technological sophistication, as well as the nature of the environment, which in turn makes possible other social organizational and ideological responses. These components of cultural materialism, with its emphasis on causality, in turn provide the trajectory on which human civilization moves forward in time.

ASSESSMENT

This review of anthropological approaches to culture and environment has been by necessity much briefer than one would prefer, since the presentation here is but a bare-bones summary of what is a very long historical development in the discipline. It should not also be implied that an anthropological approach to understanding the ecological conditions of human life has been consistent over the years. Certainly, it could be argued that "cultural ecology ... constituted a massive repudiation of historical particularism" (Barrett, 1996, p. 92) and Boas's unconvincing rejection of environmental determinism.

Cultural ecology and its later manifestation in the form of cultural materialism also aspired to a certain scientific or nomothetic status, but not everyone would agree that this aspiration was successful. Nonetheless, it is particularly evident that anthropologists have made a sustained effort for well over a century to clarify the interrelationships between environment and culture—Boas's possibilism, Kroeber's culture area concept, Forde's habitat and economy, Steward's cultural ecology, and Harris's cultural materialism. No one should suggest that this relationship is an easy one to depict, as the troubled history of anthropology in this regard well illustrates.

It should also be noted that anthropologists have not fallen into the trap of rejecting environment altogether as a causal factor, in the same manner that some geographers have rejected the role of culture. Anthropologists have not been seduced by a notion of "cultural determinism" (Sidky, 2004, pp. 120–22), even though it could be argued that the Boasian paradigm of historical particularism came close to following in this direction. Boas's early ethnographic research in Baffin Island in the 1880s was initially based on an interest in the importance of geographical factors in the life of the Inuit; however, after the publication of *The Central Eskimo* (1888), Boas was never again to place any prominence in a culture's geographical setting.

As a student of Boas's, Kroeber (1935) remarked that the Inuit Baffin Island study was "the only one in which the geographical setting is given other than perfunctory or minimal consideration" (p. 543). Therefore, as Harris (1968) concluded, "It is thus clear that in shifting over from geography to ethnography, Boas was moving away from a belief in geographical determinism" (p. 266). Boas (1948) himself made perfectly clear his position on geographical explanations with the statement that "it is fruitless to try to explain culture in geographical terms" (p. 266).

The history of anthropological theory, from its early beginnings, could therefore be seen as an attempt to chart a reasonable course between geographical determinism on one extreme and the excesses of Boas's historical particularism on the other. The task for anthropologists has been to formulate coherent statements concerning the interaction between culture and environment without reverting to the untenable deterministic schemes of geography, which make little provision for cultural variables, or of cultural deterministic schemes (culture only comes from culture), which discount the importance of human-environmental relationships.

After this lengthy discussion concerning anthropology's theoretical struggles relating environment and culture, we now turn again to Diamond's treatise on the rise of human civilizations. To refresh the reader's memory, we repeat Diamond's (1999) central point in writing *Guns, Germs, and Steel*: "History followed different courses for different peoples because of differences among peoples' environments, not because of biological differences among peoples themselves" (p. 25). However, the issue is not the juxtaposition of environment and biology as Diamond suggests, but between environment and culture. Since he does not want to suggest that human behaviour is determined by biology (or race), we are left with geography as the only alternative, as if geography and biology exhaust the range of explanations for human behaviour.

Diamond (1999) then back tracks, as a means of drawing the reader in: "Yet geography obviously has *some* effect on history; the question concerns how much effect" (p. 26; emphasis in original). Of course it is true that geography must have *some* effect on human history. He then lists other scientific disciplines that can contribute new information on the subject of human history: genetics, molecular biology, epidemiology, and linguistics (p. 26). Curiously, anthropology is not mentioned as a discipline contributing to knowledge about human history. The point is clearly made by Diamond, and just as clearly, issues of culture do not enter into this logic. The reason that anthropology is not mentioned is that if culture were given its due regard then the explanatory role of geographical influences on human history would by necessity be significantly diminished.

In the later portion of his discourse, Diamond then marshals the support of fellow colleagues who are equally adamant about the primacy of geographical factors as the single most important variable in providing explanations of human history. In response to the question "Why Europe, not China?" Diamond (1999) rejects "historical" influences, which he refers to as "proximate factors," such as differences in religion, the rise of Western science, or the emergence of European capitalism. In other words, as Diamond concludes, "I suggested that the underlying reason behind Europe's overtaking China was something deeper than the proximate factors suggested by most historians" (p. 430).

As one might expect, Diamond's "something deeper" explanation for the prominence of Europe over China involves an environmental basis. A colleague of Diamond's, Graeme Lang, in the afterword states unequivocally that "differences between Europe and China in ecology and geography helped to explain the very different fates of science in the two regions" (p. 432). Also mentioned are the favourable amounts of rainfall in Europe that produced a growing agricultural surplus, whereas in China irrigation agriculture lead to stifling state-controlled bureaucracies. Thus, "the geography of China, unlike that of Europe, did not favor the prolonged survival of independent states. Instead, China's geography facilitated eventual conquest and unification over a vast area.... The resulting state system suppressed most of the conditions required for the emergence of modern science" (p. 432). In addition, with regard to the question "Why were Europe and China different with regard to those social and cultural factors?" Diamond maintains that "explanations rooted ultimately in geography and ecology ... have reached bedrock" (p. 432).

To be fair, not all anthropologists find Diamond's work objectionable. Brian Ferguson (1998), in a review in *American Anthropologist*, laments the absence of a focus on changes in political economy. However, he suggests that anthropologists could learn a great deal from Diamond about bringing significant academic issues to a public forum. If anthropologists, for example, see their job as explaining variation and similarity in different cultures, then Diamond's book could be used as an exemplary case study. Diamond's work is also an example about how to "illuminate big questions, questions that make a difference, questions that a non-anthropological public cares about" (Ferguson, 1998, p. 901).

Diamond's conclusion, then, at least in relation to the prominence of Europe over China (an unresolved issue in itself), and by extension more broadly as to other similar historical questions of one civilization dominating another, is that social and cultural factors are not as significant as environmental ones. Thus, over a century of ethnographic and theoretical study by anthropologists into the characteristics of the relationship between environment and society is discounted in the space of a mere page. A final question therefore remains; while Diamond's book may be seductive reading for a popular audience, and has even achieved a certain degree of notoriety by winning a Pulitzer Prize, we nonetheless are compelled to ask, is it reputable science?

PUBLIC APPEAL AND REPUTABLE SCIENCE

In fact, a conference was convened in 2006 at the annual meeting of the AAA comprising archaeologists, cultural anthropologists, and historians to analyze the validity of Diamond's conclusions and case studies (McAnany & Yoffee, 2010; Lewis, 2010). The various chapters reporting the results of this conference were written for the wider public, rather than the more narrow focus of specialists, in an attempt to discuss the immense popular appeal of Diamond's *Guns, Germs, and Steel* (1999) and his later work *Collapse: How Societies Choose to Fail or Succeed* (2005).

The participants in this conference are guarded in their assessment of Diamond's work, and are "not a collection of indignant scholars dwelling on factual inaccuracies or 'Diamond-bashing'" (Lewis, 2010, p. 413). In any event, the scholars are quite clear in their assessment that environment is not the only significant factor that societies must cope with in order to remain sustainable. The contributors also were concerned with "Diamond's troubling propensity to overlook the real and powerful influences of cultural ideologies on the paths that civilizations took" (Lewis, 2010, p. 413). Human societies, they point out, also exhibit a significant degree of resilience that allows them to adapt to changing ecological conditions and to develop coping strategies, such as abandoning their settlements in favour of new habitation sites or developing approaches that better fit their economic, social, or cultural needs.

In other words, human societies are not just hapless victims of their environments, as Diamond appears to suggest.

ENVIRONMENTAL EXPLANATIONS
FOR EUROPEAN DOMINATION

The implied geographical determinism in *Gun, Germs, and Steel* is certainly a troubling epistemological point of contention, but at a deeper level the manner in which biology and race are dealt with is an even more salient matter. As has been previously reiterated, Diamond stresses in the beginning of his book (1999, p. 25) that the different trajectories in history of different societies are due to differences in people's environments, and not biological differences. Thus, Diamond would appear to disengage himself from any charge of racial determinism as an historical explanation for the differing success of the various societies discussed in his book. Unfortunately, not everyone would agree.

Kathleen Lowrey (2005) suggests that *Guns, Germs, and Steel* is so popular because it "lets the West off the hook." As she explains, "This is a punch line about race and history that many white people want desperately to hear.... It poisonously whispers: mope about colonialism, slavery, capitalism, racism, and predatory neo-imperialism all you want but these were/are nobody's fault. This is a wicked cop-out. Worse still, it is a profound insult to all non-Western cultures/societies.... Such an assertion tramples upon all that anthropology holds dear, and is a sham sort of anti-racism" (n.p.).

Similarly, in a very lengthy review of Diamond's work in the *Journal of Social Archaeology*, Michael Wilcox (2010) concludes that *Guns, Germs, and Steel* is only "disguised as an attack on racial determinism ... [and] that narratives such as Diamond's are the most potent instruments of conquest" (p. 92). Wilcox's criticism is that "much of Diamond's data is drawn from archaeological literature largely written in isolation from Native American descendent communities.... The mythology of conquest and disappearance [is] grounded in a scholarship that has failed to incorporate Indigenous histories" (pp. 92–93). European ascendency and conquest is based on an ideology that is "factually incorrect," and as such is an example of "marketing conquest" (p. 115).

Wilcox's primary objection to *Guns, Germs, and Steel* is that in the retelling of traditional domination histories, Diamond's account of the factors responsible for European ascendency are largely the product of a convergence of accidental and somewhat distant history. It is as if the domination of New World societies happened as an accidental by-product of microscopic misadventure. Thus, the savage brutality of such incidents as Pizarro's seizing of the Inca Empire of Peru by perfidious means seems justified on the grounds that the Inca would have died out anyway. In addition, just because you have the capability to dominate other societies by means of technological superiority does not justify that they be used for imperialistic or colonial purposes.

Diamond, in addition, has little to say about the important political factors and decisions that were made that enabled Europeans to pursue imperialistic objectives. An analysis of the political underpinnings of European success in subjugating those who stood in the way of the pursuit of resources was at times a crucial factor in extending colonial rule. David Cahill (2010), for example, points out that in describing the heroics of Francisco Pizarro's conquest of the Inca, Diamond ignores the many thousands of Indigenous South Americans who aided the Spanish forces.

Cahill's (2010) argument is that there could never have been a Spanish empire without these sorts of political collaborations: "The arrival of the Spanish interlopers suddenly made independence from imperial rule a practical possibility. Diamond overlooks entirely not only the crucial support from non-Incan native allies, but also the overwhelming degree to which any government, Andean or Spanish, depended on a functioning tier of local, regional, and interregional ruling cadres" (pp. 215, 224). A similar point is also made by Matthew Restall (2004) in his study of the *Seven Myths of the Spanish Conquest*, who points out that the various alliances turned out to be beneficial to some sectors of the Indigenous population who, because of the political compromises they made, allowed them to live in relative amity with their conquerors.

Another area of criticism concerns geographer James Blaut's (1999, 2000) characterization of Diamond's work as an example of "a modern Eurocentric historian." The suggestion here is that Diamond misleads the reader into accepting as fact the notion that the people of Western Europe are responsible for technological innovations that actually arose in Asia or the Middle East. Blaut also argues that Diamond either ignores or misrepresents the nutritional value of crops grown outside parts of Eurasia, and that, contrary to Diamond's supposition that the main axis of diffusion is in an east-west direction, the cultivation of corn in Peru and the transmission of this cultigen into North America from Meso-America is a noted example of a north-south movement of crops. The idea that there were significant ecological constraints to the north-south diffusion of domesticated crops is therefore largely invalidated by the fact that, even before the arrival of Europeans, maize was grown as far north as Canada (Blaut, 1999, p. 395).

Blaut's (1999) main conclusion is that "environmental determinism has served to validate a Eurocentric world history for several centuries, and it continues to do so today.... [For Diamond], culture is largely irrelevant; the environment explains all of the main tendencies of history" (pp. 391–92). Similarly, Mokyr (1999) uses the term "Eurocentricty" (p. 1243) to refer to the European acquisition of useful technology which they "learned rather greedily," in contrast to the Chinese hesitancy in accepting beneficial technological improvements from foreigners. It was therefore the cultural dynamics that prevented the Chinese from benefiting from the diffusion of new technology, contrary to Diamond's contention that the key factors involved were those of ecology.

CONCLUSION

The discussion of the work of Jared Diamond presented in this chapter is meant to provide a forum or basis for debate concerning an extremely important Pulitzer Prize– winning scholarly work. As far as public anthropology is concerned, Diamond's arguments in *Guns, Germs, and Steel* pose a challenge for anthropologists to respond to the suggestion that European domination of Indigenous peoples is merely the result of environmental opportunities, as opposed to imperialistic policies and colonial suppression. The discussion in this chapter is intentionally presented in a polemical manner such that certain questions that are raised in Diamond's work might be considered in light of anthropology's current and historical issues. These issues pertain, primarily, to the role of environment in cultural development, and the basis of human biological diversity. Also at issue are such topics as the assumed ascendency of European technological development and the role of colonial and imperialistic policies in the subjugation of Indigenous populations. The point of debate concerns whether or not the reader agrees with the statement that "Jared Diamond has done a huge disservice to the telling of human history," as Antrosio (2012, n.p.) asserts. Or, as Dennie (2011) asks, "Is it worth the hype?" (n.p.).

Chapter 5

HEALTH, WELL-BEING, AND FOOD SECURITY

Public anthropology can take many forms. In this chapter, anthropological research that is conducted with more academic goals in mind nonetheless have far-reaching implications in the wider public domains of health, food security, and the understanding of disease transmission. In particular, the goal of this chapter is to study the manner in which studies in medical anthropology, and related fields of nutrition and food security, have wider impacts beyond the specific studies conducted in academic research and therefore can be understood as making contributions to the expanding field of public anthropology.

Over the last several decades, anthropology has witnessed a surge of interest in such subjects as medical anthropology, health and disease, food security, nutrition, and a variety of related research topics. A notable figure in this nexus of interest is Paul Farmer and his influential book *Pathologies of Power* (2003). He has also contributed substantially to the growth of interest in medical anthropology with his previous research on AIDS in Haiti, especially in terms of how political economy plays a significant role in negatively influencing the quality of life of the sufferers of this disease (Farmer, 1992).

Other important topics in anthropologists' interest in health and well-being include the role of traditional medicine and how it is impacted by the spread of the commercialization of Western medicine. Anthropologists have also researched threats to food security in poor countries as nutritional stress is exacerbated by a tendency for community agricultural practices to shift from local self-sufficiency to an increased reliance on foods produced outside the region.

MEDICAL ANTHROPOLOGY

Medical anthropology is one of the most highly developed areas of applied anthropology. It is interdisciplinary in nature, combining ecological perspectives, bio-cultural adaptation, epidemiology, and health care systems. Essentially, medical anthropology is a field of cultural anthropology that studies the relationships between culture and society and the manner in which these are influenced by health, nutrition, and pathology and disease issues.

The term "medical anthropology" has been in use since the early 1960s, although an interest in the relationship between anthropology and medicine extends back many decades before this period. In addition, there have been several anthropologists who have received their primary training in medicine, psychology, and psychiatry before their contributions to anthropology, such as W.H.R. Rivers (1920), who conducted a study of the "Biological Theory of the Psycho-Neuroses," and Abraham Kardiner (1939, 1959) with his "Psychosocial Studies." A psychological orientation, especially in the "culture and personality school," was particularly prominent for several decades. As Edward Sapir (1932) explained in an article entitled "Cultural Anthropology and Psychiatry," "The true locus of culture is in the interactions of specific individuals and, on the subjective side, in the world of meanings which each one of these individuals may unconsciously abstract for himself from his participation in these interactions" (pp. 432–33).

Eventually, in anthropology, an interest in the ways in which the individual personalities are shaped by cultural processes began to give way to an interest in what is termed "transcultural psychiatry" (Bibeau, 1997).

TRADITIONAL MEDICINE

Another intersection between anthropology and medicine concerns "popular" or "folk" medicine. The term has been used to describe the sorts of health practices of Indigenous people in various parts of the world. There is a strong emphasis in this area of study on ethno-botanical knowledge and the use of traditional cures to treat illness and disease. During the first part of the twentieth century, this interest in folk medicine also included a focus on religious and magical practices since in many cultures traditional healers used various methods of treatment that were not known in Western science.

Related areas of interest stemmed from this interaction between culture and medicine, such as concepts of "normality" and how these are interpreted in a bio-cultural context. Such interests are strongly influenced by cultural anthropology's strong commitment to the concept of cultural relativism. For example, there are various ailments and diseases that belong to specific cultures, such as the *pibloktoq* psychological phenomenon of the Arctic (Koerth-Baker, 2011), or the *nerva* disorder which Lock and Wakewich-Dunk (1990) describe as occurring among immigrant Greek women living in Montreal. This condition of *nerva* could not be effectively diagnosed using the conventional concepts of Western medicine.

The Greek women in this study complained about chest pains and dizziness. The investigators concluded that these symptoms were the result of the isolation the Greek women felt, and the confusion that they experienced in their situation as immigrants in a large Canadian city. These are what could be described as "culture bound syndromes" or cultural representations of disease, health, and medical care, which are a product of a specific ethnic group's historical and social processes. In other words, mental health issues are understood more effectively if they can be placed in the social and cultural context in which they occur.

Medical anthropology does not therefore seek to impose Western scientific medicine on local Native peoples. It recognizes that Indigenous beliefs have value in areas of treatment, practices, and beliefs whether or not these are recognized by scientific medicine practitioners. The aim is to attempt a synchronization of Indigenous and Western practices so that this approach brings about effective results without supplanting local health care with health systems imposed or controlled by external agencies.

MEDICAL ANTHROPOLOGY IN CANADA

In Canada, the Association for Medical Anthropology was founded in 1982 and has experienced a steady growth in its activities ever since. Significant studies have been reported in areas of nutrition, illness, disease, and other health-related issues. Speck (1987), for example, studied the politics of medical practices in British Columbia in her book *An Error in Judgement*. Health care and culture change is the topic of a report of Aboriginal experiences in the central Subarctic (Young, 1988).

In addition, Turner (1989) described the survival of Inupiaq Eskimo skills as traditional healers and shaman. Similarly, Young, Ingram, and Swartz (1990) reported on their study of a Cree healer in *Cry of the Eagle*. A wide-ranging study of Aboriginal health in Canada from historical, cultural, and epidemiological perspectives is reported by Waldram, Herring, and Young (1995). Waldram (1997) also conducted a study of Aboriginal spirituality and symbolic healing in Canadian prisons in *The Way of the Pipe*. The areas of diet, food, and nutrition have also been important areas of research for applied anthropologists in Canada (Hedican, 1990a; Feit, 2004; Waldram & O'Neil, 1989; Waldram, Herring, & Young, 1995).

PROFILE: EMOKE SZATHMARY

In 1923, Canadian medical scientist Sir Frederick Banting received the Nobel Prize in medicine for his research in developing the use of insulin in combatting diabetes. Years later, medical anthropologist Emoke Szathmary has also made significant

BOX 5.1 Diamond Jenness (1886–1969): Psychology and Culture

Diamond Jenness was born in Wellington, New Zealand, and eventually became a pioneer of Canadian anthropology. Jenness graduated with a master's degree in 1908 from New Zealand's Victoria University College. Later, from 1911 to 1912, he became an Oxford University scholar in eastern Papua New Guinea. Jenness's long career in Canadian anthropology began almost accidently when he accepted what he thought was a temporary position as an ethnologist with the Canadian Arctic Expedition from 1913 to 1916.

From then on, Diamond Jenness focused his career on First Nations research and administrative studies. From 1926 until his retirement in 1948, Jenness held the distinguished position as Director of Anthropology at the National Museum of Canada. Between 1920 and 1970, he also had an outstanding career as author of more than 100 ethnographic and archaeological works primarily focused on Canada's Inuit and First Nations peoples. Over the length of his career, Jenness conducted original fieldwork among the Copper Inuit of the central Arctic, and among the Carrier, Ojibwa, Sekani, and Salish First Nations.

FIGURE 5.1 Diamond Jenness (left)
Source: Rudolph Martin Anderson/Library and Archives Canada/C-086412

During Jenness's fieldwork among the Pacific coast Wet'suwet'en of British Columbia, an elderly woman had fallen ill with "kyan," a malady attributed to possession by "the dreaded mountain spirit." The local belief is that only those who have recovered from this affliction are capable of controlling the spirit's power and driving it from the patient's body. Such people form a highly specialized medicine society, and in this case its members convened at the home of the stricken woman.

During a ceremony in which much singing and drumming was taking place, a white school teacher objected to "their humbug," storming off to complain to the local Indian agent and police constable. The attendants then took evasive action, shifting the proceedings to a neighbour's house in a more secluded part of the reserve. According to Richling's (2012) account, "As a reflection of their considerable trust in Jenness, they asked him to join them, assuming that the presence of a white man—a sympathetic one at that—would enable him to speak authoritatively in their defense should further complaints of 'improper or harmful' conduct eventuate" (pp. 177–78). It turned out that Jenness described this event as "the most ethnographically insightful experience" of his five months of fieldwork with the Wet'suwet'en.

This single event apparently did much to reduce Jenness's skepticism about Native medicinal practices. In addition, he came to believe that there was nothing fictitious or consciously self-induced by the treatment, and that Wet'suwet'en medicine, even though much unlike its Western counterpart, nonetheless ultimately provided an efficacious result. In fact, in 1929, Jenness even consulted Sir Frederick Banting, a recent Nobel laureate for his treatment of diabetes, during a meeting of the Royal Society, who suggested the work Jenness conducted "stood to make a valuable contribution to mental health theory and practice and urging its submission to a Canadian medical journal to gain maximum exposure" (Richling, 2012, p. 178).

Jenness's resulting scholarly paper, entitled "An Indian Method of Treating Hysteria" (Jenness, 1933), would appear to anticipate the field of psychological anthropology, or at least the "culture and personality" school advocated by Ruth Benedict in her influential text *Patterns of Culture* (1934). Irving Hallowell's fieldwork among the Ojibwa of the Berens River area of northwestern Ontario as depicted in his highly regarded work in *Culture and Experience* (1955) also could be seen as an extension of Jenness's interest in a psychological orientation to culture change.

contributions to diabetes research. Szathmary was born in Hungary and, after immigrating to Canada, earned a PhD in 1974 from the University of Toronto. Her research has largely focused on type-2 diabetes, especially concerning the microevolution of this disease among Subarctic and Arctic Aboriginal populations. In recognition of her research in the fields of genetic biology and medical anthropology, Szathmary has served as editor-in chief of both the *Yearbook of Physical Anthropology* (1987–1991) and the *American Journal of Physical Anthropology* (1995–2001).

Szathmary was also named the president and vice-chancellor of the University of Manitoba (1996–2008). In other academic posts, she has been chairperson of the Department of Anthropology at McMaster University, returning later to serve as McMaster's provost and vice-president. She has also served as the Dean of the Faculty of Social Science at the University of Western Ontario. Szathmary's research has earned her many awards and accolades because of her contributions to public health and the study of human genetics. For example, she was named a distinguished lecturer by the American Anthropological Association in 1998. This acknowledgement is the highest recognition given by the anthropological discipline for a lifetime of exemplary scholarship. In the public sphere, Professor Szathmary was appointed a member of the Order of Canada in 2003, and was named a fellow of the Royal Society of Canada in 2005. In 2007, she was awarded the Manitoba Lieutenant Governor's Medal for excellence in public administration (see the *Winnipeg Free Press*, 3 November 2009).

Szathmary's field research has been conducted among the Ottawa, Ojibwa, and Dogrib First Nations of Ontario and the Northwest Territories (Szathmary, 1990, 1994a, 1994b; Szathmary, Ritenbaugh, & Goody, 1987). A study of the geographical distribution of diabetes among the Native population of Canada examined such variables as culture area, language families, and geographical isolation (Young, Szathmary, Evers, & Wheatly, 1990). Of the more than 5,000 cases of diabetes examined in First Nations communities, these cases ranged from 0.8 per cent for the Northwest Territories, to 8.7 per cent in the Atlantic region. Among the Inuit, the cases of diabetes were the lowest in all of the Canadian Native population at 0.4 per cent. The conclusion was that both genetic and environmental factors were responsible for this distribution.

A more focused study of diabetes among the Dogrib of the Northwest Territories, where incidences of diabetes are relatively low, examined the important factor of dietary change (Szathmary et al., 1987). Among the Dogrib, the traditional food base is relatively stable. When new foods are introduced to the diet they do not replace traditional foods, but are added to it, which results in an increase in caloric intake.

Szathmary's studies of diabetes and Native food consumption have important policy implications. Her research has shown that diabetes among Native peoples is highest in areas in which a greater amount of non-traditional foods are consumed. Generally these non-traditional foods are high in calorie-laden carbohydrates and low in protein. Conversely, in the Northwest Territories, where traditional foods continue to form a high percentage of consumption patterns, the diet is typically one low in carbohydrates and high in protein. In other words, incidences of diabetes tend to increase when low-quality, non-traditional foods are consumed.

The policy implications of these studies are that it is desirable that traditional hunting, fishing, and gathering be continued wherever possible because of the health advantages over a low-quality diet introduced from outside the community. Government programs could be introduced to encourage traditional food use, such as preventing clear-cut forestry practices that increase habitat loss for animals, especially such large herbivores as moose, deer, and woodland caribou. The pollution of lakes and rivers, such as the tragic case of the Grassy Narrows and White Dog communities of northern Ontario inflicted with mercury contamination, provide less favourable environments for fish and aquatic mammals (Hedican, 2008, pp. 126–35).

In conclusion, it is research such as that conducted by Szathmary that has contributed immeasurably to the scientific basis of knowledge concerning the relationships between disease, health, and environmental factors among the Canadian Native population. Her research also has wider implications in the arena of public policy because it informs us of the dietary risks of the modern person's consumption patterns, which are predominately based on a high-fat, high-carbohydrate, low-protein, and high-glucose intake.

These dietary characteristics have been shown to increase incidences of diabetes, but also heart disease, as well as certain types of gastrointestinal cancers. In other words, Szathmary's research makes an important contribution to public anthropology because it illustrates the importance of returning to a healthier, more traditional diet among humans in the modern age. The wider impact of her research extends beyond medical anthropology far into the public realm, because it has the potential to influence the daily lives of people as they attempt to achieve healthier ways of living through nutrition, diet, and exercise.

MERCURY POISONING IN NORTHERN ONTARIO

A study described by Shkilnyk (1985), entitled *A Poison Stronger than Love*, detailed the effects of mercury pollution in the Aboriginal communities of Grassy Narrows and White Dog in northwestern Ontario near the Manitoba border. Grassy Narrows is an Ojibway or Anishenabe First Nation reserve situated about 80 kilometers north of Kenora, Ontario. Their reserve, officially designated as English River 21, is located on the Wabigoon-English River system, which was the site of a chlor-alkali processing plant. This plant was operated by the Dryden Chemical Company, which had been discharging mercury-contaminated effluent into the river system for many years.

Eventually, the Dryden plant was bought by a British multinational corporation called the Reed Paper Limited, and it continued to discharge the dangerous waste into the river system (Michalenko & Suffling, 1982; Bueckert, 2003).

Eventually, in 1961, the Reed Paper company purchased an old pulp mill in Dryden, also near Kenora in northwestern Ontario. In 1969, mercury pollution was first detected downstream from the old mill; however, measures were not enacted at that time to stop the pollution. Altogether, it has been estimated that over 10 tons of mercury, which is a shocking amount, was dumped or leaked into the Wabigoon-English River system, and another 15 tons of mercury was never accounted for.

It was not until 1970 that some control measures were finally introduced, and commercial fishing in the river system was terminated the previous year. Surprisingly, sport fishing was allowed to continue, on the rationale that the tourist industry was a vital financial asset to the area, and the fishermen would not eat enough of the mercury-contaminated fish to injure their health, since they were probably only infrequent visitors. In addition, tourist camps were also allowed to continue their operation in the area despite the high levels of mercury contamination. The problem for the Aboriginal residents of the area was that they had little choice but to continue eating the contaminated fish because the hunting and trapping economy had fallen into decline and as a result there were few alternatives for local food consumption. In addition, the commercial fishery provided just about the only alternative for not only food but also employment income.

A Japanese researcher named Masazumi Harada began conducting tests for mercury in the Wabigoon-English River system in the 1970s, and he was the first to diagnose eight Grassy Narrows residents with what he termed "Minimata disease." According to Harada, this is a neurological disorder also found in Japanese communities where mercury pollution is prevalent. The symptoms were similar, he claimed, characterized by blurred vision, shaking limbs, slurred speech, and poor muscle coordination. Initially, several of the reserve residents were thought to be drunk because of the similarity of the symptoms of excessive alcohol consumption and mercury pollution.

In one study that was reported in the news media (Bueckert, 2003), in a sample of 60 First Nation people living in the Grassy Narrows and White Dog reserves, 42 (70 per cent) showed evidence of this neurological disorder. The Ontario government responded by telling the local residents to stop eating the fish in the mercury-polluted river and to close their commercial fishery. Unfortunately, without other means of employment and generally lacking other sources of locally available food, many Aboriginal residents felt that they were forced to ignore the government warning and to continue eating contaminated fish.

Fish from the Wabigoon-English River system provided much needed protein. Given the fact that the Aboriginal residents suffered from 90 per cent unemployment in the area, closing the commercial fishery caused great economic and nutritional stress for the local population. Eventually, in 1985, the Canadian government compensated the residents of the Grassy Narrows and White Dog reserves with a $16.6 million settlement. This compensation, while providing much needed relief, did nothing, however, about the contamination of the river system as the mercury was never removed. Such a move also did little to improve the economic conditions of the area, or provide a viable source of sustained employment for the Aboriginal population.

Mr. Harada revisited the local Aboriginal reserves some 30 years after his initial study in order to conduct some follow-up research. He wanted to find out if the mercury levels had been reduced or remained the same after these three decades. Harada discovered that the mercury levels in the river system had actually increased over this period and therefore the pollution problem was becoming even more severe. The hope was that over the intervening three decades, during which time there was no more mercury effluent discharged in the river system by the pulp and paper companies because these operations had been shut down, the contamination problem would have been eliminated.

Mercury is a heavy metal and therefore it is probable that it will not simply be washed away by the actions of the river flow, but will have settled in the river bottom. One theory as to the reason for the mercury problem becoming more severe is that the clear-cut forestry practices have contributed to an increase in mercury pollution. The reasoning, which has not been substantiated by scientific research, is that incinerators and coal-fired power plants in the region contribute to an increase in airborne mercury. This mercury might normally be contained by the forest foliage, but with the removal of large stands of trees, the forest's ability to confine the mercury has been substantially reduced. The suggestion then is that intensive logging in northwestern Ontario is responsible for the accumulation of mercury in the river systems. Pollution in particular, and the industrial exploitation of northern resources, is therefore seen as the cause of much nutritional and other health-related problems for residents of the area.

TRADITIONAL MEDICINE: THE LIFE OF A CREE HEALER

Russell Willier, also known by his Cree medicine name of *Mehkwasskwan* or Red Cloud, became an Aboriginal healer after receiving a vision which foretold his role as a traditional Cree medicine man. In his vision, Red Cloud saw himself standing in front of a number of Aboriginal people who could not speak because they had no tongues; therefore, he was selected to speak on behalf of his people because he was the only one with a tongue. Throughout his career, Red Cloud has used a combination of sweat lodge therapy, herbal remedies, and other traditional techniques to treat chronic and stress-related conditions as well as various other physiological dysfunctions (Young, 1988; Young, Ingram, & Swartz, 1988, 1990).

Red Cloud believes that his healing methods are successful because of the aid of his spirit helper, the eagle. The eagle represents far-sightedness and symbolizes much of what his vision has come to mean. For example, Red Cloud envisions himself promoting Native ways, which to him does not mean returning to the old days, but moving toward a synthesis or metamorphosis that will strengthen the role of Native people in society. The eagle aides in this role by encouraging strength, majesty, and courage in Red Cloud's healing techniques. An important aspect of his knowledge is derived from traditional ways, especially his knowledge about the contents of medicine bundles that were obtained from several Cree elders in the area. However, Red Cloud is also willing to innovate by incorporating knowledge derived from many different sources.

One of the most important sources of his knowledge is derived from his great-grandfather Moostoos, who was a noted healer and leader who signed Treaty 8, and who later passed his medicine bundles down to Red Cloud's father, and then down to him. According to the legends passed down through his people, Moostoos was one of the few medicine men powerful enough to kill the *wittiko* or cannibal spirit. On one occasion, Moostoos killed a *wittiko* with an axe after this evil spirit had threatened members of his band. Moostoos was also well known for conducting the shaking tent ceremony. In this ceremony, the medicine man sits at the bottom of a cylindrical tent constructed of vertical poles with an opening at the top. It is through this opening that spirits enter the tent, which begins to shake violently because of the swirling interaction of these entities.

Amid much prayer and chanting, the medicine man attempts to ascertain the cause of various ailments suffered by members of the band. People approach a small flap at the bottom of the tent and ask the medicine man to speak with the spirits on their behalf about some worrying condition. Often a single cure is not specified, but the cause of an aliment is seen as the result of breaking some cultural mores, such as a man who has become overly friendly with his sister-in-law, or has not honoured the ancestors with gifts of tobacco.

Red Cloud himself is a specialist in the treatment of various skin diseases, such as psoriasis, and migraine headaches and backaches. In a treatment for psoriasis, for example, Red Cloud first sprinkles tobacco in a circle around the patient's feet while praying in Cree. He then begins to apply an herbal remedy made from goose grease that he has previously prepared, and then chants a prayer with a steady shaking of his rattle. However, as one patient commented, "The stuff stinks like heck, but who cares as long as it gets rid of the psoriasis.... It's really hard to put it on all the time because I have two night classes. The smell is so bad that one day I washed with tomato juice to try to get rid of it" (Young, Ingram, & Swartz, 1990, p. 103). Additional sessions require patients to spend time in a sweat lodge which opens up the skin's pores, allowing the treatment solution to seep into the infected skin area.

Red Cloud also participated in what was termed the Psoriasis Research Project, in which non-Native patients were treated with traditional Cree remedies. The results were mixed, as some people reported a lessening of their skin condition, while others claimed that no change had occurred. In the future, Red Cloud suggested, non-Native patients should visit his Sucker Creek Reserve so that they could receive the same three-day treatment as their Native counterparts.

Red Cloud's participation in this psoriasis project was the cause of some controversy within the Native community because sacred rituals were involved. Some Native people felt that Red Cloud should not have disclosed sacred knowledge that ought to have been kept within the Native community. Their concerns stemmed in part from a fear that the values and principles of traditional Native medicine would be exposed to ridicule and exploitation. Some Native people even expressed the view that if herbal cures were revealed then large Western drug companies would use them for profit. There were also some negative concerns about traditional Indigenous medicine expressed by health care professionals.

It was noted by medical anthropologists that "criticism of the research project [the Psoriasis Research Project] from within the Western medical system arises from lack of understanding of the context and scope of native therapy, which is considered to be outside the boundaries of modern 'scientific' medicine" (Young, Ingram, & Swartz, 1990, p. 110). In addition, they note that the medical anthropologists received a copy of a letter from the president of the Dermatological Association of Alberta which was addressed to the University of Alberta medical school questioning the use of university research funds for what the dermatological association described as "unscientific activities."

In summary, this anthropological study of a Cree healer illustrates the inability, or even the unwillingness, of many doctors to accept the role of traditional Native therapy and medical practices in the health care system. In response to the apparent intransigence by medical doctors in recognizing Native therapeutic approaches to health care, Aboriginal people have responded by organizing what their own association called the Traditional Native Healing Society. The goals of the Healing Society are as follows:

1. Promote, encourage, and teach Indian culture, customs, and values.
2. Provide for the treatment and prevention of diseases and ailments, incorporating traditional Indian remedies and practices.
3. Experiment with adapting traditional healing practices and remedies to the modern situation in terms of professional services and facilities for patients and families. (Young, Ingram, & Swartz, 1990, p. 131)

It should be noted that this society has been granted charitable status by Canada's federal government, a move which could be interpreted as implying that the government recognizes the value of Native medical approaches. The Healing Society has the potential to act as a bridge between Native and non-Native cultural traditions. Thus, practitioners of medical anthropology have a role in attempting to bring these two areas together for their mutual benefit.

PROFILE: PAUL FARMER

Paul Farmer is a renowned medical anthropologist and physician known for his humanitarian work, especially in bringing modern heath care to so-called Third World peoples. As described in the biographical work entitled *Mountains Beyond Mountains* (2003) by Pulitzer Prize–winning author Tracy Kidder, Farmer is particularly known for his fight against tuberculosis in Haiti, Peru, and Russia.

In 2012, he was appointed as United Nations Secretary-General's Special Adviser for Community-Based Medicine, and is co-founder of Partners in Health, which is an international health and social justice organization. Dr. Farmer was also named chairman of Harvard Medical School's Department of Global Health and Social Medicine in 2009. He is furthermore known for his influential books, especially *AIDS and Accusation: Haiti and the Geography of Blame* (1992), *Pathologies of Power: Health, Human Rights, and the New War on the Poor* (2003), and *Global Health in Times of Violence*, co-edited with Barbara Rylko-Bauer and Linda Whiteford (2009).

In an interview by Mary Carmichael in *Scientific American* (March 2011), Farmer outlines his recent research on cancer in the developing world. In 1970, 15 per cent of diagnosed cancers occurred in developing countries. By 2008, that number had increased to 56 per cent. The death rates from cancer are nearly 50 per cent higher in lower-income countries than in those countries with higher incomes. He also points out that by 2020 there will be more than 15 million people worldwide who will have cancer, according to estimates provided by the World Health Organization. This figure refers to the new cases projected to arise during that year, not to the total number of people afflicted by the disease.

Cancer in the developing world has become increasingly common; treatments are costly and often difficult to obtain. There is also the factor of "lifestyle" issues in developing countries that could be associated with certain risk factors, such as pollution and exposure to toxic chemicals, which could increase the incidences of cancer. In addition, in developing countries, life expectancy is increasing, which gives people more time to die of malignant tumours. With survival rates increasing, there are also treatment problems because of drug-resistant tuberculosis or HIV, according to Farmer.

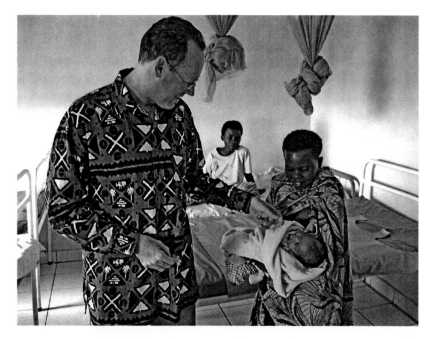

FIGURE 5.2 Dr. Paul Farmer
Source: Reprinted by permission of the Boston Globe

Farmer has also written about the expansion of cancer care in the medical journal *Lancet* (2 October 2010), in which he notes that nearly two-thirds of the 7.6 million cancer deaths on a global basis occur in countries with low- or middle-income levels, but only about 5 per cent of the cancer resources available worldwide are spent in these countries. Farmer is part of a team from the Global Task Force on Expanded Access to Cancer Care and Control in Developing Countries. The goals of this organization are centred on increasing access to medical resources in developing countries. These goals are aimed at decreasing the cost of cancer drugs, raising funds, and determining new ways to deliver cancer drugs to the patients who need them. As he explained, "With cancer, the need to integrate is especially clear, because there's not just one way to approach the disease ... so you need to get different institutional players in medicine involved" (Carmichael, 2011, p. 66).

AIDS and Accusations

Farmer, in his study *AIDS and Accusation* (1992), demonstrates that people in Haiti suffering from HIV/AIDS can be negatively influenced by the constructions of sickness and the general political economy. He points in particular to the role that "accusations" play in negatively influencing Haitians' quality of life of those infected with the virus.

In the mid-1980s, Farmer was working as a doctor in the village of Do Kay. Haiti and the United States were the first countries in the Western hemisphere whose populations suffered the initial appearance of AIDS/HIV. Some scientists even suggested that the disease originated in Haiti, and so Haitians suffered from stigmatizations as AIDS carriers and a consequent social seclusion in such areas as education and employment. The tourist industry also declined as a result of this stigmatization, leading to a further increase in poverty.

Farmer's approach is less an attempt to refute the accusations surrounding the AIDS phenomenon than to explore the underpinning power relationships that have fashioned the development of the disease. The accusations began in 1983 when the Center for Disease Control referred to Haitians as a high-risk group. This designation was based on scant evidence, yet the popular media and even some in the scientific community began to blame Haitian immigrants as the cause of the epidemic outbreak of the disease in North America. Further research demonstrated that in fact the main risk factor was associated with gay North American tourists.

Farmer explains that the accusations against Haitians were not based on sound epidemiological evidence, but on pre-existing folk models in the imaginations of the American public. This folk model is based on the notion that the typical Haitian is a black person who is engaged in voodoo rituals and a multitude of sexual relationships. HIV was seen to be endemic in Haiti because these social, racial, and religious factors were seen as responsible for fuelling the epidemic.

These various factors were important aspects in diverting the attention of North Americans from the fundamental underlying factors responsible for the spread of HIV. Farmer suggests that the real reasons for the spread of HIV infections in Haiti has nothing to do with voodoo rituals or the frequency of sexual encounters, as believed by many North Americans, but is attributable to the horrendous unemployment rates in the country, which have led to a burgeoning prostitution industry. In turn, the poor in Haiti have sexual encounters with infected gay North Americans, thus exacerbating both the health and the economic difficulties in Haiti. Therefore, it is the North American exploitation of Haitians that is the fundamental cause of the AIDS-related problem. Farmer's conclusion is that the political economy of exploitation of the Caribbean is the ultimate cause of the HIV problem and serves to function as rhetoric that blames the victims and not the exploiters.

Farmer's case for examining the political economy of exploitation is built on historical factors. In 1915, for example, Americans began an occupation of Haiti in which vast tracts of land were expropriated. There was also a brutal suppression of the peasant resistance to the occupation. Haiti's main source of foreign exchange was eliminated with the destruction of the pre-independence of the nation's sugar industry. Multiple foreign interventions have also destroyed Haitians' ability to make their own decisions and have prevented the country from developing alternative sources of income.

By the 1970s, the Haitian economy had virtually collapsed, leading to the export of workers as cheap labour elsewhere or as prostitutes servicing foreign tourists. Farmer argues that it is this dependency on remote metropolitan areas outside the country that is responsible for the rapid spread of the HIV infection throughout Haiti. As a medical anthropologist, Farmer is thus able to link the local experiences of the HIV pandemic of the village of Do Kay with the wider narrative of dependency in Haiti, in which there are wide-ranging connections with global processes, poverty, and illness.

Pathologies of Power

Farmer's later study entitled *Pathologies of Power* (2003) further explores the interrelationships between health, disease, and poverty as these are situated in the nexus of the global world political economy. He uses his experiences as a physician and medical anthropologist to study such diseases as tuberculosis and AIDS in particular locales to wider processes, especially in the case of military dictatorships.

The exercise of power is a key factor in creating the condition in which health-related problems flourish. The problem of poverty is initiated by a breakdown of subsistence activities caused by the forced relocation of peasant farmers away from fertile government-controlled land. The displaced farmers are forced to attempt a living on much less fertile land, resulting in malnutrition, starvation, and various social problems. Thus, poor health and poverty are ultimately related to the various economic and political structures of domination and exploitation, far removed from the plight of local peasant farmers. Farmer refers to this phenomenon as *structural violence* (Farmer, 2004).

The case that Farmer makes is that structural violence is embedded ultimately in the "pathologies of power" by which US foreign policy aid and military regimes collaborate in creating circumstances underlying the poverty, disease, and starvation of people in poor countries. Farmer's study is based first of all on the moral premise that health care is a universal human right. In this regard, Farmer is particularly critical of what he refers to as the "market approach" to health care. He argues that there is a need for a moral priority that places health and the lessening of suffering ahead of the market economics of the health care industry.

As far as anthropology is concerned, Farmer is also critical of the cultural relativist position which is so prevalent in the discipline. He suggests the relativist tendencies in anthropology tend to abandon the poor to their own devices because of the anti-advocacy tendencies held by many anthropologists. Furthermore, this lack of advocacy on the part of the poor is maintained by ambivalence about becoming involved in the suffering of the disadvantaged by those in the anthropological community.

A global process that suppresses the poor and creates nutritional problems is certainly an important issue, but another is the breakdown of traditional medicines and other local healing techniques. Farmer suggests the roots of the diminishing of traditional medicine can be found in the proliferation of industrialized modern medicine. The health of the world's population has been negatively affected by the growth of global capitalism and the unrelenting pursuit of economic growth at whatever cost. The quest for unlimited economic expansion is also interrelated with the expansion of Western models of health care around the world. There is also an uncritical approach to the apparent benefits of Western-based medical practices, which ultimately serves to undermine health care practices in traditional societies.

The strength of Farmer's study is that he is able to link global inequality, exploitation of the poor, and the increasing domination of Western medical practices that undermines traditional knowledge. The emerging global capitalist system also tends to undermine the development of local self-reliant health care and tends to create a dependence on technologically driven modern medicine. The result is a continuation or strengthening of dependency relationships between the rich and poor areas of the world, and a move away from sustainable solutions to health care based on local resources and expertise.

FOOD SECURITY

The nutritional problems that form the basis of much of Farmer's research are closely related to the requirements of food security and sovereignty. Food sovereignty can be defined as "the right of each nation to maintain and develop its own capacity to produce the staple foods of its peoples, respecting their productive and cultural diversity" (Menezes, 2001, p. 29). Similarly, the related term "food security" has been defined by the Food and Agriculture Organization of the United Nations as "the availability at all times of adequate world food supplies of basic foodstuffs to sustain a steady expansion of food consumption and to offset fluctuations in production and prices" (Patel, 2009, p. 664). However, in today's world, the food sovereignty of many nations is endangered by various processes that threaten peoples' access to quality food in sufficient quantities to maintain adequate health and nutrition.

While the processes that threaten food security are quite diversified, one can mention at least the large-scale destruction of local habitats and natural resources by multinational corporations. There are also drastic changes in eating habits through the enforcement of national eating standards, or the use of food provisions as an economic tool to enforce political objectives by using sanctions to block access to certain supplies of food.

Certain economic policies that have been developed that work to the disadvantage of poor countries also pose a problem for attaining food security, as well as the imposition of trade regulations which have been imposed externally, and the creation of regional trading blocs which serve to protect their own interests to the disadvantage of others. In addition, there has been a proliferation in recent years of an increasingly internationalized food organization that has negatively impacted peasant- or family-based agriculture.

These various factors that threaten global food security have caused Francisco Menezes (2001) to argue that food sovereignty reaffirms the rights of people to their autonomy, since it affects the ability of people to make their own decisions about what foods they decide to produce and consume. Food security is therefore seen in the context of social equality, since access to good quality food should be seen as a basic human right. Thus food should also be seen in the context of cultural preferences and be nutritionally adequate for the maintenance of basis health.

VIA CAMPESINA

In this context, which is to say from the perspective of globalization processes, food security becomes pitted against bio-piracy and the patenting of genetic resources. An important aspect of food sovereignty involves a resistance to expropriation of natural resources at the local level. This particularly concerns stores of local seeds, as well as access to adequate water and land. As stressed by members of the Via Campesina organization, "Genetic resources are the outcome of millennia of evolution and belong to all humankind. Patenting and retailing genetic resources by private companies should be banned" (Menezes, 2001, p. 32). There is a fear that genetically modified foods represent a threat to food sovereignty because of the increasing control over seed supplies by transnational corporations.

In fact, the Via Campesina organization was founded as a means to resist what has been perceived as autocratic policy making implemented by the World Bank in association with local elites (Desmarais, 2007; Ishii-Eiteman, 2009). Via Campesina adheres to a policy that no members of their organization should be allowed to dictate policy to any other member of the organization, which is consistent with a central feature of the organization's values that spurns policies imposed from above.

In fact, Via Campesina's position is that food sovereignty must be viewed as a necessary precondition for the existence of food security, as indicated by the following statement: "Long-term food security depends on those who produce food and care for the natural environment. As the stewards of food producing resources we hold the following principles as the necessary foundation for achieving food security.... Food is a basic human right. This can only be realized in a system where food sovereignty is guaranteed.... We have the right to produce our own food in our own country" (as cited in Patel, 2009, p. 665).

Thus, questions concerning food security can be seen in the context of power relationships, especially to the extent that discussions of food sovereignty should be viewed in the realm of the power politics of global food production systems. This means that food security and political process are interconnected in certain fundamental ways. As Raj Patel (2009) states, "The language of food sovereignty insets itself into international discourse by making claims on rights and democracy, the cornerstones of liberal governance" (p. 665).

CASE STUDY: THE KOLLI HILLS, SOUTHERN INDIA

Anthropologists are situated in an ideal position to study issues of food security, diet, and nutrition. First of all, their research usually places them in fieldwork situations at the local level that allows them a firsthand view of conditions "on the ground," in contrast to perspectives seen from government ministries or externally to the country itself. Also, research techniques of interviewing and possibly also participant observation allow for direct discussions with local residents concerning their agricultural practices and management of local resources. This sort of research is an invaluable asset when one wishes to compare the views and behaviour of local residents with that sometimes espoused by government officials in the agricultural ministries of capital cities.

Ethnographic research into the political economy of dietary transitions in the Kolli Hills region of southern India, for example, illustrates the wider economic patterns that effect local agricultural decision making (Finnis, 2007, 2008). The Kolli Hills are home to about 37,000 Malaiyali farmers who are engaged in household economies and grow a variety of crops such as coffee, bananas, millet, and spices. A significant agricultural transition has taken place in recent years in which farmers have decided to abandon millet cultivation in favour of growing the cash crop of sweet cassava. This research therefore provides important insights into the relationship between local subsistence economies in which traditional crops are grown primarily for local consumption, and the wider globalization processes that underlie decisions to engage in the commercialization of food production.

There are important impacts on local productive and consumptive patterns as a result of these sorts of decisions. For example, producing new crops for a regional commercial market may generate much needed cash, while traditional, and possibly more nutritious, crop production may decline, leading to health concerns. This is especially the case in the event that a portion of the new cash earned is then spent on less nutritious food sources. In the Kolli Hills region of southern India, this transition involves a decline in the production of traditional millet crops with an increase in cassava production for external markets. As a replacement for the shortfalls in millet production, rice is increasingly relied upon as a staple in the local diet. However, rice is accessed through public distribution ration shops, or purchased from private sources, and has therefore become the staple dietary grain.

As Finnis (2007) explains, "An agricultural shift that abandons minor millets as a food resource reflects environmental changes and household economic aspirations. Such an analysis has implications for the creation of practical food security projects through the recognition and incorporation of small-farmer experiences, voices, and priorities" (p. 343). The nutritional issue illustrated by ethnographic research in the Kolli Hills region is not so much the replacement of millet with rice, or even replacing local crops with those imported from outside the community; rather, it has to do with the role of political economic forces in encouraging a shift away from locally sustainable food production to an increasing reliance on external economic forces. Thus, this reliance on external market forces tends to increase dependency on the outside world while simultaneously decreasing local food security.

Of course, there are always trade-offs in an evolving food consumption and production system, which is what economists refer to as "opportunity costs." Normally, farmers cannot pursue two goals simultaneously, so that decisions to precede along one path means that one must forgo the pursuit of other objectives. In the case of the Kolli Hills, an attempt to generate much needed cash through sweet cassava production leads to a reduction in millet production. Since millet has traditionally been relied upon as the local food source, the pursuit of cassava production leads to the need to replace locally grown millet with a diet of rice which, for the most part, is imported from outside the community.

Beyond the Local Community

If we then step back from this view of local communities in the Kolli Hills region of southern India, we see that there are large-scale transitions occurring that link small centres to the more extensive global community in which the availability of supplies and services are determined by market conditions. There are drawbacks to the production of sweet cassava in the case of the farmers of Kolli Hills, such as the fluctuating market prices that make their incomes less predictable than they might wish. There are also the effects of uncertain yields because of weather conditions and the increasing amount of chemical fertilizers that are used to counteract the effects of soil depletion. Cassava production does, however, provide a virtually guaranteed income for farmers and this crop can be grown in uncertain environmental conditions such as unpredictable rainfall.

The change to a market crop such as sweet cassava is largely driven by a desire by local residents for goods and services not locally available. For example, people need the income from cassava production for building new homes, installing electricity in their domiciles, sending their children to higher levels of education, or throwing lavish wedding parties. The cost of these new economic transitions is a reduction in agricultural biodiversity at the local level and a corresponding decrease in household dietary variety.

There is also the possibility of a less nutritious diet that results from a reliance on a single crop such as rice, which replaces a wider variety of locally grown traditional crops. Since money is in short supply, villagers have a tendency to purchase only a limited variety of foods to supplement their new rice-based diet, whereas previously there were many more vegetables and legumes produced and consumed in the local communities. Meat and meat products, once consumed on a somewhat regular basis, are now only rarely prepared during such functions as weddings or other similar ceremonies.

The Dynamics of Household Economies

This case study of the Kolli Hills region of southern India illustrates the growing development and integration of household economies into larger spheres of production and exchange. It is also about the changing ways of using land and the attempts by local farmers to reduce their uncertainties and anxieties about food production, while at the same time attempting to generate cash through the market economy for goods and services which are now considered necessities. There are health considerations brought about by these changing patterns and preferences, such as concerns about the continued and long-term use of chemical fertilizers in the face of a growing condition of soil nutrient depletion. Farmers are worried that the economic stability of their households will be threatened by this drive for a more prosperous lifestyle.

There is therefore a reorganization occurring about the knowledge of local farming. This reorganization is also part of the larger restructuring of the national agro-industry, which in turn emphasizes a focus on monoculture and high yields, as opposed to an emphasis on health and nutritional preferences. The trouble with this change is that an increasing dependence on one crop, such as cassava production, tends to reduce agricultural flexibility, and provides less of a protection against crop disease and market volatility. Ultimately, all of these factors, while providing certain economic advantages, could nonetheless also pose a threat to local food security in the long term.

GLOBAL FORCES AND LOCAL EFFECTS

Medical anthropology began with a psychological or psychosocial orientation which focused on acculturation studies. Such studies noted the stresses experienced by non-Western peoples in their culture contact with the increasing impacts of the outside world. Later, the emphasis in anthropology began to shift from a psychological focus to the impacts of global capitalism and transnational corporations on such aspects as disease, nutritional stress, and food security.

In northern Ontario, for example, the Aboriginal population in the Kenora region has experienced harmful effects of mercury pollution, widely attributed to the contaminated effluent of pulp and paper companies that operated in the area for many years. Other studies of Canada's Aboriginal populations examined the spread of diabetes, such as that conducted by the research team led by Emoke Szathmary, and the effects of Western medicine on traditional Cree healing practices.

The various aspects of health and well-being discussed in this chapter also illustrate the ever increasing dependency of local communities on global forces. While it could be argued that these forces have beneficial effects, such as increasing living standards in certain respects, there are also increased concerns about a diminishing biodiversity, food security, and the nutritional basis of human life. Farmer's studies of disease and poverty furthermore exemplify the role of political forces, or what he refers to as "structural violence," that place certain people in the role of victim, and others as collaborators in the spread of sickness and ill fortune.

In the case of AIDS research, anthropology attempts to clarify the dynamic relationship between infected people and the political, economic, and cultural environments in which such people live their lives. Anthropologists are interested in the links between cultural and social systems and the larger structural forces in which the HIV problem is situated.

In this context, the research of Paul Farmer demonstrates the manner in which aspects of political economy can have negative influences on the people of Haiti, who are infected due to misleading information about the causes and spread of HIV infections. In the type of research conducted by anthropologists, a combination of approaches are used that link the historical contexts of disease, the larger structures that may influence its spread, and the local understandings and practices of the health problem at the local community level.

This theme of establishing the wider structural context of disease is also an important aspect of Farmer's other study on the *Pathologies of Power* (2003). Farmer is highly critical of what could be termed the "market approach" to health care and the effects of such a system on the poor people of the world. He argues that the Westernized approach to health care is technologically based and is inherently hierarchical. Third

World poverty, Farmer suggests, is the result of the exploitation of global capitalism, which allows despotic regimes to profit from the suffering of a country's poor. In addition, the exercise of power and the technological domination of medical and health care systems have also led to the demise of traditional medicine and arts of healing.

Food security is a related aspect of health and well-being that is affected by the spread of global capitalist systems. This refers to what Patel (2009) has called the "power politics of the [international] food system" (p. 665). The Via Campesina organization is a major contributor to the debate about food security because of its insistence on the rights of people to define their own food and agriculture objectives, under domestic agricultural protection, and the promotion of programs aimed at achieving sustainable development objectives.

On the other hand, ethnographic examples such as research in the Kolli Hills region of southern India illustrate agricultural transitions that have resulted in the near disappearance of traditional staple foods. This research also demonstrates the effects of the degradation of local environments by an overuse of chemical fertilizers, and an ever increasing dependence on a cash economy, often resulting in nutritionally less beneficial diets for local farming communities. In sum, the loss of traditional food crops is a result of the spread of market economies and the increasing integration of local agricultural systems into the expanding network of global capitalism.

CONCLUSION

All of the topics discussed in this chapter have important implications for the developing field of public anthropology. These topics discussed, and the profiles of the various anthropologists, demonstrate that the type of research conducted by anthropologists in medical anthropology and related areas of interest, such as nutrition and food security, illustrate the manner in which this research can be used outside of academic settings and into the public sphere. Therefore, it is reasonable to conclude that the research that is discussed in this chapter has a wider impact than just the publication of results in academic journals; it affects ordinary peoples' lives in very fundamental ways, concerning the manner in which they cope with disease, nutrition, and food security in different parts of the world.

Chapter 6

FORENSIC ANTHROPOLOGY

Forensic anthropology is a field of study combining physical (biological), medical, and cultural anthropology. The term "forensic" refers to a subfield of science that is applied to a court of law. It could be considered a field of public anthropology because it is often practised in the public domain, primarily outside of academic settings; however, this is not exclusively the case. While practices may vary, however, most forensic anthropologists work in the academic field and engage in crime scene consulting work on a case-by-case basis as casework arises. This is also an aspect of anthropology that is associated with crime scene investigations and therefore also has a wide public appeal, as evidenced by the popular *CSI* television series.

THE SCOPE OF FORENSIC ANTHROPOLOGY

The term "forensic" originally meant a place where justice was administered. It is derived from the Latin word *forum*, meaning a "public space" such as a market. Thus, the word *forensis* in Roman times referred to legal trials, sentencing, and executions that took place "for the public to view." Today, the term "forensics" refers to any scientific research that aims to analyze and interpret evidence that is involved in a legal investigative process. Forensic evidence can be derived from a variety of sources, from accounting to zoology, and either manufactured or occurring in nature (Klepinger, 2006, pp. 19–23; Nafte, 2009, pp. 5–6).

Using scientific methodology in a legal investigation is a relatively new approach to solving crimes. Fingerprinting techniques were developed by 1892, blood groupings shortly thereafter (1898), and a system for performing autopsies not long after that. During the mid-1940s, blood tests were used to exclude paternity, although a mother's testimony might be chosen by jurors over conclusive test results. Sometimes the tears of an unwed mother took precedence over scientific evidence (Thomas, 1974).

The American Academy of Forensic Sciences (AAFS) was founded in 1948. This body also held meetings in other countries, such as Argentina, Canada, and Cuba, providing an international organizational base for the interrelationship between science and the legal system. The popularity of forensic anthropology as a specific field of study began in the 1970s, when there was a need for pathological evidence in cases that were brought to court long after the crime had been committed, when the victim's remains were already in an advanced stage of decomposition. Forensic anthropologists could use anthropological and archaeological techniques to analyze and recover human remains in an effort to determine if a person had died from violent trauma, disease, or accidental causes. Thus, they could give evidence on the ethnic or cultural background, sex, age, and stature of a victim, thus filling a void in criminal investigations, which usually focus on more recent cases.

A variety of definitions have been proposed for this field, some more restrictive or expansive than others. Snow (1973), for example, defines forensic anthropology as "the application of the physical anthropologist's specialized knowledge of human sexual, racial, age, and individual variation to problems of medical jurisprudence" (p. 4). He admits that "this definition is broader than the usual ones ... which restrict the scope of forensic anthropology to the identification of human skeletal remains" (Snow, 1982, p. 128). Stewart's (1979, p. ix) approach is an example of the more limited view of the subject matter.

LEGAL AND CRIMINAL INVESTIGATIONS

In a similar vein, Nafte (2009) indicates that "forensic anthropology involves the processing and analyzing of human skeletal remains within the context of a legal investigation" (p. 33). Therefore, "a **forensic anthropologist** is a physical anthropologist, specifically an **osteologist**, who has become part of the legal investigative process" (p. 31, emphasis in the original). The American Board of Forensic Anthropology (ABFA) also defines forensic anthropology in an analogous manner, as "the application of the science of physical or biological anthropology to the legal process. Physical or biological anthropologists who specialize in forensics primarily focus their studies on the human skeleton" (www.theabfa.org).

The extent of and specialization in forensic anthropology is a matter of some debate. Snow (1982) thinks that "it would be most unwise to permit students to specialize in forensic anthropology at the expense of more traditional areas of anthropological knowledge. Overspecialization in anthropology, as in organic evolution, is a pretty sure road to extinction" (p. 113). Of course, such views and the ensuing debate

FIGURE 6.1 Clyde G. Snow
Source: Reprinted by permission of the Associated Press

about the scope of anthropology have been going on for some time. Snow's opinion is that the "four-field" approach in anthropology still has considerable merit, because a more extensive training in anthropology, he argues, lays the foundation for "talents that come in handy when making-a-living time finally comes around" (p. 113).

There is little doubt, despite this precaution, that there has been a trend toward increased specialization within the discipline for at least the last generation of anthropologists. In social or cultural anthropology, for example, there are not many field-workers who would consider the more traditional "ethnography in the round" in this day and age.

Today, forensic anthropologists work with homicide detectives and pathologists. They usually lack certain legal authorities, such as determining an official time of death, but their opinions are often taken into consideration by a medical examiner. Facial reconstruction may be one of the techniques used by a forensic anthropologist, but such a technique is not admissible as evidence in American courts of law (Christensen & Crowder, 2009; see also the American Board of Forensic Anthropology, www.theabfa.org).

FORENSIC ARCHAEOLOGY

Forensic archaeology is a related field of forensic science and could be defined as the application of archaeological principles, techniques, and methodologies in a legal context (Hunter & Cox, 2005; Connor, 2007; Blau & Ubelaker, 2009). Forensic archaeologists are frequently employed by the police or other investigative agencies in order to uncover evidence from the past in homicide cases. The techniques and skills employed are those normally used in archaeological investigations, for example, the principles of stratigraphy, radiocarbon dating, and a variety of other methods of analysis, such as aerial photography and satellite imagery.

The forensic archaeologist is engaged by an investigative agency primarily to locate, excavate, and record human remains. Investigations could involve the burial of small items of a personal nature belonging to a crime victim; the surface disposal of a victim's body, concealed under rubbish, tree branches, or other materials; or mass graves that may be part of an international United Nations investigation. Such international cases may be part of war crimes indictments in the International Criminal Court, as in the investigation of genocide graves in Yugoslavia, Rwanda, and Iraq (Congram & Sterenberg, 2009). Another expanding area of study pertains to disaster victim identification, in which archaeological approaches are employed to investigate large disaster scenes (Steadman, 2009, pp. 305–06, 330–31; Sledzik, 2009), such as the 2004 Asian tsunami (Black, 2009).

ORIGINS OF FORENSIC ANTHROPOLOGY

While the history of modern forensic anthropology is relatively recent, the field can be traced to a paper written in 1878 by Thomas Dwight (1843–1911) and entitled "The Identification of the Human Skeleton: A Medicolegal Study." Dwight has been described as "The Father of Forensic Anthropology" in the United States (Stewart, 1979, p. xii), and according to Snow, "should also be honored as an early pioneer of physical anthropology as a whole" (1982, p. 99).

In 1897, forensic evidence given by George Dorsey, who had earned a doctoral degree in anthropology from Harvard, was used in the successful conviction of Adolph Luetgert, a sausage manufacturer in Chicago, who had been accused of murdering his wife Louisa (Snow, 1982, pp. 99–100; Stewart, 1978). Luetgert claimed that his wife had disappeared because she ran off with another man, but a search of the sausage factory revealed two of his wife's rings and a corset stay. Several small bone fragments were subsequently discovered at the bottom of a large vat used for rendering meat products during the manufacturing process. The evidence presented to the court by Dorsey, an assistant curator of anthropology at the Chicago Field Museum, was instrumental in convicting Luetgert of his wife's murder. Dorsey was therefore the first anthropologist to act as a forensic expert in the United States. The case also received national attention in the news media, and for a long period people refused to purchase sausages from the Luetgert factory, believing that his wife's remains were contained in the manufactured food product. As Snow (1982) indicates rather sardonically, "Unable to dissolve his marriage, he [Luetgert] decided to dissolve his wife" (p. 100).

CRIMINAL ANTHROPOLOGY

The 1930s saw the emergence of what has been termed "criminal anthropology." Physical anthropologist Ernest Hooton was one of its main proponents. According to Hooton in his book *The American Criminal* (1939), criminals could be distinguished by certain anatomical characteristics. This approach has since been discredited and is considered to have little influence on the development of modern forensic anthropology. After this unfortunate sidetrack, during the period from the 1940s to the 1960s, the relationship between physical anthropology and the forensic aspects of this field was situated on more scientific ground.

During World War II, physical anthropologists were also recruited to identify the remains of soldiers deceased during the war. Later, during the Korean War, anthropologists were based in Japan to identify combat dead, so that their remains could be repatriated to the United States for burial. It was during this period that advances were made in identifying characteristics of skeletal remains such as sex, age, and stature. Similar activities were also performed during the later Vietnam War.

In the 1960s, W.M. Krogman (1962), who was a forensic consultant to several law enforcement agencies, including the FBI, published *The Human Skeleton in Forensic Medicine*, which soon became a standard reference work in its field and is considered the first textbook on the subject of forensic anthropology. The FBI also discovered that there was a whole coterie of physical anthropologists working at the Smithsonian Institution, which was situated right across the street from the FBI's Washington headquarters. This ease of accessibility meant that inspectors for the FBI began to make regular visits to the Smithsonian laboratories, seeking advice on osteology and sometimes even carrying various skeletal remains over for identification. The Smithsonian even offered a course on skeletal identification for crime investigators and forensic pathologists.

MODERN FORENSIC ANTHROPOLOGY

The term "forensic anthropology" began to make its appearance in the early 1970s and it was during this period that it was beginning to become recognized as a separate field of study within physical anthropology. While the majority of physical anthropologists with a forensic specialization in the discipline continued to work in universities and museums, many were branching out to play a greater role in the criminal justice system.

By 1980, the Forensic Anthropology section of the American Academy of Forensic Sciences, established in 1949, had only 43 members. At this time, only two or three forensic anthropologists were able to devote themselves full time to research, teaching, and casework in the forensics field. The majority continued to work in the more traditional areas of anthropology, while supplementing these activities with occasional forensic courses or acting as consultants to medical examiners, coroners, or law enforcement agencies. Even today, there are fewer than 100 anthropologists registered with the American Board of Forensic Anthropology (www.theabfa.org).

This situation of university-based activities in the academic field, with occasional outside consulting as it arises, remains the predominant activity for forensic anthropologists in Canada. In a review article, it was concluded that "by 2006 it was clear that forensic anthropology and its specializations had grown a great deal in terms of training and practice. However, with some exceptions, it remained a sideline of enthusiastic and socially concerned biological anthropologists whose research foci lay elsewhere" (Skinner et al., 2010, p. 193). In other words, the situation in Canada tends to mirror that of the United States, but on a smaller scale. In both countries, forensic anthropology has remained largely university based, with few individuals trained in death investigative agencies or hospital settings. Nonetheless, it is concluded that "the practice of forensic anthropology as an applied science in Canada has grown substantially" (p. 192).

A main difficulty inhibiting the growth of the field of forensic anthropology involves a marginalization of this profession from the power structures of death investigative agencies, according to the review conducted by Skinner et al. (2010). Since forensic anthropologists tend to work predominantly in university settings, they are regarded as neither police nor medical examiners. As death scene investigators, some specialists in the field may regard the participation of forensic anthropologists as optional or not necessary.

It would not be accurate to state that this is always the case, but as a general rule this tendency would appear to apply. This situation is therefore a problem, as far as public anthropology is concerned, when attempts are made by the members of certain branches of anthropology to extend their influence and activities beyond academia into public domains. One might conclude, at least as far as Canada is concerned, that "there remain areas of concern in terms of perceived role, training, facilities, support, and practice" (Skinner et al., 2010, p. 192).

CANADIAN CASEWORK

A *Globe and Mail* article suggests that "you cannot make a living in Canada in the ultra-specialized field of forensic anthropology. There just aren't enough homicides"

(Belford, 2003, p. B11). Yet, even though Canada has a homicide rate lower than that of many other countries, "Canadian citizens express dismay at horrendous homicides in Montreal, Toronto, and Vancouver that erode the confidence with which we can turn our children out to play" (Skinner & Bowie, 2009, p. 87).

Despite this concern on the part of Canadians, the maturation of forensic anthropology in Canada became more evident with its involvement in the high-profile homicide trial of Robert William Pickton in British Columbia. On June 7, 2006, both the prosecution and defence attorneys were able to call upon a number of doctorally qualified forensic anthropologists to testify in this case. Students were also initially recruited by members of the RCMP in 2001, when they attended the annual meeting of the Canadian Association of Physical Anthropology to work on the Pickton property. A hundred or more students conducted investigations of the buildings and soils of the Dominion Farm for more than two and a half years, which served to elevate the public profile of forensic anthropology in Canada.

Greater public awareness has also been made possible by such influential works as Elliot Leyton's (2003) study of serial homicide in *Hunting Humans*, which has been described as a contribution to the field of "cultural forensic anthropology" (Skinner & Bowie, 2009, p. 88). In addition, other Canadians played a significant role with their investigation of mass grave exhumations in such countries as Iraq, Yugoslavia, and East Timor (Jessee & Skinner, 2005; Kalacska & Bell, 2006).

A review of forensic anthropology casework in Canada reported that there were 1,800 cases in 2006. Of these, only about one-third of such cases were recently deceased individuals. The review also noted that publications by Canadians in forensic anthropology have increased almost threefold over the last decade. Evidence of an ever-increasing volume of research in the field was noted by papers presented during the annual meeting of the Canadian Association of Physical Anthropology held in Vancouver in 2009 (Skinner et al., 2010, pp. 193–200).

War Graves and Lost Soldiers

Among the presenters at this conference, Laura Clegg, Director of History and Heritage, Department of National Defence, reported on her research into the 27,506 Canadian service personnel who were reported missing during World War I and II, and who have no known graves. In just a three-year period so far, 48 sets of remains have been processed, and 16 cases have been recently resolved.

The majority of her cases involved soldiers' remains retrieved by the Commonwealth War Graves Commission of Pas de Calais, France. Genetic samples are secured in a mortuary facility in Canada. Clegg provides anthropological profiles to the authorities at the Department of National Defence, who may then search for the soldiers' next of kin or proceed with interring the individuals if the remains are unidentified. However, Canada no longer seeks missing personnel from past wars, and under an agreement with other Commonwealth countries, remains can never be exhumed if they are located in consecrated graves.

Simon Fraser University doctoral candidates Derek Congram and Amy Mundorff have engaged in casework involving the recovery and analysis of remains from building and car fires, and culturally buried remains. Prior to their return to the university for further study, both of them have practised as professional forensic anthropologists, working in eight countries and in a variety of situations involving execution sites, mass graves, and homicides.

False Convictions and Forensic Evidence

Congram and Mundorff discuss the controversial issue of the impact of questionable forensic science on the criminal justice system. For example, since 1981, there have been at least five false convictions and imprisonments for murder or manslaughter in Canada based on poor forensic science. This does not include the 12 cases of parents or caregivers who were falsely convicted in the deaths of infants in Ontario due to the testimony of pathologist Charles Smith. As they indicate, "There is every reason to believe that the potential for poor forensic archaeology and anthropology, due to uneven standards of practice, is greater than in well-regulated fields such as dentistry and pathology. The accreditation of individuals performing forensic archaeology and anthropology in Canada after graduation is particularly concerning ... there is also no consensus about who is most qualified to give opinions on issues of forensic anthropological import such as post-mortem interval, facial reproductions, historical analysis of bones and teeth, geophysical survey, and so on" (as cited in Skinner et al., 2010, p. 199).

THE VARIETY OF FORENSIC CASES

In other forensic work, Anne Katzenberg of the University of Calgary works as a consultant to the Office of the Medical Examiner, identifying skeletal remains in southern Alberta that have been scavenged or burnt, found in heritage material, or uncovered as a result of building activity. On average, she handles two to three cases a year, which are primarily skeletonized.

Richard Lazenby of the University of Northern British Columbia handles cases for the Office of the Chief Coroner north of the Fraser Region as well as for the RCMP. In this region, he has been involved with investigations into deaths in First Nations communities, forestry-related deaths, homicides, and deaths caused by motor vehicle accidents. He was also one of the two chief forensic anthropologists for the Pickton case, which involved several years of court testimony. Other anthropologists from Simon Fraser University, University of Western Ontario, Saint Mary's University (Nova Scotia), and the University of Alberta have used their forensic expertise to handle casework that includes the Bandidos case in Ontario; residential fires, especially trailer and cabin fires; and deaths in vehicle accidents caused by blunt-force trauma.

Thus, it is evident that forensic anthropology is a very active field practised in most areas of the country and involving a wide variety of different types of casework. As Skinner and colleagues (2010) note, "Casework is our link to the wider public. It is also the primary stimulus for research ideas" (p. 194). It is therefore evident that there is a mutually beneficial feedback effect in forensic anthropology between its academic and public settings.

This review of the practice of forensic anthropology in Canada indicates that it is a growing field, but one that is also uneven or variable across the country. It is a further fact that since the practice of forensic anthropology in Canada is typically attached to universities, not primarily in forensic science or police labs, it is somewhat marginal to traditional death investigative agencies, such as coroners, medical examiners, and the police.

Human Rights and Forensic Anthropology

Forensic anthropology has been applied increasingly over the past 15 years to human rights violations in various parts of the world, such as Eastern Europe, the Middle East, and Latin America (Nafte, 2009, pp. 165–70). There has been a dramatic increase in requests for forensic anthropologists to recover and investigate the human remains of victims of past civil wars and military regimes. In some instances, the reinstatement of democratic governments has also led to requests for assistance.

One such request involved the use of forensic anthropology as part of a 1984 human rights mission to Argentina to identify victims of the 1974–1983 civil war (Snow & Bihurriet, 1992; Doretti & Snow, 2009). Since then, various other cases of human rights investigations have been reported (Snow, Stover, & Hannibal, 1989; Gibbons, 1992; Nafte, 2009, p. 165). Forensic anthropologists usually become involved in human rights issues because of their participation in professional committees or in response to invitations from governments. Mostly, however, human rights missions from the United States and Canada take place in foreign countries.

In many cases, the investigations are part of a larger attempt to prosecute the perpetrators of "crimes against humanity." Such instances often involve interment in mass graves after victims have been abducted and executed. During the military regime in Argentina, which lasted from 1976 to 1983, it is estimated that over 10,000 people "disappeared" (Nafte, 2009, p. 167). The participation of family members is often an important part of these types of investigations, since they may be able to provide blood samples that could be used in the identification of victims, or even give eye-witness accounts that could be used in a court of law.

As Doretti and Snow (2009) remark, "Forensic investigations of human rights violations have several objectives. One is to collect, preserve, and objectively interpret physical evidence that might be used to bring the perpetrators to justice. This, of course, is not always possible, especially when the political and judicial will necessary to vigorously pursue such cases is lacking or when various forms of amnesty are implemented to protect the perpetrators" (p. 319). In other words, the political and social conditions in which forensic anthropologists work vary from country to country, at times impeding or furthering their investigative objectives.

In Guatemala, forensic anthropological techniques and methods were used to identify civilian victims of arbitrary executions that were conducted during the civil war, which ended in 1996 (Flavel & Barker, 2009). These victims were often disposed of in clandestine graves in various parts of the country. Survivor groups contacted forensic anthropologists in North America and existing forensic teams in Latin America in order to provide assistance in locating the graves and identifying the dead. It was from these early beginnings that a team of Guatemalan forensic anthropologists was formed and trained by international experts in the field, and this eventually led to the formation of the Guatemalan Forensic Anthropology Foundation (FAFG).

Human Rights Watch

Clement (2009, pp. 344–45) also reports on the activities of forensic anthropologists in gathering evidence from mass gravesites in Iraq. The evidence gathered in such investigations has been used in The Hague for the prosecution of crimes such as mass murder. Human Rights Watch estimates the number of victims who "disappeared" during the reign of Saddam Hussein in Iraq at about 300,000. Over 600,000 other deaths subsequently occurred as a result of sectarian violence after the invasion by allied forces. The Red Cross also has an international committee, called the "The Missing" project, which has been delving into the reports of persons missing as a result of civil conflicts.

The activities of forensic anthropologists in the Human Rights Watch in Iraq have also been discussed by Congram and Sterenberg (2009). They report that the political and security situations limit control of such investigations. At times, there are poorly conducted exhumations and autopsies, and graves that have been unprofessionally opened. However, they also report that the vast majority of mass graves in Iraq remained unexcavated. In 2003, a German NGO, Archaeologists for Human Rights (AFHR), was founded to continue their work in northern Iraq among the residents of local communities and the Kurdish ministries in order to assist them in

FIGURE 6.2 Anthropologists at work documenting remains from a mass gravesite in Iraq
Source: Courtesy of the Mandatory Center of Expertise for the Curation and Management of Archaelogical Collections, US Army Corps. of Engineers, St. Louis District

the recovery of remains. This group has collaborated with Human Rights Watch and other organizations to provide excavation and mortuary equipment for the Ministry of Human Rights in Erbil.

In sum, the fields of forensic anthropology and archaeology are often combined in various investigations. There is also a growing demand in the context of human rights to investigate mass gravesites that have resulted from civil conflicts, dictatorships, or other authoritarian regimes in which dissenters have been abducted. However, local political situations vary, and so the work of forensic anthropology is more successful in some countries than in others.

CONCLUSION

The relationship between anthropology and the legal system has had a long history in the discipline, dating back to the late nineteenth century. However, even with such a lengthy history, forensic anthropology practised in any systematic manner dates back only to the 1970s. This field illustrates the difficulty that anthropologists face in fully embracing employment outside academia.

For the most part, forensic anthropologists straddle the university setting and the practical or applied side in the criminal justice system. As has been pointed out in this chapter, though, the "partly in and partly out" situation should not be viewed in a negative manner, since this is a mutually beneficial situation in which the university setting is informed by applications of its theoretical knowledge to the public sphere of society and, in turn, the practical side of the discipline gains from a testing of its activities and knowledge in the theoretical arena.

In recent years, forensic anthropologists have also become more involved in human rights issues, which have taken them into a wider international public sphere. Excavations in Argentina, Iraq, and Guatemala, for example, demonstrate that the skills of the forensic anthropologist are sought in many new areas beyond local homicides, such as the investigation of mass murder gravesites and disaster victim identification. The use of forensic anthropology in human rights cases demonstrates that the recovery and documentation of physical evidence of rights violations have value in bringing to justice and prosecuting perpetrators of victim abuse charged in war tribunals. Such activities also bring a greater public awareness to the role of anthropologists in criminal investigations at the international level.

Chapter 7

RESISTANCE, RECONCILIATION, AND PUBLIC JUSTICE

The term "public" can be used in many diverse ways, and in a variety of different contexts. It is commonly used, though, in the singular form, implying that a single "public" exists. The reality, however, is that there are many "publics," depending on how one wishes to identify the constituent ethnic, economic, or political groups that populate a particular locality, provincial area, or nation state.

It is for this reason that Ronald Niezen (2010) writes in his study of the relationship between public justice and the anthropology of law that "together, the members of [a] society are popularly known as *the public*—though there is of course more than one vaguely identifiable public with more than a single repertoire of preferences, and it is usually more appropriate to use the plural term 'publics'" (p. 1). He then suggests that "looking at publics" has become the domain of anthropologists, because publics "have also become part of the social worlds of those whom it is possible to know intimately," because the manners in which people define who they are, "now often [are] negotiated and mediated in collaboration with distant publics" (pp. 1–2).

It follows, then, from this line of thought that public anthropology is a legitimate domain of investigation, because it bridges certain academic interests, such as ethnicity and identity, and the more public domains of law, indigenous rights, and collective consciousness. In addition, an interest in social and cultural identity is apt to include consideration of the manner in which the identities of diverse groups are contested in the public arena. This could furthermore involve resistance on the part of minority groups to conform to the state's image of larger public spheres through processes of integration and assimilation. As a process, resistance could lead to rebellion and ultimately to reconciliation processes, in an attempt to heal public wounds. This chapter, then, contributes to the discussion of public anthropology by outlining the various processes of resistance and reconciliation that take place in the public domain.

THE NATURE OF RESISTANCE

A significant social movement in today's world involves the efforts of certain groups to resist the hegemonic powers that seek to control them. Often, resistance is an aspect of small groups' attempting to seek autonomy from larger powers. In this chapter, the nature of resistance is explored in terms of its various characteristics, after which several examples are discussed in order to place resistance movements within a wider perspective. The focus of the chapter then shifts to attempts at reconciliation as a method of bridging the gaps between diverse populations that make up the modern, pluralistic state.

Resistance involves the refusal to comply with some pressure placed on an individual or group. It can involve providing a hindrance to some activity or acting to impede some action, often in a political context. As Allahar (1998) notes in an article, when discussing "strategies of resistance," the term "resistance" can be defined as "any action, whether physical, verbal or psychological, and whether individual or collective, that seeks to undo the negative consequences of being categorized for racial reasons.... Resistance [can] be seen as a political act ultimately tied to the wider cultural forces that frame it" (p. 338). Allahar's approach, therefore, is an attempt "to understand some ways in which the concept of race can be used or manipulated to resist or mollify the deleterious consequences of racism" (p. 338). In all, three strategies of resistance can be identified.

STRATEGIES OF RESISTANCE

One of these strategies is multiculturalism, which might not commonly be associated with resistance. However, multiculturalism can be seen as a method of resistance because it involves a strategic retreat; in other words, it involves a rejection of not only the means to achieve acceptance into the majority group (for example, by integration or other socio-cultural tactics) but also the dominant group's culture and value system. In this case, multiculturalism can be seen as a retreat into the traditional or original group's norms, values, and cultural system. In a sense, this sort of resistance can also be seen as a strategy involving a form of accommodation, especially when this strategy involves a minority group maintaining separate or culturally parallel institutions, such as churches, community centres, cultural organizations, and private schools (Allahar, 1998, pp. 338–52).

The politics of assimilation is another identified strategy of resistance. In this case, the strategy involves members of a minority group being willing to accept the value system of the dominant society as a means of passing into this larger society. This strategy can be seen as following the path of least resistance. It conforms to the definition of resistance given above because it is a strategy that seeks to undo the negative consequences of racial or ethnic categorization. Even though this strategy is essentially a rejection of multicultural policies, which accentuate the distinctiveness of certain groups, this second strategy is nonetheless political in nature because it is an attempt to negotiate the terms under which the minority group is accepted into the social structure of the dominant society.

As an example of this sort of assimilative strategy, Aboriginal authors Taiaiake Alfred and Jeff Corntassel (2011) note, "In Canada today many Indigenous people have embraced the Canadian government's label of 'aboriginal,' along with the concomitant and limited notion of postcolonial justice framed within the institutional structure of the state ... 'aboriginalism' is a legal, political, and cultural discourse designed to serve an agenda of silent surrender to an inherently unjust relation at the root of the colonial state itself" (p. 140). Their point is that this "agenda of silent surrender" has involved some Aboriginal people giving up on their cultural heritage by succumbing to the political and social agenda of the dominant society.

In Canada, it is the legal apparatus administered through the Indian Act that determines who is entitled to the status of Indian, and thereby who is also entitled to receive the benefits associated with this status. Those Aboriginal people with official status as "Indians" would probably also suggest that their adherence to this status is in itself a form of resistance because it keeps them separate from the dominant society in various legal and political ways.

A third strategy of resistance pertains to neither assimilation nor accommodation (as in multiculturalism) but instead involves a direct confrontation with those regarded as oppressing a certain group. This form of resistance is often not particularly coordinated or well planned, at least in the initial periods, because its objectives have usually not been articulated in an effective manner; a clearly articulated vision of the new social order that the group hopes to achieve through their resistance is generally lacking.

The lack of coordination characteristic of this form of resistance is due to its predominantly spontaneous nature and the absence of effective leadership capable of controlling the emergence of acts of violence. It is possible also that violence may turn inward as members of the resistance group struggle for control over the decision-making process and arguments ensue over which strategies to adopt and the most effective means by which the group can achieve its goals.

Resistance, therefore, involves not only contests between dominant and minority groups; the vision, the coordination of efforts, and the strategies adopted (or not adopted) are also matters of dispute. For this reason, Frantz Fanon argues in *The Wretched of the Earth* (1963) that decolonization is of necessity a violent process, because in the early phases of resistance the colonized may be unable to direct their frustration and anger at the colonial power. When one is unable, for various reasons, to directly confront those holding the positions of power because of inequities of population size or resources, then the resisters may direct their anger inward, against other members of their own group. In Fanon's view of resistance, violence and colonialism are inseparable phenomena. In time, as the struggle builds and gains momentum, a realization may begin to take hold that the colonial power is not inherently superior to the Indigenous group, and this discovery "shakes the world in a very necessary manner" (Fanon, 1963, p. 45).

RESISTANCE AND REINVENTION

The relationship between colonialism and resistance can lead to a "reinvention" of members of certain social groups who have been dominated by colonial regimes. Emma LaRocque, for example, refers to the "new Natives"—people forced to find their own way through a maze that is neither Western nor tribal. It is for this reason, LaRocque (2010) explains, that "we cannot accept that human progress begins and ends with European culture. Because it does not" (p. 157). This observation is similar to that of Frantz Fanon (1963, p. 45), who suggests that there is a certain inevitability of reinvention associated with resistance because it plays a role in mobilizing human creativity.

While reinvention may appear inevitable, it may not always be possible to predict in what manner or from which direction this reinvention will take place. "I believe we must reinvent ourselves," LaRocque (2010) argues, "[but] by reinvention, I do not mean prefabrication or myth-making, I mean, among other things, throwing off the weight of antiquity, and, by doing so, offering new possibilities for reconstruction" (p. 158). However, colonial regimes are not so easily "thrown off," and much destruction may take place in the process.

In addition, resistance to oppression can take many shapes. In some cases, it may take the form of violent confrontation; in others, a more passive form of noncompliance; or in others, a certain blending of these. In a very real sense, there is a form of a binding relationship between the colonizer and the colonized, forming a sort of complex in which power shifts back and forth between these groups through their interaction.

RESISTANCE AND CULTURAL REPRESENTATION

Resistance is a reply that emerges from, or is born out of, a troubled relationship over a contested ground, which may be physical in the sense of a certain territory, or conceptual in terms of a particular ideology. Acts of resistance, then, are struggles over not only power and its distribution but also the minds of people and the manner in which they conceive of their social relationships. Resistance is also a form of cultural representation, at least to the extent to which an Indigenous group resists their portrayal in the literature of the dominant society. This literature may be based on dehumanizing characterizations, such as the depiction of Indigenous people as savages or less culturally developed compared to the colonizers. Thus, "this developing counter-discourse may be best understood as a resistance response to gross representation" (LaRocque, 2010, p. 4).

Derogatory depictions of Indigenous groups tended to benefit the dominant society because it served their material and ideological ends, which, in turn, justified the exploitation of the colonized. As an example, when European settlers discovered sophisticated burial mounds in the Eastern United States, these mounds were generally attributed to lost tribes or other non-Indigenous peoples. The impoverished Aboriginal people living in their midst were not thought to be capable of such constructions, so external explanations were sought.

Ironically, it was the very treatment of the Indigenous groups by the European settlers that was largely responsible for this impoverishment; various treaties and unscrupulous land deals had removed local tribes from the better agricultural areas or other favourable subsistence areas. A sort of self-fulfilling prophecy was at work here; when the Aboriginal groups were seen as not responsible for the mound constructions, they could similarly be regarded as not autochthonous to that area. This could then be used to justify their exploitation, and they could be removed from their existing lands or territories—as occurred with the Indian Removal Act of 1830, when tribes living in the southeastern United States were relocated to land west of the Mississippi River.

RESISTANCE AS RACIAL POLITICS

Resistance can, therefore, be at least partly explained as a response to what may be viewed as a reaction to flagrant misrepresentation in terms of a distortion or falsification of the rebelling groups' motives. The colonizer or settler population has various ideological and material ends that it wishes to achieve as part of the process of European colonization and the various textual writings serve these ends and justify the exploitation of the colonized. In this sense resistance can also be understood as a form of racial politics, in addition to being seen as a struggle over the manner in which various groups are represented and portrayed.

Resistance then is not only a struggle against misrepresentation but also a battle against racist constructions and a power struggle for control over the colonial discourse. Robert Berkhofer (1978), for example, in *The White Man's Indian*, traces the history of the way in which legal designations and the development of stereotypes were used as a way of denigrating North America's Aboriginal population. Once First

Nations people had learned the rudiments of Western literacy, they began to realize how their people were being portrayed. In response they began to challenge and retaliate against what they regarded as inaccurate or false depictions of their people, such as that of "noble savage." Of course the term "Indian" is itself a white man's invention.

If we accept the adage that words are power, then we can easily see that control over what could be called the lexicon of oppression is a significant facet of resistance. Indigenous scholars Voyageur and Calliou (2011) use Canada as an example of the far-reaching power dimensions of resistance by explaining that "Aboriginal peoples resisted control by the Canadian state in many different ways. They made—and continue to make—persistent attempts to exercise independence through political, economic, and self-governing initiatives" (pp. 206–07). In recent years a growing number of First Nation judges, lawyers, and professors have become involved in Supreme Court decisions over land claims and various other issues pertaining to Aboriginal rights, such as the legalities of treaties, and hunting and fishing entitlements.

CANADA: CONFLICTS OVER ABORIGINAL RIGHTS

In Canadian history, resistance to the federal government's hegemonic control first occurred with the Red River Rebellion of 1885, initiated by Metis leader Louis Riel, and the establishment of a provisional government. Eventually, a military force known as the Wolseley Expedition defeated Riel's forces. More than a century later, Aboriginal resistance erupted again with the highly publicized and violent Oka (Quebec) crisis of 1990. Stoney Point protester Dudley George was shot and killed by OPP officer Kenneth Deane during a confrontation at Ontario's Ipperwash Provincial Park in 1995. In 1996, Gustafson Lake in British Columbia was the site of another armed conflict, with gunfire exchanged between Aboriginal protesters and provincial police. More recent conflicts have been the clash at Burnt Church, New Brunswick, over fishing rights (2002); the Grand River land dispute in Caledonia, Ontario (2006); and the Akwesasne border-crossing confrontation at Cornwall, Ontario (2009).

These are just a few of the many conflicts between the Canadian authorities and First Nations residents. These conflicts have resulted, according to Bonita Lawrence (2011), from "the forcible and relentless dispossession of Indigenous peoples, the theft of their territories, and the implementation of legislation and policies designed to affect their total disappearance as people" (p. 69). It is evident that the struggles over Aboriginal and minority rights in Canada and other countries have involved a relentless process of dispossession and assimilation, in which Indigenous peoples have been removed from their traditional territories. The colonization process can therefore be seen as a process of invasion and land theft under the guise of "negotiated" treaties and other forms of territorial surrender.

The colonized have seen the colonization process not as a benign development but as an experience that could be characterized as racism and genocide. When minority groups engage in acts of resistance to these oppressive forces in order to protect themselves and their land, they are apt to be portrayed in the contemporary media in violent and derogatory terms. Images in the Western media of "aggressive and bloodthirsty savages ... are seen daily in movies and TV programs" (Belanger, 2010, p. 174); media images commonly depict First Nations people as warriors engaged in egregious acts of violence.

There have been few studies of Aboriginal resistance that could be used to challenge the Western media's preoccupation with the bloodthirsty imagery. Wilkes (2004), however, studied over 200 protests of active resistance nationally (from 1981 to 2000) in Canada and found a very low level of violence at such events. For the most part, the protests took the form of marches, blockades, the occupying of buildings, or other forms of non-violent demonstration. In fact, almost 80 per cent of the over 600 bands in Canada have had no significant protests at all during this time period. In addition, only a very small minority (less than 2 per cent) of such events involved violence or the destruction of property.

DECOLONIZING RESISTANCE

Identifying the colonizers, or the settler population, seen to be the cause of oppression and therefore the target of resistance, is not necessarily an easy matter. Many people are prone to see a simple dichotomy, with the colonizers comprising the European or settler population on one side, and various Aboriginal or Indigenous societies on the other. The former are seen to practise policies of oppression and initiate racial intolerance, while the latter are forced to cope by rebutting or counteracting these negative influences in various ways.

In an important article entitled "Decolonizing Resistance," Sharma and Wright (2008–09) want to know how the settler population is defined. "We challenge the conflation," they assert, "between processes of migration and those of colonialism" (p. 121). Enslaved Africans or indentured Asian workers, for example, can be seen by Indigenous groups as part of the settler population. As a result there is a call from Aboriginal scholars, such as Lawrence and Dua (2005), to form an alliance with people of colour. "Aboriginal activism against settler domination," they contend, cannot "[take] place without people of color as allies" (p. 122).

The problem with this proposed alliance is that people of colour may live on lands that were appropriated from the Aboriginal population, and these lands are therefore a contested issue in terms of land claims and other Aboriginal rights. Thus, people of colour, migrant labourers, or refugees without legal documentation are apt to be lumped together with the settler population and therefore possibly seen as peoples opposed to Aboriginal nationhood. People of colour in such an instance might therefore be seen as complicit in the appropriation of Aboriginal lands, even though they did not have any direct involvement in such land seizures. We might conclude from this imbroglio that resistance is first of all largely a matter of achieving the objectives of one's own group, and only secondly one of assessing the possibility of strengthening one's position by broadening bonds with other similarly oppressed peoples.

STRUCTURES OF DOMINATION

Political philosopher James Tully (2008) draws attention to the issue of internal colonialism, by which is meant "the historical processes by which structures of domination have been set in place … over the Indigenous peoples and their territories without their consent and in response to their resistance both against and within these structures" (p. 259). In time, these structures of domination tend to become "relatively stable, immoveable and irreversible vis-à-vis any direct confrontation by the colonized population" (p. 259). According to Tully, domination of Indigenous populations takes the form of "incorporation" and "domestication."

The term "structures of domination" refers to the various techniques that are employed by national governments as mechanisms used to combat resistance. For example, Indigenous groups in North America often expend as much energy on efforts to modify the national government's techniques of control, by attempting to achieve greater self-government, than they expend on organizing specific acts of resistance. The historically developing structures of domination force Indigenous groups into diverting attempts at resistance into the very act of survival—efforts to gain control over traditional territories that have been lost by coercive treaties and other questionable land transfers.

The ongoing processes of internal colonialism therefore divert active attempts at resistance away from direct confrontations in attempts to deal with the background structures of domination. However, as Tully (2008) suggests, "There is not a sharp distinction between structures of domination and techniques of government practice, as what appears to be part of the immoveable background to one generation can be called into question and become the object of struggle and modification by another" (p. 260).

What this suggests is that the internal processes of colonization have developed, on the one hand, by the specific struggles of Indigenous peoples for freedom both against and within their territories and, on the other hand, in response to the objectives of the members of the settler societies and the forces of the capitalistic market economy. The nearly insatiable appetite of this market economy for resources tends to place Indigenous people attempting to protect their land in direct opposition to the forces attempting to secure the resources on these lands.

POLICING RESISTANCE

What could be regarded as "capitalistic forces" is not an obscure, nebulous entity. In the case of Aboriginal land claims or other situations involving the contested ground between national governments and Indigenous societies, conflict would appear to be an inevitable result of these sorts of disputes. If negotiations break down between the disputing parties, the police or other armed representatives of the state are apt to be delegated to suppress confrontations. This means that Aboriginal protesters are likely to see their land claims become transformed into a higher, more severe, level of conflict (Hedican, 2012b, 2013).

Police forces are often used by state governments to quell dissent. In such situations, there is a tendency for violence to escalate, with the result that both protesters and members of police forces could be killed. The problem with using brute force to suppress dissent is that if the original problems at the source of the dissent are not solved, then additional protests will inevitably emerge at a later place and date, leading to further strife. Reconciliation is therefore one method that could be used to contribute to an amicable resolution of conflict.

Reconciliation can take several forms, especially when there is a willingness on the part of both parties to settle their differences in a non-confrontational manner. For example, such techniques as mediation and negotiation could prove effective, provided there is a willingness on both sides to resolve their outstanding issues. The use of manipulation, force, or other forms of intimidation usually lead to more of the same on both sides, so both parties have a vested interest in resolving conflicts, therefore saving both lives and the resources that would be funnelled into the quelling of disputes.

It is also probable that the police officers who are called upon to suppress dissent will encounter further resistance, because the members of police forces are not equipped through their training to perform in a mediatory role. Their training more specifically involves enforcing the rule of law, rather than acting as legal experts. As Pue (2007) suggests, "It can be extraordinarily difficult to mark precisely where one constitutional right—freedom of expression or Aboriginal entitlement, for example—must give way to another—[such as] the preservation of peace.... Such boundaries fuzzily demarcate the frontier between lawful and unlawful police conduct" (pp. 132–33). It is for this reason—legal boundaries are "fuzzy" in situations of resistance and dissent—that law professor Gordon Christie (2007) argues that it is "critically important when attention is paid to particular disputes [that they be understood] within the larger legal, constitutional, historical and political landscape" (p. 147).

"Fuzzy boundaries" are not particularly helpful when confrontations take place between police and protesters, especially when gunfire is exchanged between the two parties. It is also not particularly helpful if the members of police forces are unsure of what their role should be in such disputes. They are certainly not legal experts who can act as arbiters between protesters and state governments, because their training is in other areas.

What could be termed as "contextual variables," such as the constitutional, political, or historical aspects of disputes, are also particularly important when it comes to understanding the reasons that the disputes are taking place or what grievances are motivating the protesters. Altogether, the resistance that police forces encounter is apt to be the result of a complex mixture of factors, legal, historical, or otherwise, that certainly complicates any role that police forces might play in serving to reduce the possible violence that confrontations could produce.

It is evident therefore that the role of the police in suppressing resistance and the associated violence that could occur in such instances is facilitated by a stricter adherence to a code of conduct, or what could be called "rules of engagement," so that police officers are able to decide more clearly how they are to proceed in particular circumstances. Allowing police forces more leeway in such disputes, such as leaving the police with an increase in discretionary powers, is liable to result only in greater confusion over what their role should be when they encounter protesters.

A conclusion is that "what this means in the context of police-governance relations should be clear. While some discretionary leeway around the exercise of decision-making power will remain unavoidably present, in broad terms the decisions of the government about how to set appropriate police policy must be by and large settled" (Christie, 2007, p. 159). It is evident, then, that the formulation of stricter rules of engagement could serve to reduce the violence that is often a significant source of conflict between government forces and those involved in resistance movements.

GOVERNMENT RESPONSIBILITIES: THE UN DECLARATION ON INDIGENOUS RIGHTS

In 2007, the United Nations Declaration on the Rights of Indigenous Peoples passed easily, by a vote of 143 to 4. The countries that voted against this UN declaration were the United States, Australia, New Zealand, and Canada, while 11 countries abstained from voting. One factor involved in the voting was that all four of the countries voting against the declaration have sizeable Indigenous populations who would no doubt wish to use the UN declaration as a means of advancing their own causes and to use media coverage of the declaration as a platform to bring to the public's attention their own grievances (see Asch, 2014, pp. 65–68).

In Canada, the declaration was not supported by the federal government because it would appear to grant Indigenous groups wide-ranging powers that, according to the government, would contravene existing laws. For example, according to Minister of Indian Affairs Chuck Strahl, the declaration is "inconsistent with the Canadian Constitution, with Supreme Court decisions and with our own treaty negotiations and obligations.... We'd have to consult with 650 First Nations to do that [support the vote]. I mean, it's simply not doable" ("Canada Votes," 2007, n.p.).

Eventually, on 12 November 2010, Canada did become a signatory to the UN declaration; however, Canada is not legally bound by its terms (Cannon & Sunseri, 2011, p. 273). There are significant aspects of the UN declaration that are worth mentioning. For example, the declaration states that Indigenous peoples "have the right to maintain and strengthen their distinctive political, legal, economic, social and cultural institutions." However, Canadian Indian Affairs Minister Strahl comments that such wording is unworkable because "some people ... say that means we can have our own legislatures, our own council in our own language. But no one's quite sure, and that's the trouble with language like that."

Such opinions aside, from the Indigenous perspective, the UN declaration is more than just a vague expression of support. According to John Paul, director of the Atlantic Policy Congress, representing over 30 Aboriginal communities in the Maritime provinces, "To us it's like the US Declaration of Independence, because it lays out a number of inalienable truths about us as aboriginal people in the world.... It recognizes who we are, that we have these fundamental rights" (*Toronto Star*, 13 September 2007; cited in Hedican, 2013, p. 39.)

One way to look at the UN declaration is to see it as a form of resistance by which Indigenous groups attempt to push back against larger colonial powers that can be seen as suppressing them. Indigenous groups claim that they have inherent rights that a central government is obligated to protect. Often these inherent rights derive from the lands that Indigenous peoples once lived on but that were ceded to larger powers through treaties or other forms of property cessions. Sometimes Indigenous groups claim that they were tricked into giving up their land, because colonial powers misworded the treaties in such a way that a treaty of peaceful relationships was prominent, but later found that what really was happening was that the dominant power was taking control over Indigenous lands.

In cases such as these, Indigenous groups, whether their lands were taken illegally or not, argue that central governments have a fiduciary obligation to protect the rights of the members of Aboriginal groups. As Christie (2007) suggests, there are "strong guiding principles laying out general restrictions on how the fiduciary can act, and guiding the fiduciary towards a narrow range of acceptable options. Ranging over the particular principles and guideposts is one over-arching fiduciary principle: the fiduciary must act in the best interests of the beneficiary" (p. 159).

In other words, when colonial powers take over Indigenous lands, these powers have an inherent obligation to deal fairly with the original inhabitants of these lands

FIGURE 7.1 The grounds of the Qu'Appelle Indian Industrial School
Source: O.B. Buell/Library and Archives Canada/PA-118765

and not exploit them by taking their resources. Resistance on the part of Indigenous groups can therefore be understood, at least partly, as a reaction against what is perceived to be suppression and a denial of their inherent rights.

It is this perception—that the colonial-Aboriginal relationship is an unjust one—that could lead Indigenous groups to dispute the jurisdiction of the state in their internal affairs. The very relationship between the state and First Nations is therefore in itself a particularly contentious issue. The role of the judiciary in conceptualizing state-Indigenous relationships further complicates matters because not all Aboriginal peoples are willing to accept the premise that they live under the sovereignty of the state government. Aboriginal peoples might hold to the position that various treaties did not necessarily lead to a relinquishing of their sovereignty and, on this basis, dispute the jurisdiction of the state in their internal affairs.

When the state-Indigenous relationship is a contested one, jurisdictional matters are particularly problematic, especially when the police, on behalf of the state, attempt to exert the enforcement of state laws on Indigenous lands. What is evident in such cases is a form of neo-colonialism, because the treaty rights and land claims of the Aboriginal groups are controlled by the state and its courts. In such a relationship, it is difficult to imagine that the rights of Aboriginal groups could be protected on the assumption that these rights are guarded by the courts, as an impartial agent of the state.

It would therefore appear inevitable that conflicts would develop between Indigenous groups and the state when the judicial system is purported to simultaneously act in the best interests of both the state and its Indigenous inhabitants. If reconciliation is to take place between the two parties—the state and Indigenous groups—then institutional structures need to be put in place that would allow for the expression of conflict without resulting in either the suppression of Indigenous groups by the police forces of the state or armed insurrection by the less dominant groups. These sorts of structures are what Williams and Murray (2007, p. 176) have referred to as "a decolonizing framework of action." This framework, they explain, embodies the core values identified by Aboriginal peoples: truth, reconciliation, reparation, and the reconstruction of the relationship between Aboriginal peoples and the state.

CANADA'S TRUTH AND RECONCILIATION COMMISSION

The Indian Residential Schools Truth and Reconciliation Commission (TRC) was officially established on 2 June 2008. The residential school system is often considered the most outstanding act of cultural genocide ever inflicted on Aboriginal peoples in Canada. The truth and reconciliation approach is seen as a form of restorative justice, which differs from the sorts of adversarial and retributive justice based on fault finding and punishment of the guilty parties (see Hedican, 2013, pp. 46–47; Henderson & Wakeham, 2013; Niezen, 2013).

On 11 June 2008, shortly after the announcement that the Truth and Reconciliation Commission had been constituted, Prime Minister Stephen Harper delivered a historic speech in the House of Commons, apologizing on behalf of all Canadians for the harm that had been done to Aboriginal peoples of this country because of the Indian residential school system. Prime Minister Harper (2008) said, "The government of

FIGURE 7.2 Students and staff at the Qu'Appelle Indian Industrial School
Source: O.B. Buell/Library and Archives Canada/PA-1182246

Canada sincerely apologizes and asks the forgiveness of the Aboriginal peoples of this country for failing them so profoundly. We are sorry" (p. 2). He also stated, "Today, we recognize that this policy of assimilation was wrong, has caused great harm, and has no place in our country" (p. 1).

Restorative justice is an approach that seeks to heal or "restore" the relationships between offenders, community members, and the victims of the offences that have taken place. This approach is especially favoured by Aboriginal peoples living in small, relatively isolated communities; offending persons need to be forgiven for their offences because they often return to their communities and need to be integrated back into their social settings.

The TRC is part of the court-approved Residential School Settlement Agreement, which was negotiated between the legal counsel of former students, government representatives, church members, the Assembly of First Nations, and other Aboriginal organizations. In March 2008, Aboriginal peoples and church officials embarked on the "Remembering the Children" tour, which went from city to city listening to Aboriginal peoples' experiences with the residential school system. In addition, in January 2009, King's University College of Edmonton, Alberta, convened an interdisciplinary studies conference on the subject of the Truth and Reconciliation Committee.

Remembering these past horrific events was not easy for the former students of residential schools. The various hearings reveal physical and sexual abuse of Aboriginal students on a wide scale. Since Aboriginal students often spent long periods of time away from their parents, siblings, and other community members, there was also the experiences of what could be termed "cultural disassociation," which prevented traditions from being passed down to succeeding generations.

Unfortunately, it did not take long for conflicts to emerge in the TRC hearings. Harry LaForme, a Justice of the Ontario Court of Appeal, was appointed the first commission chair, but he resigned in October 2008 ("Seeking Truth," 2008). A member of the Mississaugas of the New Credit First Nation in southern Ontario, Justice LaForme cited what he thought was undue political interference by Grand Chief Phil Fontaine of the Assembly of First Nations, the organization that represents all of the status Indians in Canada.

Justice LaForme claimed that Grand Chief Fontaine wanted the TRC to abandon the reconciliation approach and take a more political stance against the federal government. In the midst of this controversy, several of the commissioners resigned. However in June 2009, a reconstituted Commission was established, headed by Justice Murray Sinclair, the first Aboriginal judge in Manitoba's history. A conclusion that could be made here is that attempts at societal reconciliation have important political dimensions. Or, as Niezen (2010) states, "Public apologies and truth and reconciliation commissions have become like confessionals for states" (p. 179).

The term "the politics of reconciliation" is used by Bashir and Kymlicka (2008) to refer to a process that discredits older practices of exclusion and marginalization of Indigenous groups. Instead, there is recognition that in modern democracies, these punitive measures of the past—which were meant to control or even eradicate minority groups who were in opposition to state policies—only generate further conflict. Reconciliation in the long term is a more effective process for resolving grievances and healing old wounds because it is based on the development of new, cooperation-based relationships.

Two modes of reconciliation can be identified—the political and the legal. As Walter (2008) suggests, "It is usually assumed that reconciliation offers to political discourse something that the liberal concepts of democracy, justice, equality, and the rule of law cannot—in particular, ideas of repentance, forgiveness, healing, and harmony. But the features of reconciliation that make it a powerful political ideal also make it controversial" (p. 165). However, some might see processes of reconciliation as undermining certain liberal values, such as justice, in favour of truth or personal moral convictions.

FIGURE 7.3 A world map of Truth and Reconciliation Commissions in Santiago, Chile

Source: Photo by Wikimedia user Warko. Licensed under the terms of CC-BY-SA 3.0

It is possible, then, for attempts at reconciliation to be regarded as conflicting with democratic values of liberalism. For reconciliation between minority groups and central state authorities to work, a compromise might need to occur between the legal traditions of the state and those of Indigenous societies, whose members are apt to have their own law-making traditions.

John Hatch's (2008) work entitled *Race and Reconciliation* explores this topic further. From his perspective, "reconciliation puts *justice* into play with the exercise of rhetorical *judgement*," which he illustrates in a discussion of apartheid in South Africa. In his opinion, "reconciliation precedes ... the laws that govern both state and struggle [against apartheid]" (p. 51; emphasis in original). Reconciliation opens a new "middle time," to use Hatch's term, between the past and the future, which is seen as an alternative to continued violence. In South Africa this "middle time" allowed for a cessation of state-initiated violence. Reconciliation, though, is an ongoing historical process not achieved in a short period of time. When centralized governments refuse to recognize the rights of minority group members, resistance and rebellion are apt to prevail.

CASE STUDY: RECONCILIATION AND REVENGE IN POST-APARTHEID SOUTH AFRICA

The African National Congress (ANC), leader of the first post-apartheid government, has adopted human rights as a central element of its new governmental project (Wilson, 2000). The social effects of the human rights initiative has had varied results. Religious values, for example, have converged with the human rights discourse around the notion of reconciliation which, in turn, has been articulated by the country's Truth and Reconciliation Commission (TRC). However, there are nonetheless clear divergences between notions of justice and expressions of human rights, especially as these are expressed in the local township courts, called *lekgotla*, which emphasize punishment and retribution.

In post-apartheid Africa competing discourses around justice and reconciliation stem from several sources. For example, Christian discourses on forgiveness are advocated by TRC officials. These discourses have a persuasive effect at hearings, but they are also at times in conflict with the retributive notions of justice in local township courts. An ethnographic case in point illustrates this issue. The South African Council of Churches sponsored a street-theatre performance in which a black minister presents a white Afrikaans-speaking police officer to his congregation. In this scene, the policeman confesses that he was present at the torture and murder of an African man. The confession is made to the daughter and widow of the deceased man, with the policeman saying, "I'm sorry. I was afraid. I would like to reconcile with you." The women react violently. "You deserve to die," they say.

The minister in this performance then places himself between the two parties as a way of protecting the policeman. One of the relatives of the deceased, an old man, then steps forward and begins to quote from the Bible. He says that he forgives the policeman, saying "I want to build a new Africa." The minister extols his virtue, indicating that he has set an example for the others. The women are sent to a trauma centre (Wilson, 2000, p. 75).

In another instance, illustrating the desire for justice, the case of Duma Kumalo, reveals details of the alternative side of reconciliation in South Africa. In 1986, Kumalo had been sentenced to death along with five others for the murder of a local councillor, a crime that he claimed he did not commit. The trial of the "Sharpeville Six" received international media attention, and the case was taken to the United Nations. The case became a symbol of the lack of justice for blacks under the apartheid system. Eventually Kumalo was released in 1993 after serving seven years on death row. When released, he demanded a retrial, but this was not granted.

Then, in November 1996, Kumalo staged a 27-day sit-in at the Sharpeville police station. After the sit-in, the police took him to meet with the chief prosecutor and a white magistrate, who indicated that because there was no new evidence in the case, a retrial could not take place. The denial of the retrial seemed to spur Kumalo into an act of revenge. He hid an axe in his coat and entered the Vereeniging court while it was in session. Kumalo then began to lash out with the axe, smashing desks, chairs, and other furniture, but he did not attack any people. When armed police arrived, Kumalo calmly put the axe down and put his arms in the air. "I just wanted justice," he said (Wilson, 2000, p. 75).

These two incidents—the street-theatre performance meant to emphasize the need for reconciliation in post-apartheid Africa, and the trial of Duma Kumalo after which he later seeks justice—illustrate the often dualistic or dichotomous nature of post-revolutionary events. In the case of South Africa, both reconciliation and revenge are counterposed in a discourse about justice and legal pluralism. Clearly, the introduction of human rights in post-apartheid South Africa has had varied social effects.

Religious values emphasize the need for reconciliation and human rights as a basic value orientation. However, in the legal system and other governmental state institutional structures, notions of justice are a prevailing ideology. In this system, it is not reconciliation that is sought so much as punishment and retribution. As Wilson (2000) concludes, "The plurality of legal orders in South Africa results not from systemic relations between law and society but from multiple forms of social relations seeking to alter the direction of social change in the area of justice within the context of the nation-building project of the post-apartheid state" (p. 75).

ANTHROPOLOGY AND LEGAL PLURALISM

In the wider arena of academic debate, the South African case further illustrates the ambiguous nature of anthropological interpretations of human rights in the context of political violence. Anthropologists, for example, have been at odds with certain other academics, such as colonial historians, over the nature of the relationship between state law and informal moralities and mechanisms of adjudication, which have been referred to as "customary law." A key notion in the debate concerns the concept of "legal pluralism," a term meaning the existence of more than one legal system in a single political unit. Anthropologists have preferred to use this term, but colonial historians object to it.

The wider question posed by this case study concerns the utility of the legal pluralistic concept in the context of the dismantling of the apartheid system and the institutionalized regime of dominance and racial segregation. It is important to note, however, that even within the discipline, complete agreement over the nature of legal pluralism in legal anthropology has not emerged. Certainly Malinowski (1926) argued against legal monism, suggesting that in non-state societies social norms perform the same regulatory functions as legal norms, thus elevating the former (uncodified social rules) to the same status as law. The argument posed by Malinowski and others in favour of legal pluralism is that state law is not always absolute and is perhaps not even central to the normative operation of society.

The opposition to the pluralistic legal notions favoured by a sector of anthropologists is derived from those who view legal pluralism as a neglect of the colonial state. Legal anthropologists in a colonial context often view state law and informal law as coexisting, but employing different procedures and moralities. In other words, two systems of law (state and informal) prevail in the anthropological discourse concerning human rights: two systems that can be seen as unconnected spheres of authority. The opposition to the anthropological notion of legal pluralism is provided by historians who argue that customary (informal) law is transformed and integrated into the administrative apparatus of the colonial state.

ANTHROPOLOGY AND RESTORATIVE JUSTICE

It is not the point of the present discussion to engage in an evaluation of the merits of one side or another in this debate. The point is that anthropologists have a role to play in the discourse of justice and reconciliation issues. However, notions of "reconciliation" in the context of human rights discussions are themselves a matter of dispute. Anthropologists have possibilities for engagement in these discussions, first because of their long-term historical fieldwork in the countries involved, and second, because of their propensities to view merging social and political matters from a wider, possibly more objective, stance. This sort of perspective can be a valuable aid in emerging countries that have become polarized, as in the case of post-apartheid South Africa, over issues of reconciliation and revenge.

Granted, these two categories are not necessarily mutually exclusive; there can, for example, be retribution without vengeance. Anthropologists can attempt to make explicable the dialectical relationship between emerging state institutions and local normative orders that take place in the aftermath of tumultuous social and political upheaval such as occurred in post-apartheid South Africa. In this instance, it is evident that anthropologists have a constructive role to play in the public sphere.

REBELLION AND REVOLUTION

When reconciliation between state governments and minority groups is not possible, then violence is apt to take place in the form of rebellion and revolt. The case of the Sandinista revolution in Nicaragua, and the Zapatista uprising in Mexico, illustrate the results of ruling elites' refusing to acknowledge the political, cultural, and economic rights of minority groups under their authority.

Many rebellions result from resistance to the authority of a dominating power. The American Revolution resulted initially from unfair taxation (the Boston Tea Party) and then expanded to a full-scale revolt against British domination. In Russia, the Bolshevik Revolution was also initially precipitated by internal economic conditions of poverty, unemployment, and food shortages. Other revolutions are more political in nature, taking the form of localized resistance to internal authority imposed from the outside by colonial regimes. The American Revolution also falls into this category, as does the Algerian revolt against French domination. Many resistance movements in the world today are between centralized state governments and internal populations seeking more control and authority in their lives. In addition, most rebellions today occur in the economically poor countries of South America, Africa, and Asia.

Two classic studies of rebellion in anthropology, Max Gluckman's *Custom and Conflict in Africa* (1956) and his later *Order and Rebellion in Tribal Africa* (1963), promote the view that conflict not only is a normal course of events but also can have positive results. Known as the "conflict model," this approach was also criticized as promoting a "disguised equilibrium model" because "conflict was seen as functional; it contributed to the maintenance of society" (Barrett, 1984, p. 33). Other approaches to conflict are more explicitly Marxian influenced, such as Marvin Harris's (2001) cultural materialism, because it emphasizes conflicts of interests between those who control the means of production in the society and those who do not. However,

BOX 7.1 Max Gluckman (1911–1975): Understanding South African Conflict

Max Gluckman was born in South Africa and therefore had a better comprehension of African conflict than those who viewed this phenomenon from an outsider's perspective. Gluckman was an outstanding student, earning a Rhodes Scholarship at Oxford during the 1930s. Later, when Gluckman became more established, he led the famous Manchester School of anthropology in Britain. While Gluckman did attend Malinowski's seminars at the London School of Economics on occasion, his intellectual persuasions were more in line with the anthropology of Radcliffe-Brown and the latter's search for generalizations using the comparative method than they were with Malinowski's functionalist orientation (see Sidky, 2004, pp. 183–99). In addition, as was also the case with Malinowski, Gluckman had no aversion to speaking out about the public issues of his time, especially the South African government's policy of segregation.

In a historical context, Max Gluckman's (1940) innovative essay, "Analysis of a Social Situation in Modern Zululand" (commonly referred to as the "Bridge Paper"), has come to be recognized as "one of the most significant anthropological critiques of segregationist policy in South Africa in the first half of the twentieth century" (Cocks, 2001, p. 739). Gluckman's essay was intended as a critique of the idea that social anthropology could be used as a key source for the scientific justification of segregation. In fact,

FIGURE 7.4 Max Gluckman
Source: Reprinted by permission of the Royal Anthropological Institute

he argued, the so-called native problem was exacerbated by a segregationist policy because South Africa was really a single social and economic system (see Gluckman [1975] for a further amplification of this point).

From Gluckman's perspective, any segregationist policy for South Africa was bound to fail. At the time this was a bold idea, because it placed social anthropology itself on trial in terms of its ability to deal with the segregation issue and, furthermore, the discipline's ability to carve out its usefulness in helping to understand the future of social relationships in South Africa. In his so-called Bridge Paper, Gluckman suggested that a symbolic moment had been achieved in support of the concept of a "single social system" theory because the bridge had been "planned by European engineers and built by Zulu labourers ... [and] ... was opened by European officials and the Zulu regent in a ceremony which included not only European and Zulu but also actions historically derived from European and Zulu cultures" (as cited in Cocks, 2001, p. 752). In fact, the historical importance of the Bridge Paper has also recently been noted by Andrew Bank, who indicates that "'The Bridge' ... has come to be recognized as *the* moment when South African and African anthropology recognized the need to incorporate colonizer and colonized, European and African, into a wider, and what is now accepted as more modern, ethnographic framework" (Bank & Bank, 2013, pp. 1–2; emphasis in original).

The main point that Gluckman was making was that a segregationist policy for South Africa ignored the fact that both whites and blacks were part of the same system; that the basis of their integration was precisely what tended to separate them. While on the whole each group had different customs and beliefs, the individuals in both groups nonetheless were dependent upon each other. The groups, Gluckman suggested, needed to cooperate with each other, and their patterns of behaviour were determined by their mutual need to adapt them to each other's patterns of behaviour. As Gluckman notes further, "The Zulu desire for the material goods of the Europeans, and the Europeans' need for Zulu labour and the wealth obtained by that labour, establishes strong inter-dependent interests between them" (as cited in Cocks, 2001, p. 753).

The fundamental strengths of Gluckman's critique of segregationist policies derive from his anthropological analysis of social and cultural processes. The genius of Gluckman's analysis is that it has largely stood the test of time. The "single social system" approach, while not fully achieved in South Africa today, has nonetheless outlasted the impetus for segregationist policies. Although Richard Wilson's (2000) paper on reconciliation in post-apartheid South Africa, for example, does not make reference to Gluckman's innovative ideas, it is evident that today's African National Congress government has embarked upon a nation-building project for South Africa that is largely predicated on the social integrative processes conceived by this early pioneer of anthropology so many years before.

unlike Gluckman's approach, a Marxist type of conflict model leads to change, even revolutionary change, rather than simply a continued maintenance of the existing socio-political system.

PUBLIC ANTHROPOLOGY AND INTERPRETING SOCIETAL CONFLICT

Protests against state authorities and other forms of resistance are a topic that has not been addressed in a satisfactory manner in anthropology. Part of the problem has to do with the manner in which conflict has historically been viewed in the discipline. Conflict has often been viewed as something pathological, as disruptive to the proper "functioning" of the state apparatus. When studies of conflict have been conducted in anthropology, as in the case of Max Gluckman's African studies, the view presented is one suggesting that conflict acts as an ameliorative measure, interspersed between states of relative harmony.

The view that conflict could be seen as an endemic state in the modern world would not appear to fit well in the history of anthropological theory. Anthropology appears to be in a state of intellectual paralysis as to which direction should be followed. Yet, as Barrett (1984, p. 32) summarizes, "There is no evidence that would prove whether society is primarily harmonious or whether it is rent by strain. The history of anthropology is peppered with polarized and seemingly arbitrary arguments. In no small measure this is due to the irresolvable conceptual opposites, such as conflict versus harmony, that pervade the discipline."

In the meantime, while some anthropologists puzzle over the possibility of returning conceptually to the innocent days of assumed equilibrium or harmony as a model to guide studies of society, or whether they should fully embrace a conflict model, such as an explicit Marxist approach or some other non-Marxian model, life goes on nonetheless, despite this internal perceptual angst. If a conflict model is embraced, then a change of attitude must of necessity take place: one in which conflict is seen as normal and is generated by the internal dynamics of society itself. If this attitude is taken, then one might view conflict as necessary even to the maintenance of society.

Reconciliation in the aftermath of conflict poses another difficult conceptual issue in anthropology. There is a long history in the discipline, from at least Malinowski onwards, of viewing legal pluralism as a reaction to an exclusionary state centralism that regarded only state law as valid, as suggested by colonial historians; concepts of state law are pitted against the anthropological notion of "customary law," suggesting that there exists more than one legal system in a single political unit. This debate between legal pluralists and those who deny the validity of uncodified social rules and norms as having the same status as state law is a central point of contention in the analysis of processes of reconciliation in post-apartheid South Africa.

From the legal pluralist perspective, reconciliation can take many forms—such as, for instance, street-theatre performances that build on shared values of forgiveness and healing. From the state perspective, the stress is on establishing justice within the context of the nation-building project of the post-apartheid era. Thus, anthropological notions of pluralistic legal systems contribute to a fuller understanding of the systemic relations between law and society, and illustrate the sources of societal conflict as various concepts of reconciliation, healing, revenge, and justice become juxtaposed against one another in the emerging legal structure of a multiracial nation.

It is nonetheless apparent in this age of global conflicts that the approaches to society prevalent in the days of Robert Redfield's "little community" are not workable today. In the modern nation states, there are simply too many conflicting demands for resources, and too many opposing interest groups, for a society to be viewed as a single unit of analysis held together by common bonds of *societas* or united by common values. In view of this, rather than seeking values that are central to a social system, the focus could be on the internally generated contradictions that make up the modern world. For it is these very contradictions upon which hinge the propensity toward terror in contemporary society, and the resulting resistance that is generated against attempts to suppress the influence of hegemonic power systems.

In the introduction to Timothy Findley's historical novel *The Wars*, Guy Vanderhaeghe (2005) comments that he finds the book's title "eccentric." "It may suggest," he ponders, "that war is an endless continuum, the natural state of humankind, and that peace is the real anomaly" (p. xiv). Can anthropologists not offer their insights on this question, without resorting to intellectual hyperbole or other forms of obfuscation?

CONCLUSION

The discussions in this chapter on resistance, rebellion, and reconciliation are all important aspects of public anthropology because they seek to understand significant social and political processes beyond the realm of strictly academic discourse on these subjects. This chapter has been inspired by Max Gluckman's critique of segregation in South Africa. It demonstrates that anthropologists have a long history of studies that are publicly engaged. This has been especially the case with more recent studies of truth and reconciliation efforts in various countries as anthropologists attempt to weld their research to current public issues.

Chapter 8

GLOBAL TERROR, MILITARISM, AND COUNTERINSURGENCY

The writing of this chapter began three days after the Boston Marathon bombing on 15 April 2013. US President Barack Obama appeared on national television a day later, offering condolences to the families of the dead and wounded, and vowing that the perpetrators of this heinous crime would not escape justice.

He looked weary. While this had not been as substantial an attack as the one on the World Trade Center in 2001, you could almost read on his face a certain resignation to the idea that the so-called war on terror would never be a passing phenomenon. Later in the week, after the perpetrators had been apprehended, the president appeared once again on national television and asked a very pertinent question, paraphrased here: How is it that two young men, both raised in America, should hold such animosity towards their fellow citizens that they should cause such harm?

Regrettably, such attacks as 9/11, on a larger or smaller scale, have now become part of the global "culture." For the purposes of this book, one is led to ask, What does anthropology have to say about global terror and counterinsurgency? And how have anthropologists contributed to an understanding of this global phenomenon? The purpose of this chapter is to explore possible answers to these questions. It also seeks to understand another aspect of public anthropology having to do with the engagement of anthropologists in various militaristic settings. There are, therefore, very important practical and ethical dimensions in public anthropology when anthropologists become directly engaged in their government's counterinsurgency measures in the so-called war on terror.

THE AFTERMATH OF 9/11

The tenth anniversary of the events of 11 September 2001 has now passed into history. In one assessment of the aftermath of 9/11, it has been suggested that this event "altered the meaning and direction of public anthropology, [it] has had a profound and lasting effect on the public aspects of our discipline" (Checker, 2011, p. 491). Initially, many forensic anthropologists and archaeologists volunteered with recovery and site excavations, but the city officials directing the operations at Ground Zero declined the offer of their services. A change of mind happened five years later when anthropologists and archaeologists from the New York City Office of the Chief Medical Examiner were placed in charge of all continued excavations and recovery efforts at Ground Zero.

Forensic anthropologists participated in a nine-month mortuary operation, triaging fragmentary human remains before they went through the identification process. The experts included 33 anthropologists, who engaged in a wide variety of roles in the mortuary operation. During this process, for example, over 20,000 fragments of human remains were analyzed, of which nearly 60 per cent have now been identified. In addition, other forensic anthropologists worked to recover and identify the remains of victims of the Flight 93 crash in Shanksville, Pennsylvania, and those in Washington, DC, who had died in the attack on the Pentagon. In recognition of the significant contribution of forensic anthropologists in the Disaster Victim Identification (DVI) program, the New York City Medical Examiner's office now employs eight full-time anthropologists. In addition, many other medical examiners' offices around the United States, in recognition of the potential contributions of forensic anthropologists in DVI operations, have also created a number of full-time positions for other forensic anthropologists.

The extreme fragmentation of the World Trade Center meant that identification of victims was a difficult process. Anthropologists were also therefore a key factor in the reconciliation process as well, since they were able to reassemble dozens of pieces of human remains to a single victim. However, there were also important media aspects to consider as people around the world grappled with the motivation behind the attack on the World Trade Center. Anthropologists were called upon to comment on such topics as the rise of Islamic fundamentalism, the significance of shrines, and male bonding.

ANTHROPOLOGY AND GLOBAL TERROR

One of the anthropologists who made frequent appearances in the media was William Beeman, then director of Middle East Studies at Brown University. Beeman's research in the Middle East had been ongoing since the mid-1960s, and he had already written extensively on terrorism and religious fundamentalism, both in mainstream publications and academic journals. A frequently asked question in his media appearances was why Americans were so hated by Islamic extremists (Beeman, 2001). He was also asked about the possible success of US military actions, to which he responded as follows:

> The Bush administration's projected war on terrorism is designed to eradicate and delegitimize terrorists. Both aims are futile. The grievances of the terrorists who committed the horrendous attacks on New York and Washington on September 11 have deep and persistent roots going back more than 150 years. The terrorists harbor a hatred that will not die, and their grievances cannot be delegitimized through military attacks. (Cited in Checker, 2011, p. 493)

Conservative commentators regarded Beeman's opinion as "unpatriotic." Nevertheless, Beeman continues to speak out against what he regards as negative generalizations about Islam and against US military activity in the Middle East.

In the weeks and months following 9/11, many anthropologists across the United States urged that their fellow citizens foster a climate of multicultural understanding. Various public forums and teach-ins were organized. In one event, held in January 2002, a public event was organized at the New York Museum that involved young Arab women speaking about their lives in post–9/11 New York. Despite these various educational efforts, occasional heavy criticism of such endeavours remained nonetheless. For example, the American Council of Trustees and Alumni issued a report entitled "Defending Civilization: How Our Universities Are Failing America," in which academic institutions were censured for critiquing the war on terrorism and for engaging in anti-American activities. This report also named 40 professors, including 7 anthropologists, who were deemed to be "short on patriotism" (Gonzalez, 2004).

The teach-ins that took place in the aftermath of 9/11 are reminiscent of similar educational activities that took place during the Vietnam War era. For example, in 1965, Eric Wolf and Marshal Sahlins joined with other scholars at the University of Michigan in a teach-in movement against the war (Sahlins, 2009). Heyman (2010) suggests that the teach-in movement "can be characterized as an affirmative engagement of anthropology with politics, in the sense of trying directly to influence the course of political struggle and public policy" (p. 288). In 1970, Wolf and several other academics also attempted to bring to the public's attention the involvement of anthropologists in Thailand. This involvement, which potentially could have supplied data about individuals and specific communities to the military, was kept secret (see Wakin, 1992). Thus, during the Vietnam War era there was a division among anthropologists between those opposed to the war on one side and those who were involved in aiding the military on the other.

ESOTERIC SOPHISTICATION

In an assessment of the effectiveness, or lack of it, of anthropological participation in engaging public issues, University of London (England) anthropologist Nicholas De Genova asserts that "in the aftermath of the events of September 11, 2001, anthropology as a discipline was not particularly well positioned to make any meaningful intervention in public discourse.... Ten years on, I don't believe that this dilemma has dramatically changed" (cited in Checker, 2011, p. 494). Several reasons are given for this ineffectiveness, such as an inability within the discipline to counter the general stifling of public debate in the United States, and the discipline's propensity to bank too heavily "on the exchange value of esoteric sophistication." The result has therefore tended to be a discipline which has "inoculated itself," to use De Genova's term, "against the sorts of sociopolitical pertinence that might facilitate greater public visibility" (p. 494).

The argument could be put forward, then, that anthropology's reliance on an "esoteric sophistication" has kept the discipline out of touch with world events. Apparently little has changed in the over 70 years since the publication of Malinowski's 1941 article "An Anthropological Analysis of War," in which he was highly critical of anthropologists' understanding of war and peace. He noted, for example, that "anthropology has done more harm than good in confusing the issue by optimistic messages from the primeval past, depicting human ancestry as living in the golden age of perpetual peace" (1941, p. 521). However, Malinowski was also critical of those supporting the contrary view, which is to say that "war is an essential heritage of man" (p. 521). He suggests that war is not natural and that each specific situation of conflict should be understood in its own particular circumstance without resorting to grand generalizations.

RESEARCHING GLOBAL TERROR

Contemporary anthropologists also echo De Genova's concern about anthropology's ability, or lack of it, to effectively study global terror. Werbner (2010) asks, "Can there be an engaged public anthropology of global Islamic terror? Arguably, anthropology was not meant to be a study of clandestine networks or unreachable social groups secretly plotting sudden cataclysmic international crises" (p. 193).

The problem posed by any anthropological research into the arena of global terror, counterinsurgency, militarism, and related areas is that anthropology's conceptual tools need to be stretched beyond their original limits. Anthropology was designed, and is best suited, for the study of local communities and small-scale societies. Anthropology's conventional methodology primarily involves intensive, in-depth interviews and participant observation. The approach is most often an inductive one; general

BOX 8.1 Bronislaw Malinowski (1884–1942): Social Critic and Anti-Militaristic Scholar

Malinowski embarked on a lecture tour of the United States in the 1930s in an attempt to alert the American public to the threat posed by the rise of Nazism in Germany (Stone, 2003). This tour was another of Malinowski's attempts to apply anthropological knowledge to the current public issues of his time. Malinowski (1941) argued, for example, in an article entitled "An Anthropological Analysis of War," that war was not biologically determined, but rather that it was violence that was abnormal among the human species.

Malinowski suggested further that Nazism's claim that war was a fundamental human need was also shown to be a false assumption based on anthropological studies. In an Oxford lecture in 1933, he made this argument forcefully by stating,

The hero of the next war, the man who from the air destroys a whole peaceful township in its sleep with poison gas, is not expressing any biological characteristics of his organism, nor showing any moral virtues. In a remarkable way, he matches the head-hunter, who surprises in their sleep a village of peaceful neighbours and kills them ruthlessly, without discrimination and without personal feelings. (Cited in Stone, 2003, p. 206)

FIGURE 8.1 Bronislaw Malinowski
Source: From LSE Library's Collections MALINOWSKI/3/18/2. Courtesy of LSE

Fighting on a large scale, according to Malinowski signals "a breakdown of personality and culture" (cited in Stone, 2003, p. 206). Engaging in large-scale fighting is not the result of a built-in aggressive impulse; rather, people "organize for fighting because, through tribal tradition, through teachings of a religious system, or of an aggressive patriotism, they have been indoctrinated with certain cultural values which they are then prepared to defend, and with certain collective hatreds on which they are ready to assault and kill" (pp. 206–07).

The rise of Nazism, according to Malinowski's reasoning, does not represent the manifestation of the primal drives of German people, but a perverting of German culture. "Nazi Germany," in Malinowski's words, "developed a system of values which could, through the technique of modern propaganda and under the sanction of a perfectly organized police, be made to become the doctrine of the whole nation" (cited in Stone, 2003, p. 207). It therefore logically followed, he argued, that if the rise of Nazism was something that could be artificially manufactured, then it also followed that it was a phenomenon that could just as easily be prevented.

propositions are made on the basis of specific observations, as opposed to the deductive approach (logical reasoning from the general to the particular) commonly found in sociology and other disciplines in the social sciences.

Everyday research in anthropology starts mostly from the bottom, from the small places in the world. To attempt the adoption of a whole new conceptual approach in an attempt to deal with the impact of global events is a problematic methodological concern. Since 9/11, anthropologists want to become more engaged in understanding contemporary social issues, but are their disciplinary tools capable of undertaking this task?

ANTHROPOLOGISTS AS EXPERTS

Even for anthropologists who have been studying Muslim societies in the West, the aftermath of 9/11 has raised serious questions about what specifically constitutes expert knowledge in the discipline. Anthropologists may have conducted ethnographic studies in such predominately Muslim countries as Afghanistan or Pakistan, or the immigration of Muslims to Britain, America, or elsewhere in the West, but what can be said about 9/11 from the vantage point of previous research? During the course of this research, would an anthropologist likely encounter an Islamic terrorist?

An anthropologist who is an expert on the Muslim diaspora and who is frequently asked to speak to various groups in the hope that this research could throw light on Pakistanis' involvement in Al-Qaeda terror networks had to admit that she "had never encountered a Pakistani terrorist, young or old" (Werbner, 2010, p. 194).

Anthropologists may cultivate an aura of possessing "insider" knowledge because of their research, but when they express their opinions, are they doing so as anthropologists or as public intellectuals? The distinction between the two is difficult to ascertain in most cases. Opinions may also combine the two perspectives, as could be the case with so-called citizen-scholars, who have professional knowledge that is subsequently expressed in a public forum. Anthropologists who are experts on the Middle East and its politics, history, and religion would have credibility that others would not have because of their expertise, but whether or not this capability adds extra insights into the media's view of global terror and security is another matter.

There are anthropologists who suggest that it is about time that the discipline develop what Daniel Goldstein (2010) refers to as an "anthropology of security." "While matters of security have appeared as paramount themes in the post-9/11 world," Goldstein explains, "anthropology has not developed a critical comparative ethnography of security.... I call for the emergence of a critical 'security anthropology,' one that recognizes the significance of security discourses and practices to the global and local contexts in which cultural anthropology operates" (p. 487).

The idea behind this suggestion is that security themes today underlie many of the historical issues that have preoccupied anthropology in the past. It is suggested, for example, that a decline in neoliberalism has coincided with a rise of the security paradigm as a framework for organizing contemporary social life.

According to this perspective, the security paradigm affects the subjects of anthropological work and shapes the contexts within which such work is conducted. The terrorist attacks of 9/11, Goldstein (2010) argues, did not initiate a "security moment" in world history per se, but they did intervene in the gradual disintegration of the neoliberal social and political order (pp. 498–99). The rights of citizens can therefore be seen to be undermined by the failure of the neoliberal state to create security for local communities. For anthropology, with its emphasis on comparative ethnography, the discipline is offered an opportunity to contribute to the understanding of the contemporary global reality of the security discourse (Albro, 2007; Selmeski, 2007; Sterpka, 2007).

THE ANTHROPOLOGY OF WAR AND PEACE

It is important to stress that anthropologists as a group are not of one mind when it comes to issues of war and peace. The discipline is varied in nature, and this is reflected in the multidirectional responses that those in the discipline have brought to the legacy of 9/11 on public anthropology. Some anthropologists, for example, were embedded in military actions in Afghanistan and Iraq through the Human Terrain System, a program funded by the US Department of Defense (Gonzalez, 2009; Forte, 2011). There are also those in the discipline who have been strongly opposed to such engagements.

The basis for such opposition has been both personal and academic. There are those who believe that anthropologists could do more at a personal level to counter the negative generalizations about other cultures or those holding religious beliefs such as those found in Islam. Certain anthropologists, such as David Price (2012), have made a long-term commitment to critically scrutinizing US militarism and to "exposing" the wider socio-political impacts of what are regarded as US imperialistic policies. In this vein, such anthropologists as De Genova have criticized those in the discipline for failing to produce ethnographies of the United States and its role as a global imperial power. Such studies would focus on "the ways in which military actions since 2001 have had a profound effect on both the lives of individuals and on social life broadly conceived" (cited in Checker, 2011, p. 495).

There are also anthropologists who are vociferous opponents of American militarism. Chalmers Johnson, President of the Japan Policy Research Institute, has been

FIGURE 8.2 David Price
Source: Photo by Midge Price. Courtesy of David Price

PUBLIC ANTHROPOLOGY

critical of the war in Iraq, calling it "very possibly the most serious self-inflicted wound in the history of American foreign policy. It was caused by American imperialism and militarism" (2005, p. 10). He also points out that America has over 720 military bases in about 132 countries around the world. The American military, according to Johnson, also deploys well over half a million soldiers, spies, technicians, and other civilian contractors in other nations, which he refers to as "a new form of empire—an empire of military enclaves rather than of colonies as in older forms of imperialism" (p. 10).

Studying Militarism

Johnson furthermore suggests that there is a role for scholarship in studying the impact of the US military bases in the various countries that harbour them. Related subjects of interest could be the associated environmental degradation associated with military activities, the exploitation of women, and the general social and economic impacts of military bases. Other anthropologists, such as Catherine Lutz (2005), also call for "ethnographies of militarization." "For anthropologists," she suggests, "the global distribution of [military] bases, the cultural and transnational processes they involve ... provide an opportunity for the comparative and critical methods of the discipline to contribute to an understanding of the ongoing crisis of militarization" (2005, p. 11).

This is not to suggest that anthropologists' interest in this "new militarization" is solely a direct result of 9/11. However, in the days following 9/11 there were internal changes within the anthropological community as a response to the tragedy and its aftermath. The American Anthropological Association, for instance, drafted a statement on human rights, which has been posted online with an accompanying resource guide (www.aaanet.org/404.html). The AAA was also quick to embrace more support for public anthropology across the discipline. *American Anthropologist* launched a Public Anthropology review section under the editorship of Tom Boellstorff. In addition, long-time advocate and activist for human rights, Barbara Johnston (Johnston & Barker, 2008) was appointed the AA associate editor for public anthropology.

At the level of ethnographic research, there has also been increasing concern since 9/11 about anthropologists working in violent settings (Gill, 2005). In their research, anthropologists place a high value on participant observation, and the new realities of fieldwork, because it may be conducted in unstable situations that require special considerations. During the course of their research, anthropologists may also witness possible human rights violations perpetrated by security forces. Gill (2005) comments that human rights issues encountered during the course of research among Latin American peasant coca producers were a prominent aspect of the fieldwork setting, all of which "forced [her] to think more critically about the relationships that anthropologists develop with their research subjects" (p. 12).

This research initially began in southern Georgia at the US Army's School of the Americas (SOA), which is a counterinsurgency training centre for Latin Americans. Gill's access to the SOA was made possible through SOA Watch, a human rights group that organizes opposition to the school. Eventually, in the later 1990s, the US House of Representatives cut the school's funding because of charges that the school condoned the use of torture during the US "war on drugs" campaign. Pervasive instability, especially in Colombia, made prolonged participant observation an impossible task. In addition, ethnographic research in such violent settings tended to blur the boundaries between traditional ethnography, human rights reporting, and journalism.

ANTHROPOLOGICAL KNOWLEDGE AND STATE SECURITY

In the history of anthropology, there have been various instances in which anthropological knowledge has been used in the context of counterinsurgency operations. One of the most well-known of these, referred to as Project Camelot, was an effort to use anthropologists in counterinsurgency operations (Beals, 1967; Horowitz, 1967). This project, which sought to "assess the potential for internal war within national societies," was eventually terminated due to the widespread opposition that resulted when its aim became known (Horowitz, 1967, p. 4).

Ralph Beals (1967) investigated the extent of US intelligence agencies' involvement with American anthropologists. His investigation uncovered various instances in which anthropologists who had been working in the Soviet Union, China, or other nation states with communist connections were contacted by intelligence agency personnel about their research. Project Camelot came to the public's attention in 1965, when it was revealed that the US Special Operations Research Office (SORO) had attempted to hire anthropologists as well as other social scientists to work with the US Army in Chile and a few other countries. Beals's report was partly a response from the American Anthropological Association to the fallout from the revelations of Project Camelot's efforts to use anthropologists for clandestine research operations.

Laura Nader (1997) referred to restraints on academic freedom during the Cold War era as the "phantom factor." During this period, anthropologists who were working on controversial topics, such as poverty, racial discrimination, or post-colonialism, tended to modify their analyses in order to avoid arousing suspicion. The McCarthy era taught academics that they could avoid public humiliation by steering clear of certain topics of research or limiting their analyses in certain ways so as to curtail possible criticisms of the state security apparatus.

A lesser-known attempt than Project Camelot to use anthropological knowledge in a military context was referred to as the M-VICO system (Price, 2012). The M-VICO system was an early counterinsurgency project, eventually aborted, which sought to utilize anthropological research on a much broader scale than was envisioned under Project Camelot. The essence of the M-VICO system (an acronym derived from the categories of Matrix, Vulnerabilities, Insurgency, Counterinsurgency, and Outcomes) was to build on the various structures, methodologies, and categories that were used in the Human Relations Area Files (HRAF). The project sought to employ anthropologists to encode cross-cultural data on various forms of behaviour; the data would subsequently be used by security services for strategic purposes. In other words, the HRAF files would be employed to produce a counterinsurgency database for US military and intelligence personnel (Price, 2012, pp. 16–20).

HRAF and Military Intelligence

The Human Relations Area Files are an anthropological database founded in 1949 at Yale University in New Haven, Connecticut, primarily employed to test hypotheses in a cross-cultural perspective, as illustrated in George Peter Murdock's (1949) *Social Structure*. As Barrett (1996) explains, "Initially called the Cross-Cultural Survey [launched at Yale in 1937], the HRAF provided systematic data on more than 250 cultures. They were intended to elevate cross-cultural analysis to a fully scientific exercise, one amenable to quantitative analysis" (p. 78). Incidentally, the HRAF system was virtually ignored in Britain, and even in the United States not a great number of anthropologists used it, possibly because of a preference in the discipline for developing data from original fieldwork, as opposed to what was considered by some as "library research."

George Murdock was not only an anthropologist but also a Lieutenant Commander in World War II, during which he attempted to tailor the data created in the HRAF's predecessor, the Cross-Cultural Survey, to serve the needs of the Office of Naval Intelligence. This was especially the case with data on cultures encountered by US forces fighting on the Pacific Front (Murdock, 1961, p. xii; Price, 2008, pp. 91–96). According to David Price (2012), HRAF "went on to flourish with substantial funding from the US military and intelligence organizations, as well as university sponsorships. During the 1950s, HRAF received millions of dollars in military contracts" (p. 16).

According to the financial information provided in Price's (2012) article, by "the early 1950s, HRAF was receiving support from the government at the level of $200,000 a year. The Navy, the Army, the Air Force and the Central Intelligence Agency each contributed $50,000 a year to support research" (p. 17). During this period in the 1950s, Price concludes, more than 85 per cent of HRAF's funds came from military contracts, while less than 15 per cent of its funds derived from other sources, such as membership dues, gifts, and grants. The projects funded by the US military apparently included such activities as compiling bibliographies, translating data from foreign sources, organizing data according to certain criteria, and preparing profiles on more than 50 countries in the Soviet orbit, the Middle East, and Asia.

Use of the HRAF files is what could be called "dual use" research, in that it involves a mixture of theoretical interests and what was once called "pure science" with military applications. Usages of this type are common in other academic disciplines, such as physics, chemistry, computer science, or communication studies, but in anthropology they remain a controversial aspect of the discipline. Nonetheless, such applications of anthropological knowledge, while not widely discussed within the discipline, allowed the military to use what it needed from the ethnographic data compiled in the HRAF files, while anthropologists could continue with their own interests in pursuing cross-cultural correlations of kinship, residence patterns, and so on without being tied to any specific military agenda or military interference. However, one could reasonably conclude that all this money was spent on promoting the research conducted under HRAF auspices because anthropology was viewed "as a useful tool for infiltrating and controlling local populations with the aim of advancing the interests of the American military" (Price, 2012, p. 18).

The Human Terrain System

Anthropologists have been recruited to provide "cultural knowledge" for the purpose of achieving more effective counterinsurgency in Iraq and Afghanistan (Albro, 2010; Forte, 2011). This recruitment was part of the US Army's Human Terrain System (HTS) program, whose purpose was to "employ rapid appraisal-type ethnographic techniques to address a deficit of 'socio-cultural knowledge' on the part of Army and Marine field commanders" (Albro, 2010, p. 22).

The HTS program created conflicts and debate among HTS advocates and anthropological critics. The controversy involved such issues as the role of anthropological research in war, the ethics of research, harm to the discipline of anthropology, and the possibility that anthropological fieldworkers could be mistaken for US spies. Advocates for HTS claimed that the program actually helped to save lives and could serve as a key factor in helping anthropology become more relevant (Forte, 2011, p. 149).

The controversy concerning HTS activities also became a focus of concern for the American Anthropological Association's (AAA) executive board in 2009. A comprehensive assessment was conducted over a two-year period by the Association's Commission on the Engagement of Anthropology with the US Security and Intelligence Communities (CEAUSSIC). (This report is available for download on the AAA website at www.aaanet.org/issues/policy-advocacy/CEAUSSIC-Releases-Final-Report-on-Army-HTS-Program.cfm.) The 72-page assessment was particularly concerned with activities of the Human Terrain Teams (HTT), which was the aspect that generated the most controversy among anthropologists (Gonzalez, 2008, pp. 21–26).

HTTs were composed of squads comprising both military and social science personnel embedded with US military units in the field. The knowledge generated by the social scientists was intended to help improve decision making by commanders on the ground in order to avoid "kenetic engagements," a military euphemism for the use of lethal force (McFate & Fondacaro, 2008, p. 27). The CEAUSSIC final report issued in 2009 focused specifically on the Human Terrain System. The report neither opposed nor endorsed HTS engagements but did note the general lack of familiarity within the discipline with expanding arenas of security, since such issues have not become prevalent since the Vietnam War era. The report also noted concern over the absence of an ethical framework for the HTS program, and the inability of HTS members to provide reliable controls over the use of the data that is collected under such a scheme. There is a high probability, the report mentions that such data collection would put the research subjects in harm's way and that data collected under battlefield conditions would probably be used as military intelligence.

The report sums up the conclusions of AAA's executive board:

> When ethnographic investigation is determined by military missions, not subject to external review, where data collection occurs in the context of war, integrated into the goals of counterinsurgency, and in a potentially coercive environment—all characteristic factors of the HTS concept and its application—it can no longer be considered a legitimate professional exercise of anthropology. (Commission on the Engagement of Anthropology with the US Security and Intelligence Communities, 2009, p. 3)

In short, the idea of anthropologists scooting around a war zone in Humvees in an attempt to gather cultural knowledge that would probably be used by the US military seems to be a flawed approach, as judged by the AAA executive board.

Research versus Intelligence

In the context of the HTS program, there are further areas of concern for the discipline. First, there is a lack of clarity over the key distinctions between "research" as normally conceptualized by social scientists, and "intelligence" as they might be understood in a military context.

Second: In what ways is the overt or clandestine collection of cultural knowledge constrained by ethical codes of conduct? As Forte (2011) observes, "The bulk of the criticism from anthropologists ... has been directed at the [HTS] program's perceived failure to abide by even the most basic principles of ethical research" (p. 151). Distinctions that are drawn in this military context of research, one would presume, are therefore crucial ones for anthropologists and would have to be dealt with directly in an open forum of debate.

Third: In what sense would such data collection as that which would take place in an HTS project be properly regarded as "anthropology," since there would appear to be little opportunity for an engagement with a community of social scientists in any capacities other than military ones?

Fourth: Would the priorities of military commanders be the ones adopted as guidelines for research? This would not necessarily provide any guarantees that research would be conducted in good faith or that proper field methods would be applied in any sort of rigorous manner. In sum, then, a military-driven systems approach to cultural problem-solving, which utilizes culture as one of the key variables and in which priorities are established by combatant commanders, is an approach fraught with many conceptual and epistemological difficulties for anthropology (Albro, 2010, pp. 23–24).

ANTI-TERRORISM AND ACADEMIC FREEDOM

While there is much discussion in anthropology about an involvement with military activities, such as the Human Terrain System program, there is also an important concern about a controversial American anti-terrorism law and the possibility that this law could threaten academic freedom and human rights (M. Price, Rubinstein, & Price, 2012). Federal law in the United States prohibits providing "material support or resources" to a terrorist group. Civil libertarians, for example, are concerned that a "material support" law could be arbitrarily applied to criminalize humanitarian aid programs, charitable activities, or other such laudable endeavours.

As far as the academic community is concerned, this type of law also has the potential, as indicated in a *New York Times* editorial ("Editorial: A Bruise," 2010), of curtailing freedom of speech and criminalizing certain types of academic research. There is concern therefore among some anthropologists that their research may be regarded as working with groups designated as terrorists or populations who could be influenced by such people. There is a prohibition against supplying support to any group designated by the US State Department as a "foreign terrorist organization." The problem is that it is difficult to ascertain exactly who is contravening this law. For example, it could be difficult to differentiate among the actual members of a group, those who intend to support its illegal activities, and those who do not.

Support could also possibly take place during the course of anthropological research. The law applies to not only American citizens but also non-citizens who may live and work entirely outside of the United States. Granted, it may be difficult to prosecute cases in which persons outside the country are deemed to support a terrorist group; however, there is clearly a deterrent inherent in the "material support" law that could inhibit contact with "suspicious" persons or groups. The concern is that such a broad possible interpretation to the material support law raises "the likelihood that a wide range of normal ethnographic activities could be illegal under this law" (M. Price et al., 2012, p. 3).

Several questions emerge here. For example, are such concerns justified? What sort of ethnographic research would be of concern under the material support law? For starters, it is a fact that anthropologists must communicate with the subjects of their studies in order to perform the tasks involved in responsible research. This communication would probably involve direct personal interaction with the members of the particular culture under investigation, characterized by the commonly used methodology of participant observation in social events and in-depth interviews conducted with informants.

If an anthropologist conducted extensive interviews with individuals regarded as belonging to an organized insurgency and published the results in an academic journal, there is the possibility that such scholarly work would be regarded as a contravention of the material support law. M. Price et al. (2012, p. 3) give the example of an anthropologist trying to understand Palestinian responses to the pervasive violence that surrounds them in their daily lives, and participates by walking alongside marchers in a "martyr funeral." If the funeral was organized by a designated terrorist group, then this sort of research could be deemed in violation of the material support law. Furthermore, Richard Norton's (2007) study of Hezbollah could hardly have been conducted without some sort of contact with the members of this organization.

More examples of this variety of research could be given, but it is evident that there is more than a little uncertainty concerning the boundary between acceptable and unacceptable research with regards to US anti-terrorism law. Is it even possible, for example, that an ethnographic study could be conducted on the use of suicide bombing? Hage (2003), commenting on such a research scenario, notes that "an anthropology of the practice of suicide bombing is of course a highly unlikely endeavor. It would require the anthropologist to go into the technical and institutional processes of the practice and would involve fieldwork within such organizations as Hamas and Islamic Jihad" (p. 69). Issues such as these are also an important facet of Scott Atran's (2010) book titled *Talking to the Enemy*, which Spencer (2012) suggests tells us much about "the rather puzzling problem of anthropology and its political engagement with policy-makers and the military establishment" (p. 2).

As a result of the possibility, albeit even a remote one, of conducting studies of suicide bombers and associated controversial subjects, anthropologists could think about lobbying for an amendment to the material support law that would lessen the likelihood of certain types of ethnographic research becoming criminalized. Spencer (2012) suggests that researchers might need special review boards for their proposals that can handle "potentially tricky research into highly sensitive topics ... boards which could draw up guidelines for handling non-typical research subjects" (p. 5). Clearly, in this age of counterinsurgency, more discussion needs to take place among anthropologists about the possible legal constraints on their research activities and possible infringements on their academic freedom.

CASE STUDY: NATO MILITARY BASE PROTEST

In the late 1970s, the North Atlantic Treaty Organization (NATO) was given permission by the Canadian government to construct a military base in central Labrador at Goose Bay. The purpose of the base was to support low-level test flights (Lackenbauer, 2007; Wadden, 2001). The Aboriginal population of this area call themselves the Innu, although in the ethnographic literature they have been frequently referred to as the Barren Ground Naskapi. In his ethnographic study, Georg Henriksen (1973) described the Innu as living "on the edge of the white man's world." The Innu have lived a largely traditional lifestyle, hunting caribou in the winter months, and migrating to the coast region of Davis Inlet to fish and hunt sea mammals.

In Henriksen's (1973) assessment, in a section of his ethnography entitled "The Future of the Naskapi," he comments that "in this confrontation [with industrialized nations], they are fighting a losing battle for their social and cultural integrity. In my opinion, a most important problem is how to protect these cultures from disintegration and at the same time help them to attain an effective bargaining position *vis-à-vis* the outside world" (p. 115). In other words, the encroachment of the outside world on the Innu hunting and fishing lifestyle has severely threatened the Innu's ability to maintain a traditional social and economic way of life.

The construction of the military base has not been the only threat to Innu subsistence activities. In the 1960s, the Innu were forcibly removed from their traditional territories in the Labrador interior and resituated to the coastal areas of Sheshatshiu and Davis Inlet. Living in this new community brought on many social and economic problems: there was little wage employment for the Innu residents, housing conditions were deplorable, they were not able to access their caribou hunting areas, and contaminated drinking water led to many additional harmful health effects (Ryan, 1988).

Further impacts on the Innus' traditional activities occurred in 1972 with the construction of the Churchill Falls hydro-electric project, which diverted major waterways and caused flooding to over 4,000 square kilometres in Innu hunting and burial grounds. Furthermore, in 1994, nickel deposits were discovered in an area that the Innu claimed belonged to them. Subsequently, in the late 1990s, the construction of a highway was begun between Churchill Falls and the Labrador coast, disrupting the migration routes of the caribou upon which the Innu depended for food (Alcantara, 2007;

Armitage, & Kennedy, 1989). These various projects overwhelmed the Innu, so they decided to stage a protest against the low-level flights out of Goose Bay by occupying the military base.

The jet noise emanating from the low-level flights out of Goose Bay by the NATO exercises was a terrifying experience for the Innu hunters and their families. An anthropologist conducting fieldwork among the Innu during this period provided the following account of this experience:

> … as if hit by an abrupt, incredible blast of noise. The tent canvas shook. I fell back on the floor, ears ringing, and I felt my heart begin to pound painfully. Before I had time to recover I heard Janet scream my name.… Another blast of noise struck, and the recorder's volume meter jumped crazily in the split second it took another jet to fly over us. I felt shaken and stood up unsteadily. My initial fear changed to anger.… The twenty-tonne jet bomber had swooped just thirty meters above our heads, flying at 900 kilometers an hour. (Wadden, 2001, p. 36)

It was obviously impossible for the Innu to live and hunt under such conditions. The caribou were driven from the Innu hunting territory of Nitassinan (meaning "our land") by such ferocious noise. The Innu initially took action by expressing their dissatisfaction with the military flights. For example, a delegation of Innu travelled to West Germany in an attempt to seek support from the Green Party. In an ironic twist, the West German government had been promoting the low-level test flights in Labrador as a means of protecting the German environment. The reasoning was that such flights would take place over unoccupied Canadian territory, rather than over populated areas in Germany. Apparently, little thought had been given to the Aboriginal residents of Labrador who had lived and hunted in this area for many thousands of years.

The German Green Party was able to provide contacts with other environmental and Aboriginal support groups who were capable of bringing the Innu cause to the attention of a wider audience. However, matters became more severe for the Innu when a $550-million expansion to the Goose Bay facility was approved by NATO despite the Innu protest. In addition, an Innu request to meet with the NATO team that was to arrive at Goose Bay to coordinate the expansion plans was turned down. The Innu community then planned to take more direct action. As a result, 75 members of the Innu community began an occupation at one of the Goose Bay airstrips, resulting in the arrest of two of their leaders, as reported in a series of articles on the protest in Toronto's *Globe and Mail* (Cox, 1990a; 1990b).

The arrest of the Innu leaders led to an escalation of the protest as about 200 members of the Innu community set up a campsite just outside the fence of the main Goose Bay runway. The occupation then began to receive national and international media attention; however, the low-level flights were suspended reputedly due to cold weather, resulting in an interruption of the Innu occupation. In the following spring, the protest resumed, bringing with it many more arrests. Five of the Innu protesters were even handed jail sentences. Four of these convictions were eventually overturned, with the judge ruling in favour of the Innu argument that the Aboriginal protesters had not been trespassing on the airbase, because they believed that they had never surrendered title to the land on which the military base had been built.

Eventually, NATO announced that their plans had changed and the planned expansion to the military facility would not be constructed after all. Low-level flights continued, however, and in the period from 1992 to 1994, the Innu resumed their protest. During this period, NATO did reduce the number of flights and avoided Innu caribou hunting areas using a satellite monitoring system. NATO claimed that the reduction, and then the eventual obsolescence of low-level flights was the result not of Aboriginal protests but of a change in strategy, which made the military facility at Goose Bay less important than it had been previously.

The Innu protest was a learning experience for not only them but other Aboriginal groups as well. They learned about the effectiveness of political mobilization and the far-reaching effects of enlisting the help of international support groups. The Innu were successful in protecting themselves and the surrounding wildlife from the harmful effects of the low-level bombing flights. Innu leaders learned to develop new strategies for coping with pressures of the outside world that might be useful should further confrontations develop in the future. Innu leader Daniel Ashini (1990), in an article entitled "David Confronts Goliath," summed up these learning experiences:

The Innu will continue to use civil disobedience and will continue to fight for our rights in Nitassinan. We will continue to appeal to Canadians' sense of justice. We will not simply disappear off the cultural face of this world without a fight. (p. 70)

Evidently, this is the sort of bold statement that anthropologists who are interested in public issues should take note of. There are many Indigenous groups around the world who are in need of the same wider political, economic, and media support as the Innu. However, the manner in which this support is rendered by anthropologists remains an unresolved issue within the discipline.

CONCLUSION

The relationship between anthropology and the military is a precarious one, fraught with pitfalls and many unresolved issues. Originally designed for small-scale community studies, cultural anthropology appears ill equipped for research on global terrorism, counterinsurgency, and military alliances. Among the various problems that anthropologists have encountered in their attempts to delve into terrorism, for example, are ethical issues of confidentiality. How can one's sources of information be protected, especially when these sources could pose a threat to national security? Methodological concerns are also important. Participant observation, the hallmark of cultural anthropological research techniques, is apt to contravene American material support laws if research is conducted with groups deemed as terrorist ones. So many other possibilities, such as research into suicide bombing, also fall into this category.

An important concern that cannot be overlooked is the traditional stance of cultural relativism, which has been such a pillar of anthropology's theoretical foundation since the Boasian days nearly a century ago. Do anthropologists feel comfortable with choosing sides when it comes to supporting the military or acting against terrorism and counterinsurgency? Again, as discussed earlier, are there human rights issues that should override cultural relativism?

There is no doubt that public anthropology needs to tread with great caution as it proceeds into the future of global issues. One is reminded of the old adage "Fools rush in where angels fear to tread." Anthropology needs to keep up with the times as it evolves alongside changes in human societies in the modern world. The predecessors of modern anthropology—Boas, Mead, and Malinowski—could never have predicted a world of global terrorism and the unprecedented threats to human life posed by atomic bombs in the hands of those with malevolent intentions toward others. There is no doubt that 9/11 changed the world in so many ways, yet anthropologists need to reassess how they fit into this new human culture of seemingly quotidian violence.

Pnina Werbner (2010) refers to the "anthropological blues in the face of global terror." The dilemma for modern anthropology is summarized in an articulate manner: "Anthropologists may choose to speak out eloquently and persuasively on global terror as public intellectuals or citizen scholars, even without regional expertise, but the question is, what particular anthropological theoretical or analytical insights can they bring to bear on an event produced by a hidden world of clandestine plotting and scheming beyond their knowledge?" (p. 194). Seeking answers to this significant question would appear to be a necessary prerequisite, a beginning point for today's public anthropologist.

Chapter 9

MEDIA, THE INTERNET, AND OUR GLOBAL VILLAGE

As far as public anthropology is concerned, the media and the Internet have expanded the discourse about anthropological topics and interests out to the entire globe. As far back as 1997, it was exclaimed, no doubt with some trepidation about what the future would hold, that "the Internet as a topic has taken over our professional lives" (Ogburn, 1997, p. 286). More recently, it has been remarked that "virtual communities are often more real to their users than certain constructed communities from the so-called real reality" (Gordana, 2011, p. 17).

The media and its associated forms, such as the Internet, are a relatively new area of research that deserves anthropologists' complete attention as they engage more fully in public issues. Indeed, "after long decades of neglect," Postill (2009) exclaims, "the anthropological study of media is now booming" (p. 334). There are recent studies of digital ethnography (Zorn, 2013), the role of media in studies of ritual and religion (Engelke, 2010; Sumiala, 2013), the anthropology of news and journalism (Bird, 2010), experimental film (Schneider & Pasqualino, 2014), various research reports of the Internet (Hart, 2004; Saunders, 2011), as well as more general studies of the influence of media on anthropological topics (Rothenbuhler & Comar, 2005; Armin, 2010; Daniels & Feagin, 2011). The digital age and online anthropology have also had some unintended results, such as a protest from an Aboriginal South African tribe whose members objected to the multimedia images of human remains, belonging to an anthropological collection at the University of Vienna, which tribal members claimed were "gathered using unethical methods, such as grave-robbing" (Scully, 2008, p. 1155).

There is hardly a person alive today whose life has not been impacted to a significant degree by the role of media. There is also no doubt that our own life histories are framed to one degree or another by our association with media. For this author, it ranges from the pre-television era, when the whole family gathered around

FIGURE 9.1 Marshall McLuhan
Source: Library and Archives Canada

the radio after supper hour, to the present Internet age of high-speed communications in the "global village," a term coined by communication guru Marshall McLuhan.
Even though our lives are framed in a temporal sequence by media events (Kennedy's
assassination, the Apollo moon walk, 9/11), there is still much more in anthropology
that could be accomplished with a focus on the role of media in our everyday lives,
although this research situation is rapidly changing in recent years with the proliferation of social media of various genres.

   During the 1950s, when someone in my hometown wanted to make a telephone
call, they would lift the receiver, and an operator would come on the line and ask,
"Number please?" (Our home number was simply 128.) Today, my children do not
remember a time when schools did not have computers, Internet access, and word
processors. They do not remember a time before cellphones, Facebook, and texting.
This will be the last generation in the history of humanity to experience such a vast
and all-pervasive electronic revolution. From the viewpoint of anthropology, the question is, Is enough research being conducted to document this unprecedented revolution while the opportunity continues to exist?

THE MEDIUM AND PUBLIC EVENTS

Some of my earliest childhood memories involve lying on our family's living-room floor, propped up on cushions, listening to the large radio-stereo combination that was typical of the 1950s. My favourite show was *The Lone Ranger*. My mind was ablaze with images of Tonto, Silver, and runaway wagon trains. Later, when the same shows were played on our newly acquired television set, I was puzzled by my sense of disappointment. Whatever had been going on in my head when I listened to the radio did not appear to be happening when I watched what were apparently the same shows televised on our primitive black-and-white set.

This feeling of disappointment was eerily similar to what I felt when my favourite book was made into a movie. There was just so much missing in the visual version. This was a classic case of subtraction by addition, or adding more but getting less. I now realize that when I listened to the radio, my mind had a free rein to imagine whatever it wanted or was able to create. Television and movies, on the other hand, controlled everything too much: the images they offered up to my mind were too restrictive; they could not be altered, and this was at least partly the source of my dissatisfaction.

In university, I heard about Marshall McLuhan (1964) and his famous pronouncement that "the medium is the message" in *Understanding Media*. Now, this helped to clarify things for me. My dissatisfaction as a child was not with *The Lone Ranger* version portrayed on television, but with the manner in which the medium had controlled my experience. I also had a sense of the manner in which a machine could control one's life in certain fundamental ways. The television was guiding, in a particularly insidious manner, my sense of reality and, in the process, was remaking my sense of self. What I was experiencing was, in other words, this: the medium creates a symbiotic relationship between a person and a machine, which influences how a message is perceived. The form of the medium embeds itself in the message. According to McLuhan, then, it is the medium itself, and not the content it carries, that should be the focus of study and concern.

If I may fast-forward in my life history: I am seated in a high school history exam on 22 November 1963. Someone rushes into our classroom and whispers something into our teacher's ear. The teacher then scrawls on the blackboard "President Kennedy Has Been Shot." The teacher then tells us to continue with our exam, that there is no news that the President has actually died. I think, 'How ironic, such an event announced in our history class.' Later that evening, after supper, my family sat around the television, watching in disbelief as the passing of the presidential motorcade and the shooting in Dallas were played out repeatedly before us. My mother commented that even during the (Second World) War she had never seen anything so startling.

Before television, one watched heavily edited newsreels at the movie theatre, minus most of the gory details.

I missed the lunar landing of Apollo 11 on 20 July 1969, because I was working an afternoon shift in a nickel mine at Thompson, Manitoba. Everybody that I knew was up early the morning of the landing, huddled around their television sets, fully aware of the momentous event that would occur that day. And then there was 11 September 2001. Who doesn't remember where they were that morning? I was standing at the kitchen counter preparing breakfast when the phone rang.

My son was driving to school and phoned to tell me to turn on CNN as fast as I could. One of the Twin Towers was already smouldering away. Then a newscaster started yelling, pointing up into the sky, "And here's another one, look, look!" The passenger plane seemed suspended, as if travelling in slow motion, held up by invisible strings. It didn't seem to strike the tower but to pass through it. Everything happened so fast that there was a lag in my comprehension about what was going on.

I recollect a sense of confusion because we had all seen planes striking buildings in the movies, but not in real life. How could this happen in real life? The crash into the Twin Towers, ironically, appeared as if real life was imitating the media representations of such events. How was this possible? I had a flashback in which I was listening again to *The Lone Ranger* on our living-room floor, and I marvelled at how far my life had travelled from those ostensibly innocent days of the 1950s. It is apparent that our lives in the modern world are marked out in sequential fashion by significant, unforgettable events as disseminated by the media; however, Marshall McLuhan would surely have objected to this lineal depiction of media's impact on our lives.

WHAT IS A MEDIUM?

In *Understanding Media*, Marshall McLuhan (1964) proposed that it is the medium that controls and shapes "the scale and form of human association and action" (p. 9). When we are watching a movie at the theatre, for example, this medium manipulates our conceptions of speed and time. Thus, a movie transforms our "world of sequence and connections into the world of creative configuration and structure" (p. 12).

McLuhan conceptualized "medium" in a very expansive sense. As an example, a lightbulb does not have any content in the conventional sense that television has programs or magazines have stories. Yet a lightbulb nonetheless has repercussions on society, because it allows for an opening up of space after daylight ceases or is minimized. In a contemporary instance, as I am writing this chapter, the television news media reports on three women in Cleveland kidnapped and held for over decade.

What? Excuse me for asking, but what sort of human communities are we living in, when we can sit down and watch the evening news, reporting events on the other side of the planet in the most intricate detail, yet are totally unaware of what is happening next door, where three women are raped repeatedly for over a decade, one even bearing her attacker's child in the house? A neighbourhood boy notices a woman running around naked in the backyard, but doesn't see this as particularly unusual or worthy of any concern.

On the same day, Jodi Arias was convicted of murder in the brutal, sex-related slaying of her boyfriend. While the incidents reported were horrific in nature and were no doubt both heinous crimes, nonetheless the various interviews of the persons in the crowds gathered in Cleveland or outside the Arizona courthouse revealed as much about the public's attitudes toward these crimes than it did about the characteristics or particular details of the crimes themselves. In other words, the "content" of the newscasts would appear to be less important than the "message" involved, which is to say that the portrayal of such horrific crimes can become a topic of dinnertime conversation in our homes, and not much more.

The so-called content of a newscast is what we all concentrate on, because we are interested in the "juicy" details of lives lived beyond our normal experience. However, what we miss altogether is the manner in which this content is delivered to us, and the manner in which our senses are manipulated during the whole process. Granted, the process of watching television is a subtle experience, yet it transforms our cognitive and social affairs in very significant ways.

When I was a child, before television, we always ate our meals at the dining room table, and conversed about our day's activities, homework, sports at school, and so on. After a television was installed in our living room, the dining room table was used only at Christmas or on other holidays. My parents purchased a number of the popular small fold-up TV trays, and we henceforth ate our evening meals while watching the suppertime newscasts on television. We no longer conversed about anything as before, and our social interaction was no doubt diminished in the process, because we stopped learning about what was happening in each other's lives. As a consequence, when my own children were growing up, the television was not allowed to be on during mealtimes.

It took coercive measures and many arguments to counter the prevailing structural changes in our behaviour brought on by changes in our media technology. I am aware of parents of my generation who will not even allow television in their homes, much to the chagrin of their children. There are, no doubt, aspects of television programming that these parents do not approve of, such as the culture of violence, but the more astute ones are also cognizant of the wider repercussions here, that is to say, the pervasive social and psychological effects on their children, the behavioural issues and patterns of social interaction that television brings into their homes.

In response to the question, What is a medium? Eisenlohr (2011a) suggests that one first "has to confront the great multiplicity and broad range of the items and phenomena that have been considered a medium in the scholarly literature" (p. 1). First of all, the field of media greatly exceeds the domain of communication technology. In fact, in the literature it appears that just about anything can be regarded as a medium—money, power, a wheel, art, belief, or love have all been identified as media. Also, remember McLuhan's insistence that a lightbulb is a medium, albeit without content. The range of objects and phenomena labelled as media complicates any approaches anthropologists might have to the subject.

For anthropologists, the question of media is ultimately linked to debates within the discipline regarding the concept of culture. For decades, the debate focused on the so-called politics of culture, but in more recent times the notion of cultural traditions as publicly circulating entities has taken hold, as in the perception of "public culture" (Appadurai & Breckenridge, 1988; Nugent, 2001). Furthermore, Eisenlohr (2011a; 2011b) also links our current interest in media to the wider process of globalization, such that "public culture" can also be seen as part of "globally networked imaginations" which, in turn, are integral to the resulting "circulation of images and discourse." In this sense, questions about media are therefore important aspects of cultural analysis.

MCLUHAN'S GLOBAL VILLAGE AND THE INTERNET

From an anthropological focus, especially one in which media practices are understood in socio-cultural contexts, the approaches of such communication theorists as Marshall McLuhan would appear to be in conflict with long-standing concepts of "culture" in the discipline. McLuhan (1964), for example, promoted the concept of an emerging global village, suggesting that an ever-increasing reliance on electronic technology had caused a contraction of the globe into a village.

Information moves around the globe in an almost instantaneous manner; thus, it could also be proposed that McLuhan was responsible for envisioning the Internet and the World Wide Web, which he foresaw as an "extension of consciousness" long before their actual emergence as reality. In *The Gutenberg Galaxy*, McLuhan (1962) suggested, "The next medium, whatever it is—it may be an extension of consciousness—will include ... a private line to speedily tailored data of a saleable kind" (p. 6).

McLuhan's concept of the global village may be at odds with anthropological perspectives. The idea that the world's population, under the influence of electronic technology, would somehow be conflated, imploded, or otherwise contracted into the sort of villages commonly studied in anthropological community studies does not seem like a reasonable proposition. The idea relies too much on a sort of technological determinism, as if all of the social, economic, and political characteristics of a society were determined by a central core. We have seen this sort of reasoning before with Marvin Harris's cultural materialism, and even earlier with Julian Steward's core/periphery distinction.

There are so many aspects of a society that are not affected to any large degree by technological process. Certainly, economic aspects of production, distribution, and exchange are influenced by technology. However, other social or cultural aspects, such as kinship principles, family characteristics, religion, and world view are much less influenced by technology, if at all. Thus, the idea of a global village in which social and cultural variability are eliminated, or at least greatly reduced, by technological advances is an idea that needs to be tested rather than simply assumed.

In fact, anthropologists have begun to take notice of McLuhan's global village concept. In Fish's (2011) article "The Place of the Internet in Anthropology," it is noted that technological advances in information sharing are having significant impacts on the world's societies. Perhaps the most significant impact is that "space is compressed in this post-modern world and despite differences, the earth's inhabitants are closer" (p. 17). Closer, maybe, in terms of geographical distance, but apparently not necessarily closer in terms of resolving cultural, social, and political differences. Many countries regard the Internet as an example of information imperialism and have become resistant to its spread, using such tactics as censorship.

Internet Enemies

In 2010, the organization Reporters Without Borders compiled a list of 13 countries that were regarded as "Internet enemies." These countries are noted for censorship and instituting national laws that not only impact the way people engage with the Internet but also suppress free speech online. While the United States was not on this list, in the wake of Edward Snowdon's leaking of classified information, various American companies such as MasterCard, Visa, Apple, Amazon, among others, were pressured into cutting their financial support for WikiLeaks. Federal employees were subsequently blocked from viewing the leaked cables online, all of which raises the question of which countries are actually curtailing free speech and promoting censorship. It is still difficult to gauge whether Edward Snowdon is our enemy or our friend.

In Fish's (2011) opinion, "It's a myth that the Internet is immaterial as it is a myth that the Internet produces a global village" (p. 17). It may be that a global village structure is emerging because of the sharing of Internet hardware, software, and protocols, but this does not necessarily mean that the Internet is being used as a sort of Greek agora or neighbourhood coffee shop. Recent research (cited in Fish, 2011, p. 17) suggests that Internet users are becoming entrenched in "filter bubbles," in that people are paying more attention to national issues than to global affairs. The Internet, therefore, is becoming a more "place-based" phenomenon, contrary to what McLuhan might have originally envisaged with his global village concept.

FIGURE 9.2 An Egyptian citizen uses a cellphone to record events during the 2011 Arab Spring
Source: Courtesy of Dr. Heba Farouk. Reprinted by permission

Egypt's Internet Youth

What could be inferred from the study of "Internet youth" in Egypt is that electronic technology adapts to local or regional social, religious, and political circumstances, rather than acting as a deterministic factor upon these circumstances themselves. These circumstances were also influenced by emerging wealth disparities in the country, as well as ideological religious conflicts between secularists and members of the Muslim Brotherhood. When the revolution against President Mubarak's regime began to foment, it was the technologically savvy 20-something middle-class youth who mobilized on 25 January 2011 and began to bring down the 60-year-old regime.

Members of the Egyptian generation who grew up in the age of the Internet, unlike their predecessors, are plugged into a myriad of communication and information sources. When they were online, they were able to participate in a world far different than the one they were living in. An important aspect of this participation was the freedom they experienced in expressing their views. They were also able to freely associate with others on the Internet, an experience that stood in stark contrast to the suppression so characteristic of life in their home country.

Blogs, Facebook, tweets, and web chats allowed the young people in Egypt to engage in discussions of the authoritarian politics, nepotism, and police brutality that were a part of their daily lives at home. They learned about new ideas, such as social justice, human rights, democracy, and equality from global activists. It was this new influx of ideas that formed the basis of the youthful "Internet revolution," centred in Tahrir Square, against Egypt's political suppression. "Now is the time," Shahine (2011) exclaims, "for anthropologists to start asking new research questions and to engage in the dialogue that their Arab interlocutors have so articulately begun" (p. 3).

THE POLITICS OF THE RUSSIAN TALK SHOW

With the beginning of perestroika in the mid-1980s, the talk show, or *tok-shou*, began to occupy a central place in Russian radio and television (Matza, 2009). The Russian talk show can be traced to Gorbachev's policy of glasnost, which was initiated in 1985. This entailed a "revaluation of values" and took place primarily through the mass media. New television and radio programs focused on such controversial topics as prostitution, violence, drug abuse, and corruption, all of which competed with the more conservative broadcasting. These programs offered audiences new faces and novel arenas in public discourse. In one popular show, *Vzgliad*, or Viewpoint, for example, a number of young journalists sat around a table and discussed sensitive political issues, their dialogue interspersed with rock music.

The difference between Russian and American talk shows is that the Russian shows had a much diminished focus on personal detail compared to the US programs. The US shows, such as *Donahue* or *Oprah*, mainly featured tabloid-style confessionals, whereas in the Soviet Union the talk-show format could be used to push dialogue on political issues. By the early 1990s, however, personal details became more prevalent on Russian television, along with a greater degree of commercialization and more explicit violence and sexual content.

The commercialization of television in the post-Soviet era became characterized by a new media environment. Talk shows in Russia began moving in a new direction, with tabloid-style formats increasing and politically oriented shows becoming less prevalent. A focus on confession and group therapy aimed at increasing public participation increased, whereas shows focusing on questions of governance became more diluted in content.

A main attraction of such shows is that audiences are given the opportunity to speak out about the struggles of their everyday lives. These struggles often centre on the economy and politics, but other issues, such as social interrelationships, are also important. In addition, a new style of post-Soviet talk show is based on a format in which callers are offered psychological advice. Matza's ethnography of talk show media texts was based on fieldwork conducted in St. Petersburg during 2005–06. It investigates the manner in which talk shows serve to reshape "the self" in post-socialist society.

In one show called *Lolita*, pop singer Lolita Miliavskaia helps guests "change their lives," by discarding "the masks that hidden feelings lurk behind" (Matza, 2009, p. 490). In addition, professional psychologists and psychotherapists are present to provide concrete advice which could enable callers to "find the path out of their most hopeless situations" (p. 490).

In another show, *Understand, Forgive,* a guest enters an office staffed by two psychotherapists. A consultation takes place that includes an expanded investigation of the guest's life, consisting also of televised visits to his or her home or work so that viewers can understand "those places where conflict happens" (Matza, 2009, p. 490). One of the most popular television shows of this variety is called *We Will Solve Everything with Doctor Kurpatov.* Doctor Kurpatov was the first to open the therapeutic session to viewers. He sits opposite his guest(s) and offers couple therapy as well as treating irrational phobias.

Matza's study of Russian media illustrates the changing political aspects of public discourse. Changes in Russian talk shows over the last 20 years demonstrate the manner in which there has been a redirection in political dissatisfaction. What has taken place in the Russian talk show is a new emphasis on self-transformation and personal fulfillment—what has been termed "liberation therapy" (Matza, 2009, p. 503).

Yet changes in media emphasis toward a more liberal-democratic vision are not without their political repercussions. The liberal-democratic image of a future Russian civil society is nonetheless at odds with President Vladimir Putin's policies, which are essentially hostile to outspoken journalists and grassroots politics. Thus, there is a clash between the "neoliberal" stance taken in the new Russian media and the realities of national politics, in which political liberalism is viewed with skepticism.

CASE STUDY: THE YANOMAMO AND ANTHROPOLOGY'S PUBLIC REPUTATION

Media coverage of a war-like South American tribe called the Yanomamo has sparked debate in anthropology about the manner in which certain cultures are depicted in the discipline. This debate has also brought into question anthropology's reputation as an objective science, given that certain traits, such as the portrayal of the Yanomamo's apparent propensity for violence, are accentuated to the virtual neglect of other cultural characteristics.

The Yanomamo, who live in southern Venezuela and adjacent portions of northern Brazil, illustrate some of the extremes of human behaviour, especially in their preoccupation with warfare and interpersonal violence. To most outward appearances, the Yanomamo live a conventional village life in the jungle habitat of South America. They clear the forest using the swidden, or slash-and-burn, horticultural technique, and grow crops of bananas and manioc in small garden plots. They also participate in an elaborate system of marriage involving brother-sister exchange such that kinship groups become interdependent pairs of woman-exchanging kin-groups. However, despite these apparent cultural regularities, the Yanomamo also engage in forms of violence, in a graded series of aggressive activities. This behaviour ranges from inter-village raiding parties, chest-pounding duels, and club fights in which contestants try to hit each other on the head with long poles—resulting in lacerated skulls and broken fingers.

The situation of women among the Yanomamo is particularly hazardous. If a man and his wife are caught in the forest by an enemy group on a raiding party, the wife is apt to be abducted and her husband killed. The captured woman is then raped by all the men in the raiding party, and possibly also by the other men in the village. Even within her own village, a woman may be subjected to physical violence.

In one instance, a wife was punished by her husband, who cut both her ears off with his machete. As anthropologist Napoleon Chagnon (1968) indicates, "I describe the Yanomamo as 'the fierce people' because that is the most accurate single phrase that describes them. That is how they conceive themselves to be, and is how they would like others to think of them" (p. 1). One of the challenges of social anthropology, therefore, is the task of placing societies like the Yanomamo in the wider context of human behaviour, in which there are also many societies of a more peaceful nature.

One of the various issues that the ethnography of the Yanomamo has raised pertains to the role of the anthropologist as an expert on Indigenous peoples, and even occasionally as an activist on their behalf. As Stephen Nugent (2001) explains, "The complexity of that mediating role has never been well articulated. It is a source of continuing debate within anthropology itself and proves baffling to most outsiders" (p. 10).

Patrick Tierney's (2000) *Darkness in El Dorado: How Scientists and Journalists Devastated the Amazon* is a trenchant, some would say caustic, criticism of anthropologists' relationships with the Aboriginal people upon whom ethnographers depend for their cultural information. The terms used to describe anthropologists' research in the Amazon depict the discipline to the non-anthropological public in the most derisive and contemptuous manner possible. For example, the charge is made that research in the Amazon reveals "the real anthropological heart of darkness," "preposterous accusations," "ideological posturing," and an "unparalleled violation of scientific ethics" (Nugent, 2001, p. 10).

Further criticism was also made about anthropology's assumed role as a scientific or humanistic discipline. Tierney (2000) charges that the theoretical pillar of anthropology, cultural relativism, is really not much more than a denunciation of science and is seen in the discipline as just another "cultural construct." Furthermore, anthropology's association with science is not much more than an attempt to provide credible validity to what is regarded by Tierney as little more than "travel writing, tourism, exploring, adventurism and other informal links between the West and the Rest" (Nugent, 2001, p. 10).

To get to the point of Tierney's criticism about anthropology, two aspects predominate: first, the debate about anthropology as a science, and second, the question of ethical conduct in anthropological research. Space precludes an extended discussion of these two very important issues; however, several general comments can be made. One of these is that criticisms of anthropology are hardly newsworthy, as this has been going on since the very beginnings of the discipline. In the particular case of Chagnon's research among the Yanomamo, the issues here that are the most significant pertain to the accuracy of his data and the validity of the particular methods used to gather ethnographic information. The charge that Tierney specifically makes concerning Chagnon's research is that the data was manipulated in such a way as to confirm his (Chagnon's) view that Yanomamo men engaged in a culture of violence in order to maximize their access to women, that is, reproductive partners, and thereby contribute to a greater chance for their genes to disproportionately continue into the future.

So, with regard to the charge that Chagnon shaped or otherwise misrepresented his data in order to "prove" his particular theory associating men in violent cultures and the success or greater distribution of their genes in future generations: well, this is a very complicated matter. There are few instances in which anthropologists have actually re-studied a society previously the subject of other anthropologist's research. Most notably there is the famous Robert Redfield–Oscar Lewis controversy concerning the characteristics (harmonious relationships versus endemic hostility) in the Mexican village of Tepoztlan (Hedican, 2012a, pp. 142–44). Beyond this instance there is not much comparative evidence. Anthropologists do not like to revisit their colleagues' research, as doing so is considered very bad form.

As far as the internecine squabbling among anthropologists is concerned, there are certainly critics of Chagnon's neo-Darwinian perspective on the Yanomamo. On the wider front, anthropologists are polarized around the relevance of biological interpretations of socio-cultural phenomena. Certainly, Chagnon should be allowed to make his theoretical points without being subjected to such vituperative attacks as those inflicted by Tierney in *Darkness in El Dorado*. If Teirney desired to provide a truly objective criticism of Chagnon's research, then he would need to follow the proper canons of science, that is to say, conduct his own research, and then possibly arrive at a different conclusion.

One conclusion that attempts to sum up this controversy is this: "Despite early media interest, debates about *Darkness in El Dorado* have been largely confined to anthropological communities, and it seems unlikely that the circumstances will change" (Nugent, 2001, p. 14). In fact, Napoleon Chagnon has published a rebuttal to his critics, entitled *Noble Savages: My Life Among Two Dangerous Tribes—the Yanomamo and the Anthropologists* (Chagnon, 2013). It is therefore apparent that Chagnon feels the necessity to defend himself against critics both within and outside the discipline of anthropology.

Chagnon is particularly concerned that anthropology has, in his view, turned its back on science and traded its scientific mission for political activism. We will no doubt hear more about such controversial debates—science versus politics, sociobiology versus culture, and so on—in the near feature as these are played out in various media outlets both printed and visual.

MEDIA AND CULTURE

Media, from the perspective of anthropology, poses an interesting intersection of ideas. A central concern in anthropology would quite naturally appear to be the interrelationships between media and culture (Postill, 2009; Armin, 2010; Sumiala, 2013; Zorn, 2013). More specifically, the question could be asked about the influence of culture on media: is this influence simply a matter of degree, or are more profound or fundamental aspects at work in this interaction?

Anthropologists have a tendency to view all social phenomena through the lens of learned behaviour, comprising such aspects as language, economic exchange, politics, kinship and family life, and world view. In the modern world, it would be reasonable to assume that there is a symbiotic interrelationship between media and culture, with each influencing the other. The question is, To what degree? As Eisenlohr (2011b, pp. 42–43) observes in a study of media and the question of ethnic and religious pluralism, "Anthropologists have analyzed uses of new media technologies as profoundly interconnected with diverse cultural frames of reference."

The anthropology of media has a long history, which can be traced to at least as far back as Hortense Powdermaker's (1950) study of the Hollywood film industry, although this field of study did not gain any sort of prominence until the 1980s. More recently, the emphasis has been on media consumption, with media audiences playing an active role as producers of media messages. Anthropologists have shown how local audiences can drastically transform media texts and messages by relating them to local socio-cultural values. Also of interest are the practices of governance, and media's role in shaping the conflicts and politics of state institutions (Hull, 2008). A further focus is on the manner in which state-controlled television in post-colonial states influences nation-building and social reform, as illustrated by a media study on Egypt (Abu-Lughod, 2005).

Anthropologists have also shown a growing interest in the use of contemporary media in religious practices. They have studied how media technology—such as audio-cassette sermons, audio-visual media, and televangelism—creates new publics and forms of religious authority. Part of this focus has been on the reframing of established media that authenticate religious experience and reinforce established authority. Anthropologists interested in the impact of media have often taken different approaches than most media theorists, not necessarily studying the intrinsic qualities of media technologies but analyzing how media become part of specific cultural and social settings (Meyer, 2006; van de Port, 2006).

One can therefore surmise from this brief review that anthropologists regard the cultural context of media as a central factor of analysis. Eisenlohr (2011b), for example, indicates that as far as the role of media in the context of ethnic and religious pluralism is concerned, the "uses of media technologies become imbedded in different cultural and historical contexts [such that] they become subject to different ideas and expectations with respect to their functioning" (p. 52). What is meant here, then, is that media technologies may be more or less similar in a global context, but that the expectations and ideas with regard to what media is capable of doing varies greatly because of differences in social and cultural settings.

This view is not shared by all media scholars. The anthropological focus on the sociocultural contexts of media is at odds with one that stresses globalization processes in the understanding of media. For one, Mazzarella (2004) argues that differences in the study of ethnographic and indigenous media "can no longer be understood as a function of culture" (p. 360). The reason for this suggestion is that anthropologists, as the argument goes, are mistaken if they think that difference can be seen as "a measure of the distance between two or more bounded cultural worlds." Rather, difference is more cogently understood as a "space of indeterminacy ... inherent to the social process *per se*" (p. 360).

YouTube and "Bottom-Up" Ethnography

If culture is understood in its widest sense as sets of learned and shared attitudes, beliefs, and values, then would it not also be useful to include in a cultural context such "participatory" media as YouTube in this discussion of media anthropology? It has been suggested that YouTube videos have a "capacity to foster and sustain a sense of 'community' online," and that this medium represents "an emerging platform for dialogue, expressions of self and identity, constructions of meaning, and fostering of relationships" (Scobie, 2011, p. 661). The suggestion here is that YouTube, from an ethnographic perspective, offers access to people's everyday lives through a video format. People post home movies and video blogs on YouTube, illustrating what Burgess and Green (2009) have referred to as "bottom-up creativity."

In this sense—of people incorporating YouTube into their daily lives—individuals also then begin to inhabit this mediascape. In turn, people watch the videos posted by others, which suggests that YouTube has the capacity to foster community-building and play a role in identity formation. Scobie (2011) suggests that YouTube is "an important social space that warrants further research [because] anthropologists go where the action takes them." Certainly one wonders if conventional anthropology is capable in its present form, with its current theoretical orientations and methodologies, of engaging with virtual ethnography by studying "digital natives." And—perhaps most importantly—is YouTube a cultural phenomenon?

Without stretching the imagination too much, one can concede that YouTube represents a social space with its own characteristic forms of interaction. If one wishes to understand YouTube as a research site in which cultural forms take place in the context of learned behaviour, then this should be explored as well. Whatever one's opinions might be regarding the appropriateness of a virtual reality for proper ethnographic investigation, it is quite possible that anthropologists have the capabilities to study our increasingly networked society. However, on a cautionary note: anthropologists usually view culture as a multi-stranded phenomenon, which may not mesh well with the more ephemeral interconnections and relationships established in a social media context. Certainly more debate about these sorts of contemporary issues would be welcome in the discipline in the context of public anthropology.

Social Media and Academic Life

Media anthropology may be a relatively new phenomenon, not much more than three decades old, but it does allow for the engagement of debate that extends well beyond the discipline into the public realm. Take, for example, Marshall McLuhan's notion of the global village. If the idea is that the emergence of the global village is a process that diminishes cultural boundaries, then there is likely to be a lively debate about this proposal. Certainly there is evidence, as in the case of the "Internet youth" of Egypt, that media technologies are adapted to social and cultural uses that are more place oriented than global.

If we pursue this line of thinking further—that media technology impacts a society in certain fundamental ways that obscure cultural boundaries—then we might be well advised to exercise caution. Past studies of technology in anthropology have amply demonstrated that technology in itself does not tend to transform the fundamental basis of a society. People in different societies pick and choose from the outside world what is useful to them in their everyday lives. What is important is the content conveyed by any particular medium, and this idea accords well with McLuhan's "the medium is the message" idea.

Yet we should not hasten to entirely dismiss McLuhan's global village concept. Certainly, at a particular level cultural differences seem to be diminishing at an alarming rate worldwide. It seems that teenagers holding a cellphone to one ear while attempting to text and speak at the same time and wearing the same American Eagle clothing are a global phenomenon. We wonder, though, if these images simply represent superficial details, while under the surface religious, ethnic, and other worldviews are just as entrenched as they ever were.

As far as the academic community is concerned, the Internet and social media have certainly transformed the research process in ways that were unimaginable to an earlier generation of scholars. As Daniels and Feagin (2011) summarize, "New social media and other web technologies are transforming the way we, as academics, do our job. These technologies offer communication that is interactive, instantaneous, global, low-cost, and fully searchable, as well as platforms for connecting with other scholars everywhere" (p. 2). It is difficult to remember a time when academics did not do much of their research online.

Few scholars today would remember a time before the Internet when one searched through drawers of library card catalogues and bound volumes of journal articles, or read hard copies of printed books. The microfilm machines are rapidly disappearing as well, and our days of spending endless hours standing over a photocopier is also a thing of the past. Today we search online databases, and electronic access to journals and eBooks has increased to the point where this type of research is now the norm.

In turn, as we work more online, academics find themselves occupied away from their campus or college libraries. More work is conducted remotely, untethering us from our conventional offices and particular locations (Cohen, 2004). The repertoire of many scholars includes GoogleScholar and GoogleBooks, as scholarly resources become more openly available on the web. Scholars can now maintain closer collegial ties than ever before, as social media allows for new arrangements of academics. Virtual conferences are now held, which reduces the cost of much professional travel. Conversations are now held via Twitter, Facebook, Skype, and blogs that serve to maintain scholarly ties. This virtual revolution suggest that anthropologists, as with many scholars today, would do well to reflect on the manner in which rapidly changing media technologies are transforming the very epistemological basis of the way research and other forms of scholarly investigation are conducted.

Chapter 10

TRENDS AND PROSPECTS

This volume is not intended to provide exhaustive coverage of all the topics that could be subsumed under the rubric of "public anthropology." Yet it does afford a fairly comprehensive discussion of most of the major areas that one would expect to find included in a work of this nature. The purpose of this chapter is to offer summary remarks on what, admittedly, is a very wide-ranging discussion. It will also look ahead, as far as this is possible, to the future of anthropology's concern with public issues and offer some practical suggestions.

There is little doubt that anthropologists today stand on a new threshold, one that in so many ways is vastly different than what was envisioned for the discipline in past decades. The problem is that when we try to reach solutions to today's problems, the society on which these suggestions are based will already have become transformed in such a way that new and unanticipated problems will present themselves. In other words, there is a time lag involved, with social thinkers working on contemporary problems while simultaneously attempting to anticipate new issues emerging in their midst. In addition, it is evident that in order to survive in a climate of academic accountability, anthropologists need to demonstrate the value of their work to a larger audience, both within and outside the scholarly community. So, in conclusion, we must ask, What challenges does embracing public anthropology pose for the discipline? And what specific problems need to be dealt with?

PUBLIC ANTHROPOLOGY: PROS AND CONS

Historically speaking, the issue is no longer whether or not anthropology should embrace or reject involvement with social issues. The time for this debate was decades ago. As this book amply illustrates, anthropologists today are heavily involved in social issues of the modern world. Looking back in time, we see that anthropologists have often confronted the social issues of their day. Franz Boas was one of the first social scientists to confront the racist attitudes in his time. He also argued against cultural determinist ideas, suggesting that a society's norms and ideas were a relative phenomenon.

Malinowski toured America in the 1940s, attempting to warn Americans about the Nazi threat in Europe. Margaret Mead pored over Hitler's speeches in an effort to understand his personality and worldview. Many other such examples of public involvement by anthropologists in the past could be cited. In fact, one could likely argue successfully that anthropologists, for at least the last century, have concerned themselves with the public issues of their contemporary settings. In other words, public anthropology, under whatever rubric it might be known, is hardly a recent or novel phenomenon.

The spectrum of issues that anthropologists study today is truly diverse, ranging from health, food security, and forensic science to resistance movements, global terror, and media anthropology. What are the trends that bind these initiatives together, if any? The main advantage that anthropologists have is the conceptual bedrock that has been a fairly consistent guideline throughout most of the modern history of the discipline. Cultural relativism is not only a theoretical orientation but also a moral guidepost that directs research in anthropology. Of course, there are debates about the relevance of this concept, such as the nagging issue of universal human rights; however, there is little dispute about the fact that anthropologists continue to cling to this idea because it provides an ethical basis for their research.

A research methodology based on small-scale community settings, using the fieldwork techniques of participant observation and in-depth interviews, has also provided continuity to the practice of public anthropology. Without a doubt, the study of various issues requires a diversified methodology, yet anthropologists continue to make contributions to the social sciences because they have employed a fairly consistent approach, not replicated to any great extent by other disciplines, to gathering social and cultural information.

The main advantage, therefore, of an engagement with public issues today is that it tends to allow anthropologists to build upon the core strengths of their discipline. However, if we take the issue of counterinsurgency as an example, anthropologists who are best positioned to make a contribution to this field of study freely admit that access to terror groups is probably not advisable, even if it were possible. Instead, anthropologists focus on the American military and provide a critique of the long-standing issue of imperialism and its counterproductive effects.

In sum, the greatest tool that anthropologists possess is a theoretical orientation that is based on a comparative perspective. This perspective is comprehensive enough that various facets of issues, especially ones that transcend cultural boundaries, can be studied beyond the specific domains of particular societies, nations, or other bounded units. Anthropologists are in a position to investigate issues within particular communities, using such ethnographic techniques as participant observation and informant interviews. They are also equipped to adopt a larger view, based on the comparative methodology developed in the field of ethnology. These two vantage points, developed in ethnography and ethnology, give anthropology a distinct advantage, unique in the social sciences, in studying the world's problems.

LOOKING BACK, LOOKING FORWARD

The entire history of social or cultural anthropology, at least since the days of Boas, Mead, and Malinowski, has been based on the principle of ethical neutrality and objective detachment. The fundamental reason for this stance has been that interfering in the social and cultural life of the people who are the objects of study will probably change the results of such research.

The other important reason is that any interference or manipulation is apt to be seen as a reflection of anthropology's connection to a colonial past. Therefore, attempting to exert as little influence as possible on what happens during fieldwork has been an important epistemological principle of the discipline, even if interference may have been well meant and possibly justified from a personal perspective. On the other hand, more participatory and collaborative approaches are emerging in public anthropology, such that the ethnographic enterprise is more highly informed by the participants of research in terms of relationships of reciprocal interaction.

In the United States, James Mooney (1896) studied the Ghost Dance Religion, which was widespread among Western Aboriginal tribes. This was an early form of advocacy, as he provided a sympathetic portrayal of the dislocation caused by the Indian Wars and the harmful social and economic effects that confinement to reservations produced. Through his attacks on the ideas of racial determinism commonly held by the American population, Franz Boas played an important role in demonstrating the important ways that anthropology could contribute to public policy. Margaret Mead (1932) provided an ethnographic account of the deteriorating conditions of the Plains Indians that resulted from the acculturation and assimilative policies of the American government. Mead's study was a forerunner of the many acculturation studies that were so prominent in anthropology during the 1960s.

Bronislaw Malinowski was one of the early forerunners of a more proactive British anthropology. His contributions to public service extended back as far as 1918, when he presented evidence to an Australian government inquiry seeking information on the labour conditions of Indigenous populations of the western Pacific (Ervin, 2005, pp. 15–16). Malinowski (1970/1929) early in the history of the discipline encouraged a form of "practical anthropology." He suggested that anthropologists document health care conditions, aspects of land tenure, juridical matters, and changing demographic circumstances, among other topics, as part of their ethnographic research.

The purpose of the preceding discussion is not to provide any sort of definitive history of public anthropology, but to suggest that the idea of anthropologists speaking out about the social, economic, and political issues of their time is hardly a new phenomenon but can be traced back practically to the very origins of anthropology. If one takes the trouble to delve into the literature, one will find copious examples in the history of the discipline of anthropologists taking an active interest, one that extended beyond the normal course of research, in the conditions of their ethnographic subjects. All of these examples, in the context of public anthropology, serve to link anthropology's past with its present and future concerns.

PUBLIC ANTHROPOLOGISTS AS ADVOCATES

It is also worth noting that the American Anthropological Association's (2012) Statement on Ethics makes explicit mention of advocacy, which is germane to public anthropology. For example, it indicates that "anthropologists may choose to link their research to the promotion of well-being, social critique or advocacy." However, there is a caution that "anthropological work must ... reflect deliberate and thoughtful consideration of potential unintended consequences and long-term impacts on individuals, communities [and] identities." So, as far as public anthropology is concerned, these "unintended consequences" deserve considerable thought. It should also be noted in this regard that the AAA ethics code also established that one of the goals of anthropology concerns "the dissemination of anthropological knowledge and its use to solve human problems," thus reinforcing the applied or public stance of the discipline.

One can conclude that adopting an advocacy position has a very long history in anthropology and that for many decades anthropologists have spoken out against social injustice, imperialism, colonialism, and other related topics. Anthropologists would, therefore, be well advised to continue in their roles as advocates, cultural brokers, mediators, and consultants, and in other similar, analogous roles (exercising due caution, of course, in facing the dilemmas and ethical hazards that such situations have historically involved).

We might also take the advice of British social anthropologist Raymond Firth (1981), who suggested that the problem of engagement and detachment in anthropology is "to adopt the concept that there is no single best solution of a practical problem, but only some compromise between conflicting interests" (p. 199). Although this advice was written decades ago, it would nonetheless appear sound today as a practical guide to contemporary anthropology. Firth suggests that we learn as we go and that there are no perfect solutions to the various problems in cross-cultural settings in which anthropologists are actively engaged. Yet, as the AAA ethics code reminds us, anthropologists in today's world are apt to "face myriad ethical quandaries."

"STUDYING UP"

One of these "quandaries" is that if anthropologists follow Firth's reasonable advice, then the suggestion that they should be prepared to choose sides when confronted with disputes is probably ill advised. Laura Nader's recommendation that anthropologists "study up" was certainly a reasonable one. The proposal has merit because it would allow anthropologists to see two sides of a problem—one from below, with the viewpoints of local communities; and the other from above, with the perspectives of elites, government administrations, and corporate powers.

It has been at least three decades since Nader made her proposal. Unfortunately, little can be said about anthropological success in studying up. The problem has mainly been an inability, or possibly an unwillingness, to attempt studies of societies' more powerful elements. Members of societies' elites have the means to protect themselves from intrusive investigations and the ability to ward off inquiries that they might regard as not being in their best interests. A major challenge, then, for public anthropology in the future is to find the means to enter worlds previously closed to ethnographic research.

Faced with this dilemma, it is probably also not advisable to regard the elites of society as being somehow antagonistic to anthropological scrutiny. Such a position will only antagonize a powerful sector of society who might already regard anthropologists with suspicion, considering them much too allied to left-wing political interests. This raises the issue of how far public anthropologists are willing to allow their personal political interests to intrude on their academic or scholarly investigations. Anthropologists are likely to encounter greater success if they are able to separate their personal feelings and affections from their academic pursuits.

ETHICAL NEUTRALITY AND PUBLIC ANTHROPOLOGY

There are certainly anthropologists who would suggest that a position of ethical neutrality is untenable in today's world. They would suggest that anthropologists who are "fence sitters" will likely lose whatever leverage they presently enjoy with local communities whose members are constantly facing threats of environmental degradation and pollution, threats from colonial administrations, and so on.

There are myriad pitfalls here, both personal and scholarly. Is a neutral position on social and ethical issues even tenable, some might ask? Is it possible for researchers to conduct impartial interviews when they must indicate some degree of agreement with, or at least sympathy for, a particular social, economic, or political point of view? There is no doubt that the cultural relativist stance can cause a field-worker considerable strain because of informants' various opinions and points of view.

This issue of ethical neutrality has been around for many decades, yet anthropologists seem ill equipped to come to a definitive position on what their role should be. Do they defend particular causes, ones that seem perfectly justified, such as human rights, environmental protection, or poverty reduction in developing countries? On the other hand, is it even possible to express some point of view that will not offend one party or another?

Recent studies continue to grapple with these issues. Galit Sarfaty (2012), for example, in *Values in Translation*, discusses human rights issues in terms of the culture of the World Bank, suggesting (pp. 23–50) that there is an "institutional resistance" to human rights in many large, transnational organizations. However, "because of a concern for their public image and the reputational and legal risks of committing human rights abuses, some corporations are beginning to take steps toward becoming more socially responsible by adopting such tools as human rights impact statements" (pp. 23–24).

Similarly, in David Mosse's (2005) *Cultivating Development*, he refers to the "varied spectrum of positions from which anthropologists work, and their individual capacity to combine engagement with policy and critical work … this capacity depends both upon developing close connections to agencies and the policy process, *and* upon independent critical reflection. If anthropologists become too close to the policy process this potential disappears" (pp. 241–42; emphasis in original).

PUBLIC COMMITMENT AND SOCIAL RESPONSIBILITY

Margaret Mead is to be commended for anticipating several of the significant problems of modern anthropology. In her lifetime, she spoke out on social injustice, the suppression of youth, nuclear disarmament, generational conflict, and sexual and minorities rights. She had an international reputation, and people listened to what she had to say. Unfortunately few, if any, anthropologists today have achieved such prominent status that their opinions are respected even though particular interest groups may not agree with them. In a study of the generation gap titled *Culture and Commitment*, Mead (1970) wrote, "It is my conviction that in addition to the world conditions that have given rise to this search for new commitment and to this possibility of no commitment at all, we also have new resources for facing our situation, new grounds for commitment" (p. xii).

Mead recognized a dilemma that is equally present in today's world: it has become increasingly difficult for people to find themselves within the conflicting versions of our culture. These conflicts—both personal and academic—mean that it is precarious for people to make choices about which ideals, if any, they should commit themselves to. For anthropologists, this situation of conflicting values could be seen as an important opportunity to inform people about the competing ideological forces in contemporary society. It is also entirely possible, one could argue, to become "engaged" without becoming wholly committed to particular causes.

Many anthropologists today no doubt feel the stress of their occupations emanating from many sources. Accountability within the college and university setting has placed an emphasis on scholarly productivity. In fieldwork settings, an anthropologist can feel stress from both the communities in which he or she is conducting research and from those outside these communities. This "stress of involvement" can emerge from a field-worker's psychological makeup or temperament, moral or ethical position, personal political persuasion, or from pressures placed on them by local-level factions who may wish to manipulate the anthropologist for their own purposes and interests.

Under these sorts of pressures and persuasions, there are anthropologists who have become advisers for particular interest groups, who have taken up advocating minority group causes, or who see new research opportunities in the roles of consultants and advisers in emerging conflict mediation. It is obvious, therefore, that as far as public anthropology is concerned, the issue today is not so much whether or not to become involved but what effects various sorts of involvement will have on the possible shape of the discipline in the future. An additional problem that anthropologists face when they find themselves embroiled in controversy or in the midst of conflict is that they lack appropriate role models to provide guidelines on how to handle themselves in such situations (although the discipline does have such paragons of commitment as Boas, Malinowski, and Mead to show the way).

In summary, it can be amply demonstrated that throughout much of the history of anthropology, practitioners of this discipline have taken an active interest in the public social issues of their time. Especially over the last several decades, anthropologists, in their role as public intellectuals, have lent their academic expertise to illuminating a range of issues extending across the wide spectrum of global terror, food security, media relations, forensic studies, and race and science. These activities have resulted in a considerable modification in the more traditional role of the ethnographic fieldworker, such that anthropology's long-standing position on objectivity and relativism has at times become a matter of intense debate. Such airing of opinions not only is a healthy state of affairs in any academic community but also serves to more clearly define the direction in which the discipline is heading.

CONCLUSION

There will never be any definitive, cut-and-dried solutions to the sorts of problems and issues that anthropologists face today when they engage in public controversies. Nonetheless, they need to keep trying to make a contribution to the understanding of public issues, lest they become sidelined into an anachronistic discipline without any social relevance to contemporary society. The anti-advocacy position has been expressed in some circles, either with the suggestion that there are no sound academic or intellectual grounds for taking sides or based on the argument that no particular cause is legitimate in a social justice sense. Of course, there is merit to this point of view, but does the discipline as a whole need to be held hostage to a perpetual dialogue and debate about where it should be going?

Many anthropologists have no doubt asked themselves at some point in their careers if what they are doing is just a job that pays the bills, like any other economic activity, or whether, alternatively, there are more important principles involved. The fact of the matter is that the reputation and very future of the discipline are at stake, and academics should devote some soul-searching to the issue. Hiding in an ivory tower and watching the world go by will only relegate anthropology further and further to the sidelines of anachronistic irrelevance. In today's world, a sense of social responsibility is certainly needed as an integral ingredient in such a way that public anthropology moves to the forefront of the discipline. It will be up to future generations to decide on the shape of the discipline as it builds on the earlier efforts of Mead, Malinowski, and Boas. Hopefully, their legacy of scholarly commitment to making the world a better place to live in will prevail in the years ahead.

GLOSSARY

Aboriginal: Describes the indigenous or original inhabitants of a particular territory.

acculturation: The process of interaction between two societies in which the culture of the society in the subordinate position is drastically modified to conform to the culture of the dominant society.

action anthropology: A term suggested by Sol Tax and colleagues from the University of Chicago for the "Fox Project" in which the Fox tribe, or Mesquakie, are seen as co-investigators and play a prominent role in defining the direction of the course of the research.

activism anthropology: The concept that anthropologists should participate in the public political process; refers to an involvement in political causes and struggles.

advocate role: The function of promoting the social, economic, or political interests of a client group and providing an analysis of possible courses of action.

anthropology: A term derived from two Greek words, *anthropos* for "human" and *logos* for "the study of"; the scientific study of humankind from social and biological perspectives.

applied anthropology: The study of the practical applications of anthropological knowledge, especially in terms of solving social problems.

assimilation: An ethnic group's loss of identity because of its absorption into the society of a dominant group.

biological determinism: A view that race and biology are seen to determine culture and behaviour.

collaborative anthropology: One meaning refers to a combined research effort involving anthropologists and community members in a non-hierarchical relationship; a second meaning refers to a number of anthropologists combining their research efforts in one particular community setting.

colonialism: A policy whereby a nation seeks to establish a long-term socio-political and economic domination over another people, usually by the installation of an administrative structure that uses members of the dominant society to facilitate control.

consensus: A process of decision making based on negotiation and discussion, as opposed to decisions dictated by a single individual or group; usually found in societies with non-hierarchical political structures.

consulting role: The function of providing information or advice to a client on a particular course of action.

deductive method: A form of logical reasoning in which general principles are derived from particular instances; contrasts with inductive method.

dialogical approach: The use of texts to represent the encounter between native informants and ethnographers; a form of dialogue in which the voice of the Other has a priority.

ecology: A field of study pertaining to the interrelationships between living populations and their habitats.

empiricism: A perspective that holds that meaningful knowledge should be based on experience and concrete reality rather than on mental or intellectual speculation.

enculturation: The process by which the individual learns and assimilates the patterns of a culture; the patterns by which cultural traditions are transmitted from one generation to the next.

engaging anthropology: An involvement in social, political, and cultural issues in the public arena.

environmental determinism: A perspective holding that social and cultural phenomena are determined principally by mechanisms of the natural habitat in which a population is found.

epistemology: The study of the nature of human knowledge; how it is that we know what we know.

ethnocentrism: The practice of making value judgments concerning other people or their cultures on the basis of a belief in the superiority of one's way of life or cultural standards.

ethnography: A division of anthropology devoted to the descriptive recording of cultures based on research techniques such as participant observation, carried out through fieldwork.

fieldwork: In social anthropology, the main technique used to gather information on human behaviour; usually involves living for an extended period of time in a human population and conducting research by participating and observing people in different cultures.

holistic: An approach used by anthropologists that is comprehensive in scope such that all aspects of human life, biological and cultural, are considered important in understanding behaviour.

Human Relation Area Files (HRAF): An anthropological database founded in 1949 at Yale University in New Haven, Connecticut; primarily employed to test hypotheses in a cross-cultural perspective.

inductive method: A mode of logical analysis by which propositions are inferred on the basis of specific observations; contrasts with deductive method.

informant: An individual who provides information to an anthropologist during the conduct of fieldwork; especially those people with expert or specialized knowledge in their culture.

infrastructure: An aspect of the theoretical orientation of cultural materialism, such as mode of production, which exerts a causal influence on cultural and economic systems.

life histories: Cultural profiles that are created based on details in the lives of particular individuals derived from their experiences and points of view; a research approach characteristic of Boasian ethnography.

means of production: The tools and technology used during the process of production.

mediator role: The function concerned with bringing two or more conflicting persons or groups together in order to provide acceptable solutions to common problems.

militant anthropology: The idea that anthropologists should adopt a position of solidarity with informants and other community members who are seen to be the objects of oppression by outside powers; a position associated with Nancy Scheper-Hughes, who suggests that anthropologists should support the poor and powerless.

neo-colonialism: A modern version of colonial practices in which non-industrial societies are exploited for their labour or natural resources by indirect means, often in the context of multinational corporations.

Other: In postmodern terminology, "the Other" is a term used to refer to non-Western people and is based on the assumption that each culture produces unique human characteristics; contrasts with the idea of "pan-human culture"; see **postmodernism**.

participant observation: A research technique developed in social anthropology that involves living with the people of a particular culture or community over an extended period of time, such that researchers attempt to immerse themselves in the day-to-day activities of the group under study.

participatory action research (PAR): Based on the position that conventional fieldwork in anthropology is outmoded; in this approach, community members conduct most of the research and own the information that is gathered.

political economy: A theoretical orientation that stresses the role of political factors, such as power and authority, in the economic organization of production, consumption, and distribution of goods.

polyvocal: A postmodern term meaning "multiple voices," as opposed to the "single" voice of the ethnographer.

postmodernism: In anthropology, a theoretical position that rejects the idea of universal laws and objective knowledge; stresses ethnography as a literary project with multiple "truths."

practical anthropology: A term used by Malinowski that focuses on the useful aspects of ethnographic research. It is based on the idea that ethnographic information has "practical" value in understanding the internal conflict that results from the external intrusions of colonial administrations on local affairs.

public anthropology: The application of anthropological knowledge, techniques, and epistemologies beyond university and college settings to the public domain.

qualitative research: Methods of gathering information in the social sciences using research strategies of interviewing, description, and subjective understanding; see **participant observation**.

quantitative research: Strategies of information gathering that stress the collection of quantitative data; the use of statistical analysis and hypothesis testing.

relativism: In anthropology, a perspective stressing the uniqueness and individual characteristics of different cultures, particularly associated with the Boasian orientation of historical particularism.

Social Darwinism: As espoused by Herbert Spencer (1820–1903), a doctrine based on the application of the theory of "the survival of the fittest," which is used to justify and explain the inequalities of wealth, power, and oppression in societies.

social structure: The ways in which groups and individuals are organized and relate to one another; linkages between social roles in a society.

society: An aggregation of human beings (a population) living as a distinct entity and possessing a distinct culture.

sociobiology: An approach to the study of human behaviour that stresses the Darwinian underpinnings of biological or genetic factors.

state: The association within a society that undertakes to direct and organize policy on behalf of and in the name of the entire society; a centralized hierarchical political, economic, and social organization characteristic of large, sedentary populations.

tribe: A social group speaking a distinctive language or dialect and possessing a unique culture that sets it off from other tribes. It is not necessarily organized politically, nor does it have a centralized decision-making body. A tribe is usually based on an organization of kinship units consisting of unilineal descent groups; associated with horticulture or pastoralism as a subsistence strategy.

REFERENCES

Abu-Lughod, L. (1990). The romance of resistance: Tracing transformations of power through Bedouin women. *American Ethnologist*, 17(1), 41–55. doi: http://dx.doi.org/10.1525/ae.1990.17.1.02a00030.

Abu-Lughod, L. (1991). Writing against culture. In R.G. Fox (Ed.), *Recapturing anthropology* (pp. 137–162). Santa Fe, NM: School of American Research Press.

Abu-Lughod, L. (2005). *Dramas of nationhood: The politics of television in Egypt.* Chicago, IL: University of Chicago Press.

Aiello, L.C. (2010). Engaged anthropology: Diversity and dilemmas. *Current Anthropology*, 51(S2), S201–S202. doi: http://dx.doi.org/10.1086/656340.

Aiello, L.C. (2012). The biological anthropology of living human populations: World histories, national styles, and international networks. *Current Anthropology*, 53(S5), S1–S2. doi: http://dx.doi.org/10.1086/663328.

Albro, R. (2007). Anthropology's terms of engagement with security. *Anthropology News*, 48(1), 20–21. doi: http://dx.doi.org/10.1525/an.2007.48.1.20.

Albro, R. (2010). Anthropology and the military: AFRICOM, "culture" and future of human terrain analysis. *Anthropology Today*, 26(1), 22–24. doi: http://dx.doi.org/10.1111/j.1467-8322.2010.00712.x.

Alcantara, C. (2007). Explaining aboriginal treaty negotiation outcomes in Canada: The cases of the Inuit and the Innu in Labrador. *Canadian Journal of Political Science*, 40(1), 185–207. doi: http://dx.doi.org/10.1017/S0008423907070060.

Alfred, T., & Corntassel, J. (2011). Being Indigenous: Resurgences against contemporary colonialism. In M.J. Cannon & L. Sunseri (Eds.), *Racism, colonialism and indigeneity in Canada* (pp. 139–145). Oxford: Oxford University Press.

Allahar, A. (1998). Race and racism: Strategies of resistance. In V. Satzewich (Ed.), *Racism and social inequality in Canada: Concepts, controversies and strategies of resistance* (pp. 335–354). Toronto, ON: Thompson Educational Publishing.

American Anthropological Association. (1998). Statement on "Race." Retrieved from http://www.aaanet.org/stmts/racepp.htm.

American Anthropological Association. (1999). Declaration on anthropology and human rights. Retrieved from http://www.aaanet.org/about/Policies/statements/Declaration-on-Anthropology-and - Human-Rights.cfm.

American Anthropological Association. (2012). Statement on ethics: Principles of professional responsibility. Retrieved from http://ethics.aaanet.org/category/statement.

American Anthropological Association (2014). Race: Are we so different? Retrieved from http://www.aaanet.org/resources/RACE-Are-We-So-Different.

American Board of Forensic Anthropology. Retrieved from http://www.theabfa.org.

Anthony, D.W. (2007). *The horse, the wheel, and language: How bronze-age riders from the Eurasian steppes shaped the modern world.* Princeton, NJ: Princeton University Press.

Antrosio, J. (2012). *Real history versus* Guns, Germs and Steel *by Jared Diamond.* Retrieved from http://www.livinganthropologically.com/anthropology/guns-germs-and-steel

Appadurai, A. (1991). Global ethnoscapes: Notes and queries for a transnational anthropology. In R.G. Fox (Ed.), *Recapturing anthropology* (pp. 191–210). Santa Fe, NM: School of American Research Press.

Appadurai, A., & Breckenridge, C. (1988). Why public culture? *Public Culture, 1*(1), 5–9. doi: http://dx.doi.org/10.1215/08992363-1-1-5.

Armin, J. (2010). Anthropology and the media. *Current Anthropology, 51*(2), 161. doi: http://dx.doi.org/10.1086/650993.

Armitage, P., & Kennedy, J.C. (1989). Redbaiting and racism on our frontier: Military expansion in Labrador and Quebec. *Canadian Review of Sociology and Anthropology, 26*(5), 798–817.

Asad, T. (Ed.) (1973). *Anthropology and the colonial encounter.* Atlantic Highlands, NJ: Humanity Press.

Asch, M. (2014). *On being here to stay: Treaties and Aboriginal rights in Canada.* Toronto, ON: University of Toronto Press.

Ashini, D. (1990). David confronts Goliath: The Innu of Ungava versus the NATO alliance. In B. Richardson (Ed.), *Drumbeat: Anger and renewal in Indian country* (pp. 45–70). Toronto, ON: Summerhill.

Atran, S. (2010). *Talking to the enemy: Violent extremism, sacred values and what it means to be human.* New York, NY: Penguin Books.

Bair, B. (2011). Review of race and science. *Journal of Southern History, 77*(3): 744–746.

Baker, D. (1978). Race and power: Comparative approaches to the analysis of race relations. *Ethnic and Racial Studies, 1*(3), 316–335. doi: http://dx.doi.org/10.1080/01419870.1978.9993236.

Bank, A., & Bank, L.J. (Eds.). (2013). *Inside African anthropology: Monica Wilson and her interpreters.* Cambridge, UK: Cambridge University Press. doi: http://dx.doi.org/10.1017/CBO9781139333634.

Banton, M. (1977). *The idea of race.* London, UK: Tavistock Publications.

Barrett, S.R. (1984). *The rebirth of anthropological theory.* Toronto, ON: University of Toronto Press.

Barrett, S.R. (1987). *Is God a racist? The right wing in Canada.* Toronto, ON: University of Toronto Press.

Barrett, S.R. (1996). *Anthropology: A student's guide to theory and method.* Toronto, ON: University of Toronto Press.

Barrett, S.R. (2002). *Culture meets power.* Westport, CT: Praeger Publishers.

Basch, L.G., Saunders, L.W., Sharf, J.W., & Peacock, J. (1999). *Transforming academia: Challenges and opportunities for an engaged anthropology*. Arlington, VA: American Anthropological Association.

Bashir, B., & Kymlicka, W. (2008). Introduction: Struggles for inclusion and reconciliation in modern democracies. In W. Kymlicka & B. Bashir (Eds.), *The politics of reconciliation in multicultural societies* (pp. 1–24). Oxford, UK: Oxford University Press.

Battiste, M., & Henderson, S. (2011). Eurocentrism and the European ethnographic tradition. In M.J. Cannon & L. Sunseri (Eds.), *Racism, colonialism and indigeneity in Canada* (pp. 11–19). Oxford, UK: Oxford University Press.

Beals, R. (1967). Background information on problems of anthropological research and ethics. *American Anthropological Association Newsletter, 8*(1), 2–13.

Beeman, W.O. (2001). Writing for the crisis. *Anthropology Today, 17*(6), 1–2. doi: http://dx.doi.org/10.1111/1467-8322.00086.

Belanger, Y.D. 2010. *Ways of knowing: Native studies in Canada*. Toronto, ON: Nelson Canada.

Belford, T. (2003, July 14). Forensic science gains cache. *The Globe and Mail*, p. B11.

Belshaw, C. (1976). *The sorcerer's apprentice: An anthropology of public policy*. New York, NY: Pergamon Press.

Benedict, R. (1934). *Patterns of culture*. Boston, MA: Houghton Mifflin.

Benedict, R. (1946). *The chrysanthemum and the sword*. Boston, MA: Houghton Mifflin.

Benedict, R. (1960). *Race: Science and politics*. New York, NY: Viking Press. (Original work published 1945).

Berkhofer, R.F. (1978). *The white man's Indian*. New York, NY: Random House.

Besteman, C. (2010). In and out of the academy: Policy and the case for a strategic anthropology. *Human Organization, 69*(4), 407–417. doi: http://dx.doi.org/10.17730/humo.69.4.e2373565nqu46873.

Better, S. (2008). *Institutional racism: Theory and strategies for social change*. New York, NY: Rowman and Littlefield.

Bibeau, G. (1997). Cultural psychiatry in a creolizing world: Questions for a new research agenda. *Transcultural Psychiatry, 34*(1), 9–41. doi: http://dx.doi.org/10.1177/136346159703400102.

Bird, E. (2010). *The anthropology of news and journalism: Global perspectives*. Bloomington, IN: Indiana University Press.

Black, S. (2009). Disaster anthropology: The 2004 Asian tsunami. In S. Blau & D.H. Ubelaker (Eds.), *Handbook of forensic anthropology and archaeology* (pp. 397–406). Walnut Creek, CA: Left Coast Press.

Blau, S., & Ubelaker, D.H. (Eds.). (2009). *Handbook of forensic anthropology and archaeology*. Walnut Creek, CA: Left Coast Press.

Blaut, J.M. (1999). Environmentalism and eurocentrism. *Geographical Review, 89*(3), 391–408. doi: http://dx.doi.org/10.2307/216157.

Blaut, J.M. (2000). *Eight Eurocentric historians*. New York, NY: Guilford Press.

Boas, F. (1888). *The central Eskimo. Report of the Bureau of Ethnology, 1884–1885*. Washington, DC: Smithsonian Institution.

Boas, F. (1911). *The mind of primitive man*. New York, NY: Macmillan.

Boas, F. (1928). *Anthropology and modern life*. New York, NY: W.W. Norton.

Boas, F. (1940). *Race, language and culture.* New York, NY: Macmillan.

Boas, F. (1948). Changes in the bodily form of descendants of immigrants. In *Race, language and culture* (pp. 60–75). New York, NY: Macmillan. (Original work published 1912)

Bolaria, B.S., & Li, P.S. (1988). *Racial oppression in Canada.* Toronto, ON: Garamond Press.

Borofsky, R. (1999). Public anthropology. *Anthropology News, 40*(1), 6–7. doi: http://dx.doi.org/10.1111/an.1999.40.1.6.

Bourgois, P. (2006). Forward: Anthropology in the global state of emergency. In V. Sandford & A. Angel-Ajani (Eds.), *Engaged observer: Anthropology, advocacy, and activism* (pp. ix–xii). New Brunswick, NJ: Rutgers University Press.

Brace, C.L. (1964). A non-racial approach towards the understanding of human diversity. In M.F. Ashley Montagu (Ed.), *The concept of race,* pp. 103–152. New York, NY: Free Press.

Briller, S., & Sankar, A. (2013). Engaging opportunities in urban revitalization: Practicing Detroit anthropology. *Annals of Anthropological Practice, 37*(1), 156–178. doi: http://dx.doi.org/10.1111/napa.12022.

Brondo, K.V. (2010). Practicing anthropology in a time of crisis: 2009 year in review. *American Anthropologist, 112*(2), 208–218. doi: http://dx.doi.org/10.1111/j.1548-1433.2010.01220.x.

Bueckert, D. (2003, July 28). Mercury poisoning issue back 30 years later, disease signs present in Indians. *The Toronto Star.*

Burgess, J., & Green, J. (2009). *YouTube: Online video and participatory culture.* Cambridge, UK: Polity Press.

Cahill, D. (2010). Advanced Andeans and backward Europeans. In P.A. McAnany & N. Yoffee (Eds.), *Questioning collapse* (pp. 207–238). Cambridge, UK: Cambridge University Press.

Canada votes against UN Aboriginal declaration. (2007, September 13). *The Toronto Star.*

Cannon, M.J., & L. Sunseri. (Eds.). (2011). *Racism, colonialism, and indigeneity in Canada.* Toronto, ON: Oxford University Press.

Carmichael, M. (2011). Not just an illness of the rich. *Scientific American, 304*(3), 66–69. doi: http://dx.doi.org/10.1038/scientificamerican0311-66.

Carmichael, S., & Hamilton, C.V. (1967). *Black power: The politics of liberation in America.* New York, NY: Random House.

Carnegie Museum of Natural History (2014). *RACE: Are we so different?* Retrieved from http://carnegiemnh.org/exhibitions/event.aspx?id=21884/.

Carter, B., & Virdee, S. (2008). Racism and the sociological imagination. *British Journal of Sociology, 59*(4), 661–679. doi: http://dx.doi.org/10.1111/j.1468-4446.2008.00214.x.

Castellano, M.B., & Reading, J. (2010). Policy writing as dialogue: Drafting an Aboriginal chapter for Canada's tri-council statement: Ethical conduct for research involving humans. *International Indigenous Policy Journal, 1*(2), 1–18.

Commission on Anthropology's Engagement with US Security and Intelligence Communities (CEAUSSIC, American Anthropological Association). (2007). Final report on the army's human terrain system proof of concept program. Retrieved from http://www.aaanet.org/cmtes/commissions/ceaussic/upload/ceaussic_hts_final_report.pdf.

Chagnon, N.A. (1968). *Yanomamo: The fierce people.* New York, NY: Holt, Rinehart and Winston.

Chagnon, N.A. (2013). *Noble savages: My life among two dangerous tribes—the Yanomamo and the anthropologists.* New York, NY: Simon and Schuster.

Chambers, E. (1985). *Applied anthropology: A practical guide.* Englewood Cliffs, NJ: Prentice-Hall.

Checker, M. (2009). Anthropology in the public sphere, 2008: Emerging trends and significant impacts. *American Anthropologist, 111*(2), 162–169. doi: http://dx.doi.org/10.1111/j.1548-1433.2009.01109.x.

Checker, M. (2011). "Year that trembled and reel'd": Reflections on public anthropology a decade after 9/11. *American Anthropologist, 113*(3), 491–504.

Chesler, M.A., Lewis, A., & Crowfoot, J. (2005). *Challenging racism in higher education: Promoting justice.* New York, NY: Rowman and Littlefield.

Chrisman, N. (2008). Engaging anthropology: A message for graduate students. *Anthropology News, 49*(3), 21. doi: http://dx.doi.org/10.1525/an.2008.49.3.21.1.

Christensen, A.M., & Crowder, C.M. (2009). Evidentiary standards for forensic anthropology. *Journal of Forensic Sciences, 54*(6), 1211–1216. doi: http://dx.doi.org/10.1111/j.1556-4029.2009.01176.x.

Christie, G. (2007). Police-government relations in the context of state-Aboriginal relations. In M.E. Beare & T. Murray (Eds.), *Police and government relations: Who's calling the shots?* (pp. 147–172). Toronto, ON: University of Toronto Press.

Claeys, G. (2000). The "survival of the fittest" and the origins of social Darwinism. *Journal of the History of Ideas, 61*(2), 223–240. doi: http://dx.doi.org/10.1353/jhi.2000.0014.

Clarke, K.M. (2010). Towards a critically engaged ethnographic practice. *Current Anthropology, 51*(S2), S301–S312. doi: http://dx.doi.org/10.1086/653673.

Clement, J.G. (2009). Forensic odontology. In S. Blau & D.H. Ubelaker (Eds.), *Handbook of forensic anthropology and archaeology* (pp. 335–347). Walnut Creek, CA: Left Coast Press.

Clinton, C.A. (1975). The anthropologist as hired hand. *Human Organization, 34*(2), 197–204. doi: http://dx.doi.org/10.17730/humo.34.2.r700401887nt12k4.

Cocks, P. (2001). Max Gluckman and the critique of segregation in South African anthropology, 1921–1940. *Journal of Southern African Studies, 27*(4), 739–756. doi: http://dx.doi.org/10.1080/03057070120090718.

Cohen, D. (2004). History and the second decade of the web. *Rethinking History, 8*(2), 293–301. doi: http://dx.doi.org/10.1080/13642520410001683950.

Congram, D., & Sterenberg, J. (2009). Grave challenges in Iraq. In S. Blau & D.H. Ubelaker (Eds.), *Handbook of forensic anthropology and archaeology* (pp. 441–453). Walnut Creek, CA: Left Coast Press.

Connor, M.A. (2007). *Forensic methods: Excavation for the archaeologist and investigator.* New York, NY: Rowman and Littlefield.

Coon, C.S. (1962). *The origin of races.* New York, NY: Alfred A. Knopf.

Cove, J. (1987). *Shattered images: Dialogues and meditations on Tsimshian narratives.* Ottawa, ON: Carleton University Press.

Cox, K. (1990a, May 22). Innu fighting back on challenges to traditional lifestyle. *The Globe and Mail.*

Cox, K. (1990b, October 7). NATO rejects Goose Bay for base, Innu protesters claim victory. *The Globe and Mail.*

Cravens, H. (2010). What's new in science and race since the 1930s? Anthropologists and racial essentialism. *Historian, 72*(2), 299–320. doi: http://dx.doi.org/10.1111/j.1540-6563.2010.00263.x.

Daniels, J., & Feagin, J.R. (2011). The (coming) social media revolution in the academy. *Fast Capitalism, 8*(2), 1–11. Retrieved from http://www.fastcapitalism.com.

Dennie, J.O. (2011). Op-ed: Jared Diamond's "Guns, Germs and Steel": Is it worth the hype? *Digital Journal.* Retrieved from http://digitaljournal.com./article/302333.

Desmarais, A.A. (2007). *La via campesina: Globalization and the power of peasants.* Halifax, NS: Fernwood Publishing.

Dewbury, A. (2007). The American school of scientific racism in early American anthropology. *Histories of Anthropology Annual, 3,* 121–147. doi: http://dx.doi.org/10.1353/haa.0.0026.

Diamond, J. (1999). *Guns, germs and steel: The fates of human societies.* New York, NY: W.W. Norton.

Diamond, J. (2005). *Collapse: How societies choose to fail or succeed.* New York, NY: Penguin Books.

Dobzhansky, T., & Ashley Montagu, M.F. (1947). Natural selection and the mental capacities of mankind. *Science, 105*(2736), 587–591. doi: http://dx.doi.org/10.1126/science.105.2736.587.

Doretti, M., & Snow, C.C. (2009). Forensic anthropology and human rights: The Argentine experience. In D.W. Steadman (Ed.), *Hard evidence: Case studies in forensic anthropology* (pp. 303–320). Upper Saddle River, NJ: Prentice-Hall.

Doughty, P.L. (2011). Mary Lindsay Elmendorf: Citizen activist to applied anthropologist. *American Anthropologist, 113*(3), 498–502.

Editorial: A bruise on the First Amendment. *The New York Times.* (2010, June 21).

Eisenlohr, P. (2011a). Introduction: What is a medium? Theologies, technologies and aspirations. *Social Anthropology, 19*(1), 1–5. doi: http://dx.doi.org/10.1111/j.1469-8676.2010.00134.x.

Eisenlohr, P. (2011b). The anthropology of media and the question of ethnic and religious pluralism. *Social Anthropology, 19*(1), 40–55. doi: http://dx.doi.org/10.1111/j.1469-8676.2010.00136.x.

Engle, K. (2001). From skepticism to embrace: Human rights and the American Anthropological Association from 1947–1999. *Human Rights Quarterly, 23,* 536–559.

Engelke, M. (2010). Religion and the media turn: A review essay. *American Ethnologist, 37*(2), 371–379. doi: http://dx.doi.org/10.1111/j.1548-1425.2010.01261.x.

Eriksen, T.H. (2006). *Engaging anthropology: The case for a public presence.* New York, NY: Berg.

Ervin, A.M. (1990). Some reflections on anthropological advocacy. *Proactive: Society of Applied Anthropology in Canada, 9*(2), 24–27.

Ervin, A. M. (2005). *Applied anthropology: Tools and perspectives for contemporary practice.* Boston, MA: Allyn and Bacon.

Etzioni, A. (1993). Power as a societal force. In M.E. Olsen & M.N. Marger (Eds.), *Power in modern societies* (pp. 18–28). Boulder, CO: Westview Press.

Fanon, F. (1963). *The wretched of the earth.* New York, NY: Grove Press.

Farber, P., & Cravens, H. (Eds.). (2009). *Race and science: Scientific challenges to racism in modern America.* Corvallis, OR: Oregon State University Press.

Farmer, P. (1992). *AIDS and accusation: Haiti and the geography of blame.* Berkeley, CA: University of California Press.

Farmer, P. (2003). *Pathologies of power: Health, human rights, and the new war on the poor.* Berkeley, CA: University of California Press.

Farmer, P. (2004). An anthropology of structural violence. *Current Anthropology, 45*(3), 305–325. doi: http://dx.doi.org/10.1086/382250.

Farmer, P. (2010). Expansion of cancer care and control in countries of low and middle income: A call to action. *Lancet, 376*, 1186–1193. doi: http://dx.doi.org/10.1016/S0140-6736(10)61152-X.

Farmer, P., Rylko-Bauer, B., & Whiteford, L. (2009). *Global health in times of violence*. New York, NY: School for Advanced Research Press.

Feagin, J.R. (2006). *Systemic racism: A theory of oppression*. New York, NY: Routledge.

Feagin, J.R. (2010). *Racist America: Roots, current realities, and future reparations*. New York, NY: Routledge.

Feit, H.A. 2004. Hunting and the quest for power: The James Bay Cree and Whiteman in the twentieth century. In R.B. Morrison & C.R. Wilson, (Eds.), *Native peoples: The Canadian experience* (pp. 181–223). Don Mills, ON: Oxford University Press.

Ferguson, B. (1999). Review of "Guns, Germs, and Steel" by Jared Diamond. *American Anthropologist, 101*(4), 900–901. doi: http://dx.doi.org/10.1525/aa.1999.101.4.900.

Finnis, E. (2007). The political ecology of dietary transitions: Changing production and consumption patterns in the Kolli Hills, India. *Agriculture and Human Values, 24*(3), 343–353. doi: http://dx.doi.org/10.1007/s10460-007-9070-4.

Finnis, E. (2008). Economic wealth, food wealth, and millet consumption: Shifting notions of food, identity, and development in South India. *Food, Culture, & Society, 11*(4), 463–485. doi: http://dx.doi.org/10.2752/175174408X389139.

Firth, R. (1981). Engagement and detachment: Reflections on applying social anthropology to social affairs. *Human Organization, 40*(3), 193–201. doi: http://dx.doi.org/10.17730/humo.40.3.c035k82pm2651531.

Fish, A. (2011). The place of the internet in anthropology. *Anthropology News, 52*(3), 17.

Flavel, A., & Barker, C. (2009). Forensic anthropology and archaeology in Guatemala. In S. Blau & D.H. Ubelaker (Eds.), *Handbook of forensic anthropology and archaeology* (pp. 426–440). Walnut Creek, CA: Left Coast Press.

Fletcher, A.J., & Marchildon, G.P. (2014). Using the Delphi method for qualitative participatory action research in health leadership. *International Journal of Qualitative Methods, 13*.

Forde, C.D. (1963). *Habitat, economy and society*. London, UK: Methuen.

Forte, M.C. (2011). The human terrain system and anthropology: A review of ongoing public debates. *American Anthropologist, 113*(1), 149–153. doi: http://dx.doi.org/10.1111/j.1548-1433.2010.01315.x.

Frideres, J.S. (1976). Racism in Canada: Alive and well. *Western Canadian Journal of Anthropology, 6*(4), 124–145.

Fried, M. (1967). *The evolution of political society*. New York, NY: Random House.

Fromm, P., & Varey, R. (1983). *Sociobiology: Blueprint for survival* (C-FAR Canadian issues series 3).

Gibbons, A. (1992). Scientists search for the "disappeared" in Guatemala. *Science, 257*(5069), 479. doi: http://dx.doi.org/10.1126/science.1636082.

Gibel Azoulay, K. (2006). Reflections on "race" and the biologization of difference. *Patterns of Prejudice, 40*(4–5), 353–379. doi: http://dx.doi.org/10.1080/00313220601020098.

Gill, L. (2005). Empire, ethnography and engagement. *Anthropology News, 46*(1), 12. doi: http://dx.doi.org/10.1525/an.2005.46.1.12.

Gillborn, D. (2008). *Racism and education: Coincidence or conspiracy?* New York, NY: Routledge.

Gilroy, P. (2001). *Against race: Imagining political culture beyond the color line.* Cambridge, MA: Harvard University Press.

Glover, K.S. (2009). *Racial profiling: Research, racism, and resistance.* New York, NY: Rowman and Littlefield.

Gomberg-Munoz, R. (2013). Public anthropology year in review. *American Anthropologist, 115*(2), 286–296.

Gluckman, M. (1940). Analysis of a social situation in modern Zululand. *Bantu Studies, 14*(1), 1–30. doi: http://dx.doi.org/10.1080/02561751.1940.9676107.

Gluckman, M. (1975). Anthropology and apartheid: The work of South African anthropologists. In M. Fortes & S. Patterson (Eds.), *Studies in South African anthropology* (pp. 21–40). London, UK: Academic Press.

Goldstein, D.M. (2010). Toward a critical anthropology of security. *Current Anthropology, 51*(4), 487–517. doi: http://dx.doi.org/10.1086/655393.

Gonzalez, N. (2010). Advocacy anthropology and education: Working through the binaries. *Current Anthropology, 51*(S2), S249–S258. doi: http://dx.doi.org/10.1086/653128.

Gonzalez, R.J. (2004). Introduction. In R.J. Gonzalez (Ed.), *Anthropologists in the public sphere: Speaking out on war, peace, and American power* (pp. 1–20). Austin, TX: University of Texas Press.

Gonzalez, R.J. (2008). "Human terrain": Past, present and future applications. *Anthropology Today, 24*(1), 21–26.

Gonzalez, R.J. (2009). *American counterinsurgency: Human science and the human terrain.* Chicago, IL: University of Chicago Press.

Goodey, J. (2007). Racist violence in Europe: Challenges for official data collection. *Ethnic and Racial Studies, 30*(4), 570–589. doi: http://dx.doi.org/10.1080/01419870701356007.

Gordana, B. (2011). The Internet as a field and a means of contemporary ethnological and anthropological research (translation from Russian). *Zbornik Matice Srpske za Drustvene Nauke, 134*, 17–27.

Gorodzeisky, A., & Semyonov, M. (2009). Terms of exclusion: Public views towards admission and allocation of rights to immigrants in European countries. *Ethnic and Racial Studies, 32*(3), 401–423. doi: http://dx.doi.org/10.1080/01419870802245851.

Gravlee, C.C. (2009). How race becomes biology: Embodiment of social inequality. *American Journal of Physical Anthropology, 139*(1), 47–57. doi: http://dx.doi.org/10.1002/ajpa.20983.

Gravlee, C.C., & Sweet, E. (2008). Race, ethnicity, and racism in medical anthropology, 1977–2002. *Medical Anthropology Quarterly, 22*(1), 27–51. doi: http://dx.doi.org/10.1111/j.1548-1387.2008.00002.x.

Gross, D., & Plattner, S. (2002). Anthropology as social work: Collaborative models of anthropological research. *Anthropology News, 43*(8), 4. doi: http://dx.doi.org/10.1111/an.2002.43.8.4.1.

Gumbhir, J. (2007). *But is it racial profiling? Policing, pretext stops, and the color of suspicion.* New York, NY: LFB Scholarly Publishing.

Gustav, J. (2009). Intra-European racism in nineteenth century anthropology. *History and Anthropology, 20*(1), 37–56. doi: http://dx.doi.org/10.1080/02757200802654258.

Hage, G. (2003). "Comes a time we are all enthusiasm": Understanding Palestinian suicide bombers in times of xenophobia. *Public Culture, 15*(1), 65–89. doi: http://dx.doi.org/10.1215/08992363-15-1-65.

Hale, C.R. (Ed.). (2008). *Engaging contradictions: Theory, politics, and methods of activist scholarship.* Berkeley, CA: University of California Press.

Hallowell, A.I. (1955). *Culture and experience.* Philadelphia, PA: University of Pennsylvania Press.

Hardon, A., & Moyer, E. (2014). Anthropology of AIDS: Modes of engagement. *Medical Anthropology, 33*(4), 255–262. doi: http://dx.doi.org/10.1080/01459740.2014.889132.

Harper, S. (2008). Text of Prime Minister Harper's apology, 11 June. Retrieved from www.aadnc-aandc.gc.ca/DAM/DAM-INTER-HQ/STAGING/texte-text/rqpi_apo_pdf_1322167347706_eng.pdf.

Harris, M. (1968). *The rise of anthropological theory.* New York, NY: Harper and Row.

Harris, M. (1991). *Cultural anthropology.* New York, NY: Harper Collins.

Harris, M. (2001). *Cultural materialism: The struggle for a science of culture.* Walnut Creek, CA: Alta Mira.

Hart, K. (2004). Notes towards an anthropology of the internet. *Horizontes Antropologicos, 10*(21), 15–40. doi: http://dx.doi.org/10.1590/S0104-71832004000100002.

Hastrup, K., & Elsass, P. (1990). Anthropological advocacy: A contradiction in terms? *Current Anthropology, 31*(3), 301–311. doi: http://dx.doi.org/10.1086/203842.

Hatch, J.B. (2008). *Race and reconciliation: Redressing wounds of injury.* New York, NY: Lexington Books.

Hedican, E.J. (1986a). Anthropologists and social involvement: Some issues and problems. *Canadian Review of Sociology and Anthropology/La Revue canadienne de Sociologie et d'Anthropologie, 23*(4), 544–558. doi: http://dx.doi.org/10.1111/j.1755-618X.1986.tb00822.x.

Hedican, E.J. (1986b). *The Ogoki River guides: Emergent leadership among the northern Ojibwa.* Waterloo, ON: Wilfrid Laurier University Press.

Hedican, E.J. (1990a). The economics of northern Native food production. In J.I. Baker (Ed.), *The world food crisis* (pp. 281–300). Toronto, ON: Canadian Scholars' Press.

Hedican, E.J. (1990b). Richard Salisbury's anthropology: A personal account. *Culture (Québec), X*(1), 14–18.

Hedican, E.J. (2001). *Up in Nipigon country: Anthropology as a personal experience.* Halifax, NS: Fernwood Publishing.

Hedican, E.J. (2008). *Applied anthropology in Canada: Understanding Aboriginal issues* (2nd ed.). Toronto, ON: University of Toronto Press.

Hedican, E.J. (2012a). *Social anthropology: Canadian perspectives on culture and society.* Toronto, ON: Canadian Scholars' Press.

Hedican, E.J. (2012b). Policing Aboriginal protests and confrontations: Some policy recommendations. *International Indigenous Policy Journal, 3*(2), 1–17.

Hedican, E.J. (2013). *Ipperwash: The tragic failure of Canada's Aboriginal policy.* Toronto, ON: University of Toronto Press.

Hedican, E.J. (2014). Eurocentrism in Aboriginal studies: A review of issues and conceptual problems. *Canadian Journal of Native Studies, 34*(1), 87–109.

Helleiner, J. (2000). *Irish Travellers: Racism and the politics of culture*. Toronto, ON: University of Toronto Press.

Henderson, J., & Wakeham, P. (Eds.). (2013). *Reconciling Canada: Critical perspectives on the culture of redress*. Toronto, ON: University of Toronto Press.

Henriksen, G. (1973). *Hunters in the barrens: The Naskapi on the edge of the white man's world*. St. John's, NL: Institute of Social and Economic Research, Memorial University of Newfoundland.

Henriksen, G. (1985). Anthropologists as advocates: Promoters of pluralism or makers of clients? In R. Paine (Ed.), *Advocacy and anthropology* (pp. 119–129). St. John's, NL: Memorial University of Newfoundland.

Hepner, T.R. (2011). Collaborative anthropology comes to life: Catherine Besterman and the Somali Bantu experience. *American Anthropologist, 113*(2), 346–347. doi: http://dx.doi.org/10.1111/j.1548-1433.2011.01337.x.

Heyman, J. (2010). Activism in anthropology: Exploring the present through Eric R. Wolf's Vietnam-era work. *Dialectical Anthropology, 34*, 287–293. doi: http://dx.doi.org/10.1007/s10624-010-9186-6.

Hinshaw, R.E. (1980). Anthropology, administration, and public policy. *Annual Review of Anthropology, 9*(1), 497–522. doi: http://dx.doi.org/10.1146/annurev.an.09.100180.002433.

Hooton, E.A. (1939). *The American criminal*. Cambridge, MA: Harvard University Press.

Horowitz, I.L. (Ed.). (1967). *The rise and fall of project Camelot*. Cambridge, MA: MIT Press.

Howard, J. (1984). *Margaret Mead: A life*. New York, NY: Fawcett Columbine.

Howell, S. (2010). Norwegian academic anthropologists in public spaces. *Current Anthropology, 51*(S2), S269–S277. doi: http://dx.doi.org/10.1086/652907.

Huber, M.T. (1998). *Community college faculty attitudes and trends, 1997*. Menlo Park, CA: Carnegie Foundation.

Hughes, D., & Kallen, E. (1974). *The anatomy of racism*. Montreal, QC: Harvest House.

Hume, S. (1991, March). Judge prefers dusty documents to oral truth. *Proactive: Society of Applied Anthropology in Canada 10*, (1), 31–32 (orig. *Vancouver Sun*, 22 March, 1991).

Hunter, J., & Cox, M. (2005). *Forensic archaeology: Advances in theory and practice*. London, UK: Routledge.

Hull, M. (2008). Ruled by records: The expropriation of land and the misappropriation of lists in Islamabad. *American Ethnologist, 35*(4), 501–518. doi: http://dx.doi.org/10.1111/j.1548-1425.2008.00095.x.

Isaac, B. (2006). Proto-racism in Graeco-Roman antiquity. *World Archaeology, 38*(1), 32–47. doi: http://dx.doi.org/10.1080/00438240500509819.

Ishii-Eiteman, M. (2009). Food sovereignty and the international assessment of agricultural knowledge, science and technology for development. *Journal of Peasant Studies, 36*(3), 689–700.

Jacobs, S.E. (1974). Action and advocacy anthropology. *Human Organization, 33*(2), 209–215. doi: http://dx.doi.org/10.17730/humo.33.2.l38h6vt37r842687.

Jenness, D. (1933). An Indian method of treating hysteria. *Primitive Man, 6*(1), 13–20. doi: http://dx.doi.org/10.2307/3316221.

Jensen, A. (1969). How much can we boost I.Q. and scholastic achievement? *Harvard Educational Review, 39*(1), 1–123. doi: http://dx.doi.org/10.17763/haer.39.1.l3u15956627424k7

Jessee, E., & Skinner, M.F. (2005). A typology of mass grave and mass grave-related sites. *Forensic Science International*, 152(1), 55–59. doi: http://dx.doi.org/10.1016/j.forsciint.2005.02.031.

Johnson, C. (2005). Militarism in America. *Anthropology News*, 46(1), 10–13. doi: http://dx.doi.org/10.1525/an.2005.46.1.10.1.

Johnston, B.R. (2010). Social responsibility and the anthropological citizen. *Current Anthropology*, 51(S2), S235–S247. doi: http://dx.doi.org/10.1086/653092.

Johnston, B.R. (2012). Editorial work as public anthropology. *American Anthropologist*, 114(4), 576–577. doi: http://dx.doi.org/10.1111/j.1548-1433.2012.01484.x.

Johnston, B.R., & Barker, H.M. (2008). *Consequential damages of nuclear war: The Rongelap report*. Walnut Creek, CA: Left Coast Press.

Kalacska, M., & Bell, L.S. (2006). Remote sensing as a tool for the detection of clandestine mass graves. *Canadian Society of Forensic Science Journal*, 39(1), 1–13. doi: http://dx.doi.org/10.1080/00085030.2006.10757132.

Kallen, E. (1982). *Ethnicity and human rights in Canada*. Toronto, ON: Gage Publishing.

Kardiner, A. (1939). *The individual and his society*. New York, NY: Columbia University Press.

Kardiner, A. (1959). Psychological studies. *Science*, 130, 1728.

Keesing, R.M. (1994). Theories of culture revisited. In R. Borofsky (Ed.), *Assessing cultural anthropology* (pp. 301–312). New York, NY: McGraw-Hill.

Kidder, T. (2003). *Mountains beyone mountains: The quest of Dr. Paul Farmer, a man who could cure the world*. New York, NY: Random House.

Kirsch, S. (2002). Anthropology and Advocacy: A Case Study of the Campaign against the Ok Tedi Mine. *Critique of Anthropology* 22: 175–200.

Kirsch, S. (2010). Experiments in Engaged Anthropology. *Collaborative Anthropologies* 3: 69–80.

Klepinger, L.L. (2006). *Fundamentals of forensic anthropology*. Hoboken, NJ: John Wiley. doi: http://dx.doi.org/10.1002/0470007729.

Koerth-Baker, M. (2011). Pibloktoq: Psychology of the Arctic. Retrieved from http://boingboing.net/2011/05/17/pibloktoq-psychology.html.

Kunnah, G.T. (2013). Anthropology's ethical dilemmas: Forum on public anthropology. *Current Anthropology*, 54(6), 740.

Kuper, A. (2013). Out of Eden: Anthropology confronts the problems of the modern world. *Anthropology of This Century*, 8.

Kuper, A. (2014). Anthropology and anthropologists forty years after. *Anthropology of This Century*, 11.

Lackenbauer, P.W. (2007). *Battle grounds: The Canadian military and Aboriginal lands*. Vancouver, BC: University of British Columbia Press.

Lamphere, L., Rayna, R., & Rubin, G. (2007). "Anthropologists are talking" about feminist anthropology. *Ethnos*, 72(3), 408–426. doi: http://dx.doi.org/10.1080/00141840701577057.

LaRocque, E. (2010). *When the Other is me: Native resistance discourse 1850–1990*. Winnipeg, MB: University of Manitoba Press.

LaRusic, I.E. (1979). *Negotiating a way of life*. Ottawa, ON: Canadian Department of Indian Affairs and Northern Development.

Lassiter, L.E. (2005). Collaborative ethnography and public anthropology. *Current Anthropology*, 46(1), 83–106. doi: http://dx.doi.org/10.1086/425658.

Lassiter, L.E., & Campbell, E. (2010). Serious fieldwork: On re-functioning ethnographic pedagogies. *Anthropology News*, 51(6), 4–8. doi: http://dx.doi.org/10.1111/j.1556-3502.2010.51604.x.

Law, I., Phillips, D., & Turney, L. (2004). Tackling institutional racism in higher education: An antiracist toolkit. In I. Law, D. Phillips, & L. Turney (Eds.), *Institutional racism in higher education* (pp. 93–103). Staffordshire, UK: Trentham Books.

Lawrence, B. (2011). Rewriting histories of the land: Colonization and indigenous resistance in Canada. In M.J. Cannon & L. Sunseri (Eds.), *Racism, colonization, and indigeneity in Canada* (pp. 68–80). Oxford, UK: Oxford University Press.

Lawrence, B., & Dua, E. (2005). Decolonizing antiracism. *Social Justice*, 32(4), 120–143.

Lentin, R. (2007). Ireland: Racial state and crisis racism. *Ethnic and Racial Studies*, 30(4), 610–627. doi: http://dx.doi.org/10.1080/01419870701356023.

Levi-Strauss, C. (1966). Anthropology: Its achievements and future. *Current Anthropology*, 7(2), 124–127. doi: http://dx.doi.org/10.1086/200688.

Lewis, K. (2010). Did they fail? Could they choose? *Science*, 327(5964), 413–414. doi: http://dx.doi.org/10.1126/science.1184327.

Leyton, E. (2003). *Hunting humans: The rise of the modern multiple murderer*. New York, NY: Carrol and Graf.

Lindee, S., & Ventura Santos, R. (2012). The biological anthropology of living human populations: World histories, national styles, and international networks. *Current Anthropology*, 53(S5). doi: http://dx.doi.org/10.1086/663335.

Lock, M., & Wakewich-Dunk, P. (1990). Nerves and nostalgia: Expression of loss among Greek immigrants in Montreal. *Canadian Family Physician*, 36, 253–258.

Low, S.M., & Merry, S.E. (2010). Engaged anthropology: Diversity and dilemmas. *Current Anthropology*, 51(S2), S203–S226. doi: http://dx.doi.org/10.1086/653837.

Lowrey, K. (a.k.a. Ozma). (2005). Anthropology's guns, germs, and steel problem. *Savage minds—notes and queries in anthropology*. Retrieved from http://savageminds.org/2005/07/24/anthropologys-guns-germs-and-steel-problem/.

Lutz, C. (2005). Military bases and ethnographies of the new militarization. *Anthropology News*, 46(1), 11. doi: http://dx.doi.org/10.1525/an.2005.46.1.11.

MacClancy, J. (2013). *Anthropology in the public arena: Historical and contemporary contexts*. Chichester, UK: Wiley-Blackwell. doi: http://dx.doi.org/10.1002/9781118475539.

Malinowski, B. (1926). *Crime and custom in savage society*. London, UK: Kegan Paul.

Malinowski, B. (1929). *The sexual life of savages in Northwestern Melanesia*. London, UK: George Routledge.

Malinowski, B. (1941). An anthropological analysis of war. *American Journal of Sociology*, 46(4), 521–550. doi: http://dx.doi.org/10.1086/218697.

Malinowski, B. (1970). Practical anthropology. In J.A. Clifton (Ed.), *Applied anthropology* (pp. 12–25). Boston, MA: Houghton Mifflin. (Original work published 1929).

Marx, E. (1981). The anthropologist as mediator. In J.G. Galaty, D. Aronson, & P.C. Salzman (Eds.), *The future of pastoral peoples* (pp. 119–126). Ottawa, ON: International Development Research Centre.

Marx, K. (1978). *The eighteenth Brumaire of Louis Bonaparte*. Peking, China: Foreign Language Press. (Original work published 1852).

Marx, K. (1904). *A contribution to the critique of political economy*. Chicago, IL: International Library Publication. (Original work published 1859).

Marks, J. (2012). Review of "Race and Science." *Quarterly Review of Biology, 87*(1), 46–47. doi: http://dx.doi.org/10.1086/663883.

Maskovsky, J. (2013). Protest anthropology in a moment of global unrest. *American Anthropologist, 115*(1), 126–129. doi: http://dx.doi.org/10.1111/j.1548-1433.2012.01541.x.

Matza, T. (2009). Moscow's echo: Technologies of the self, publics, and politics on the Russian talk show. *Cultural Anthropology, 24*(3), 489–522. doi: http://dx.doi.org/10.1111/j.1548-1360.2009.01038.x.

Mazzarella, W. (2004). Culture, globalization, mediation. *Annual Review of Anthropology, 33*(1), 345–367. doi: http://dx.doi.org/10.1146/annurev.anthro.33.070203.143809.

McAnany, P.A., & Yoffee, N. (Eds.). (2010). *Questioning collapse: Human resilience, ecological vulnerability, and the aftermath of empire*. Cambridge, UK: Cambridge University Press.

McFate, M., & Fondacaro, S. (2008). Cultural knowledge and common sense: A response to Gonzalez in this issue. *Anthropology Today, 24*(1), 27. doi: http://dx.doi.org/10.1111/j.1467-8322.2008.00562.x.

McLuhan, M. (1962). *The Gutenberg galaxy: The making of typographic man*. Toronto, ON: University of Toronto Press.

McLuhan, M. (1964). *Understanding media: The extensions of man*. Toronto, ON: McGraw-Hill.

Mead, M. (1928). *Coming of age in Samoa*. New York, NY: Morrow.

Mead, M. (1932). *The changing culture of an Indian tribe*. Columbia University Contributions to Anthropology: No. 15. New York, NY: AMS Press.

Mead, M. (1970). *Culture and commitment: A study of the generation gap*. New York, NY: The Natural History Press.

Menezes, F. (2001). Food sovereignty: A vital requirement for food security in the context of globalization. *Development, 44*(4), 29–33. doi: http://dx.doi.org/10.1057/palgrave.development.1110288.

Mevorach, K.G. (2007). Race, racism, and academic complicity. *American Ethnologist, 34*(2), 238–241.

Messenger, J. (1989). *Inis Beag revisited: The anthropologist as observant participator*. Salem, WI: Sheffield Publishing.

Meyer, B. (2006). Religious revelation, secrecy, and the limits of visual representation. *Anthropological Theory, 6*(4), 431–453. doi: http://dx.doi.org/10.1177/1463499606071596.

Michaels, W.B. (1992). Race into culture: A critical genealogy of cultural identity. *Critical Inquiry, 18*(4), 655–685. doi: http://dx.doi.org/10.1086/448651.

Michalenko, G., & Suffling, R. (1982). Social impact in Northern Ontario: The Reed Paper controversy. In C.C. Geisler, R. Green, D. Usner, & P.C. West (Eds.), *Indian SIA: The social impact assessment of rapid resource development on Native peoples* (pp. 274–289). Ann Arbor, MI: University of Michigan Press.

Mokyr, J. (1999). Eurocentricity triumphant. *American Historical Review, 104*(4), 1241–1246. doi: http://dx.doi.org/10.2307/2649575.

Montagu, A. (1942). *Man's most dangerous myth: The fallacy of race*. New York, NY: Columbia University Press.

Montagu, A. (1963). *Race, science and humanity*. New York, NY: Van Nostrand Reinhold.

Montagu, A. (1964). *The concept of race.* New York, NY: Free Press.

Montagu, A. (1980). *Sociobiology examined.* London, UK: Oxford University Press.

Mooney, J. (1896). *The Ghost Dance religion and the Sioux outbreak of 1890.* Annual Report No. 14. Washington, DC: Bureau of American Ethnology.

Mosse, D. (2005). *Cultivating development: An ethnography of aid policy and practice.* London, UK: Pluto Press.

Mullings, L. (2005). Interrogating racism: Towards an antiracist anthropology. *Annual Review of Anthropology,* 34(1), 667–693. doi: http://dx.doi.org/10.1146/annurev.anthro.32.061002.093435.

Mullins, P. (2011). Practicing anthropology and the politics of engagement. *American Anthropologist,* 113(2), 235–245. doi: http://dx.doi.org/10.1111/j.1548-1433.2011.01327.x.

Murdock, G.P. (1937). *Statistical correlations in the science of society.* New Haven, CT: Yale University Press.

Murdock, G.P. (1949). *Social structure.* New York, NY: Macmillan.

Murdock, G.P. (1961). *Outline of cultural materials* (4th ed. revised). New Haven, CT: Human Relations Area Files.

Murdock, G.P. (1963). *Outline of world cultures.* New Haven, CT: Human Relations Area Files.

Murdock, G.P. (1967). *Ethnographic atlas.* Pittsburgh, PA: University of Pittsburgh Press.

Nader, L. (1974). Up the anthropologist—perspectives from studying up. In D. Hymes (Ed.), *Reinventing anthropology* (pp. 284–311). New York, NY: Vintage.

Nader, L. (1997). The phantom factor. In N. Chomsky, L. Nader, I. Wallerstein, R.C. Lewontin, & R. Ohmann (Eds.), *The Cold War & the university: Toward an intellectual history of the Cold War years* (pp. 107–146). New York, NY: New Press.

Nafte, M. (2009). *Flesh and bone: An introduction to forensic anthropology.* Durham, NC: Carolina Academic Press.

Nietzsche, F. (1968). *The will to power.* Edited by W. Kaufmann. New York, NY: Random House.

Niezen, R. (2010). *Public justice and the anthropology of law.* Cambridge, UK: Cambridge University Press. doi: http://dx.doi.org/10.1017/CBO9780511779640.

Niezen, R. (2013). *Truth and indignation: Canada's truth and reconciliation on Indian residential schools.* Toronto, ON: University of Toronto Press.

Norton, A.R. (2007). *Hezbollah: A short history.* Princeton, NJ: Princeton University Press.

Nugent, S. (2001). Anthropology and public culture: The Yanomami, science and ethics. *Anthropology Today,* 17(3), 10–14. doi: http://dx.doi.org/10.1111/1467-8322.00059.

Ogburn, J.L. (1997). On anthropology and the internet. *Current Anthropology,* 38(2), 286–287. doi: http://dx.doi.org/10.1086/204610.

Orr, Y.A. (2009). Public anthropology. *Current Anthropology,* 50(4), 413. doi: http://dx.doi.org/10.1086/600067.

Paine, R. (1985). *Advocacy and anthropology: First encounters.* St. John's, NL: Memorial University of Newfoundland.

Panel on Research Ethics. (2009). *Tri-council policy statement: Ethical conduct for research involving humans. Draft second edition.* Ottawa, ON: Interagency Advisory Panel on Research Ethics. Retrieved from www.pre.ethics.gc.ca/default.aspx.

Patel, R. (2009). Food sovereignty. *Journal of Peasant Studies,* 36(3), 663–706. doi: http://dx.doi.org/10.1080/03066150903143079.

Peacock, J.L. (1997). The future of anthropology. *American Anthropologist*, 99(1), 9–17. doi: http://dx.doi.org/10.1525/aa.1997.99.1.9.

Peterson, J.H. (1974). The anthropologist as advocate. *Human Organization*, 33(3), 311–318.

Pigg, S.L. (2013). On sitting and doing: Ethnography as action in global health. *Social Science & Medicine*, 99, 127–134. doi: http://dx.doi.org/10.1016/j.socscimed.2013.07.018.

Postill, J. (2009). What is the point of media anthropology? *Social Anthropology*, 17(3), 334–337. doi: http://dx.doi.org/10.1111/j.1469-8676.2009.00079_1.x.

Powdermaker, H. (1950). *Hollywood, the dream factory*. Boston, MA: Little, Brown and Company.

Preston, R.J. (1982). The politics of community relocation: An Eastern Cree example. *Culture (Québec)*, 2(3), 37–49.

Price, D.H. (2008). *Anthropological intelligence: The deployment and neglect of American anthropology in the Second World War*. Durham, NC: Duke University Press. doi: http://dx.doi.org/10.1215/9780822389125.

Price, D.H. (2012). Counterinsurgency and the M-VICO system: Human relations area files and anthropology's dual-use legacy. *Anthropology Today*, 28(1), 16–20. doi: http://dx.doi.org/10.1111/j.1467-8322.2012.00850.x.

Price, M., Rubinstein, R.A., & Price, D.H. (2012). "Material support": US anti-terrorism law threatens human rights and academic freedom. *Anthropology Today*, 28(1), 3–5. doi: http://dx.doi.org/10.1111/j.1467-8322.2012.00847.x.

Pue, W.W. (2007). Comment on the oversight of executive-police relations in Canada: The constitution, the courts, administrative process, and democratic governance. In M.E. Beare & T. Murray (Eds.), *Police and government relations: Who's calling the shots?* (pp. 131–134). Toronto, ON: University of Toronto Press.

Purcell, T.W. (2000). Public anthropology: An idea searching for a reality. *Transforming Anthropology*, 9(2), 30–33. doi: http://dx.doi.org/10.1525/tran.2000.9.2.30.

Rangasamy, J. (2004). Understanding institutional racism: Reflections from linguistic anthropology. In I. Law, D. Phillips, & L. Turney (Eds.), *Institutional racism in higher education* (pp. 27–34). Staffordshire, UK: Trentham Books.

Restall, M. (2004). *Seven myths of the Spanish conquest*. New York, NY: Oxford University Press.

Richling, B. (2012). *In twilight and in dawn: A biography of Diamond Jenness*. Montreal, QC: McGill-Queen's University Press.

Robinson, M. (2006). Joan Ryan (1932–2005). *Arctic*, 59(4), 447–448.

Rothenbuhler, E.W., & Comar, M. (2005). *Media anthropology: An overview of anthropological approaches to the study of mass media*. London, UK: Sage Publications.

Rivers, W.H.R. (1920). *Instinct and the unconscious: A contribution to a biological theory of the psycho-neuroses*. Cambridge, UK: Cambridge University Press.

Ryan, J. (1988). Economic development and Innu settlement: The establishment of Sheshatshit. *Canadian Journal of Native Studies*, 8(1), 1–25.

Ryan, J. (1995). *Doing things the right way: Dene traditional justice in Lac La Martre, NWT*. Calgary, AB: University of Calgary Press.

Ryan, J., & Robinson, M. (1990). Implementing participatory action research in the Canadian North: A case study of the Gwich'in language and cultural project. *Culture (Québec)*, 10(2), 57–71.

Ryan, J., & Robinson, M. (1996). Community participatory research: Two views from Arctic Institute practitioners. *Practicing Anthropology, 18*(4), 7–11. doi: http://dx.doi.org/10.17730/praa.18.4.8165n7kw19187181.

Sahlins, M. (1960). Evolution: Specific and general. In M. Sahlins & E. Service (Eds.), *Evolution and culture* (pp. 12–44). Ann Arbor, MI: University of Michigan Press.

Sahlins, M. (2009). The teach-ins: Anti-war protest in the old stone age. *Anthropology Today, 25*(1), 3–5. doi: http://dx.doi.org/10.1111/j.1467-8322.2009.00639.x.

Said, E.W. (1979). *Orientalism.* New York: Vintage Books.

Salisbury, R.F. (1986). *A homeland for the Cree: Regional development in James Bay, 1971–1981.* Montreal, QC: McGill-Queen's University Press.

Salzman, P.C. (1986). Is traditional fieldwork outmoded? *Current Anthropology, 27*(5), 528–530. doi: http://dx.doi.org/10.1086/203484.

Sanday, P.R. (1976). *Anthropology and the public interest.* New York, NY: Academic Press.

Sandford, V., & Angel-Ajani, A. (Eds.). (2006). *Engaged observer: Anthropology, advocacy, and activism.* New Brunswick, NJ: Rutgers University Press.

Sapir, E. (1932). Cultural anthropology and psychiatry. *Journal of Abnormal and Social Psychiatry, 27*(3), 229–242. doi: http://dx.doi.org/10.1037/h0076025.

Sarfaty, G.A. (2012). *Values in translation: Human rights and the culture of the World Bank.* Stanford, CA: Stanford University Press.

Saunders, R.A. (2011). *Ethnopolitics in cyberspace: The Internet, minority nationalism, and the web of identity.* Lanham, MD: Lexington Books.

Schensul, S. L., & Schensul, J.J. (1978). Advocacy in applied anthropology. In G.H. Weber & G.I. McCall, (Eds.), *Social scientists as advocates* (pp. 121–163). Beverly Hills, CA: Sage.

Scheper-Hughes, N. (1987). The best of two worlds, the worst of two worlds: Reflections on culture and fieldwork among the rural Irish and Pueblo Indians. *Comparative Studies in Society and History, 29*(1), 56–75. doi: http://dx.doi.org/10.1017/S0010417500014341.

Scheper-Hughes, N. (1995). The primacy of the ethical: Propositions for a militant anthropology. *Current Anthropology, 36*(3), 409–420. doi: http://dx.doi.org/10.1086/204378.

Scheper-Hughes, N. (2001). *Saints, scholars and schizophrenics: Mental illness in rural Ireland, anniversary edition, revised and expanded.* Berkeley, CA: University of California Press.

Schneider, A., & Pasqualino, C. (2014). *Experimental film and anthropology.* London, UK: Bloomsbury Press.

Scobie, W. (2011). An anthropological introduction to YouTube. *American Anthropologist, 113*(4), 661–662. doi: http://dx.doi.org/10.1111/j.1548-1433.2011.01386.x.

Scully, T. (2008). Online anthropology draws protest from Aboriginal group. *Nature, 453*(7199), 1155. doi: http://dx.doi.org/10.1038/4531155a.

Seeking truth about lost children. (2008, May 29). *The Toronto Star.*

Selmeski, B.R. (2007). Who are the security anthropologists? *Anthropology News, 48*(5), 11–12. doi: http://dx.doi.org/10.1525/an.2007.48.5.11.2.

Shahine, S.H. (2011). Youth and the revolution in Egypt. *Anthropology Today, 27*(2), 1–3. doi: http://dx.doi.org/10.1111/j.1467-8322.2011.00792.x.

Shanklin, E. (1998). The profession of the color-blind: Sociocultural anthropology and racism in the 21st century. *American Anthropologist, 100*(3), 669–679. doi: http://dx.doi.org/10.1525/aa.1998.100.3.669.

Shanklin, E. (2000). Representations of race and racism in American anthropology. *Current Anthropology, 41*(1), 99–103. doi: http://dx.doi.org/10.1086/300105.

Sharma, N., & Wright, C. (2008–09). Decolonizing resistance: Challenging colonial states. *Social Justice (San Francisco, Calif.), 35*(3), 120–138.

Shkilnyk, M. (1985). *A poison stronger than love: The destruction of an Ojibwa community.* New Haven, CT: Yale University Press.

Shore, C., & Wright, S. (1997). *Anthropology of public policy: Critical perspectives on governance and power.* London, UK: Routledge.

Sidky, H. (2004). *Perspectives on culture: A critical introduction to theory in cultural anthropology.* Upper Saddle River, NJ: Pearson Prentice-Hall.

Singer, M. (2000). Why I am not a public anthropologist. *Anthropology News, 41*(6), 6–7. doi: http://dx.doi.org/10.1111/an.2000.41.6.6.

Sjoberg, G., & Nett, R. (1968). *A methodology for social research.* New York, NY: Harper and Row.

Skinner, M.F., Clegg, L., Congram, D., Katzenberg, A., Lazenby, R.A., Mundorff, A., …, & Waterhouse, K. (2010). Taking the pulse of forensic anthropology in Canada. *Canadian Society of Forensic Science Journal, 43*(4), 191–203. doi: http://dx.doi.org/10.1080/0008503 0.2010.10768136.

Skinner, M.F., & Bowie, K. (2009). Forensic anthropology: Canadian content and contributions. In S. Blau & D.H. Ubelaker (Eds.), *Handbook of forensic anthropology and archaeology* (pp. 87–103). Walnut Creek, CA: Left Coast Press.

Sledzik, P.S. (2009). Forensic anthropology in disaster response. In S. Blau & D.H. Ubelaker (Eds.), *Handbook of forensic anthropology and archaeology* (pp. 374–387). Walnut Creek, CA: Left Coast Press.

Smedley, A., & Smedley, B. (2005). Race as biology is fiction, racism as a social problem is real: Anthropological and historical perspectives on the social construction of race. *American Psychologist, 60*(1), 16–26. doi: http://dx.doi.org/10.1037/0003-066X.60.1.16.

Snow, C.C. (1973). Forensic anthropology. In A. Redfield (Ed.), *Anthropology beyond the university* (pp. 4–17). Athens, GA.: University of Georgia Press.

Snow, C.C. (1982). Forensic anthropology. *Annual Review of Anthropology, 11*(1), 97–131. doi: http://dx.doi.org/10.1146/annurev.an.11.100182.000525.

Snow, C.C., Stover, E., & Hannibal, K. (1989). Scientists as detectives investigating human rights. *Technology Review 92*, 43–51.

Snow, C.C., & Bihurriet, M.J. (1992). An epidemiology of homicide: Ningun Nombre burials in the province of Buenos Aires from 1970 to 1984. In T.B. Jabine & R.P. Claude (Eds.), *Human rights and statistics: Getting the record straight* (pp. 328–364). Philadelphia, PA: University of Pennsylvania Press.

Speck, D.C. (1987). *An error in judgement: The politics of medical care in an Indian/white community.* Vancouver, BC: Talon Books.

Spencer, J. (2010). The perils of engagement: A space for anthropology in the age of security? *Current Anthropology, 51*(2), S289–S299. doi: http://dx.doi.org/10.1086/653421.

Spencer, J. (2012). Who is the enemy? *Anthropology of This Century, 4*. Retrieved from http://aotcpress.com/articles/enemy.

Stacey, J. (1988). Can there be a feminist ethnography? *Women's Studies International Forum, 11*(1), 21–27. doi: http://dx.doi.org/10.1016/0277-5395(88)90004-0.

Steadman, D.W. (Ed.). (2009). *Hard evidence: Case studies in forensic anthropology*. Upper Saddle River, NJ: Prentice Hall.

Sterpka, M.K. (2007). Anthropology and intelligence gathering. *Anthropology News, 48*(5), 11. doi: http://dx.doi.org/10.1525/an.2007.48.5.11.1.

Stepan, N. (1982). *The idea of race in science*. London, UK: Macmillan.

Steward, J. (1955). *Theory of culture change*. Urbana, IL: University of Illinois Press.

Stewart, T.D. (1978). George A. Dorsey's role in the Luetgert case: A significant episode in the history of forensic anthropology. *Journal of Forensic Sciences, 23*, 786–791.

Stewart, T.D. (1979). *Essentials of forensic anthropology*. Springfield, IL: Thomas.

Still, C. (2015). Comparing race and caste. *Anthropology of This Century, 12*.

Stocking, G.W. (1968). *Race, culture, and evolution: Essays in the history of anthropology*. New York, NY: Free Press.

Stone, D. (2003). Nazism as modern magic: Bronislaw Malinowski's political anthropology. *History and Anthropology, 14*(3), 203–218. doi: http://dx.doi.org/10.1080/0275720032000143356.

Stull, D.D., & Schensul, J.J. (Eds.). (1987). *Collaborative research and social change: Applied anthropology in action*. Boulder, CO: Westview Press.

Sumiala, J. (2013). *Media and ritual: Death, community, and everyday life*. New York, NY: Routledge.

Susser, I. (2010). The anthropologist as social critic: Working toward a more engaged anthropology. *Current Anthropology, 51*(S2), S227–S233. doi: http://dx.doi.org/10.1086/653127.

Szathmary, E.J.E. (1990). Diabetes in Amerindian populations: The Dogrib studies. In A.C. Swedlund & G.J. Armelagos (Eds.), *Disease in populations in transition* (pp. 75–103). New York, NY: Bergin and Garvey.

Szathmary, E.J.E. (1994a). Non-insulin dependent diabetes mellitus among Aboriginal North Americans. *Annual Review of Anthropology, 23*(1), 457–480. doi: http://dx.doi.org/10.1146/annurev.an.23.100194.002325.

Szathmàry, E.J.E. (1994b). Factors that influence the onset of diabetes in Dogrib Indians of the Canadian Northwest Territories. In J.J.R. Young & R.S. Young (Eds.), *Diabetes as a disease of civilization* (pp. 229–267). Berlin, Germany: Mouton de Gruyter. doi: http://dx.doi.org/10.1515/9783110853148.229.

Szathmary, E.J.E., Ritenbaugh, C., & Goodby, C.S.M. (1987). Dietary change and plasma glucose levels in an Amerindian population undergoing cultural transition. *Social Science & Medicine, 24*(10), 791–804. doi: http://dx.doi.org/10.1016/0277-9536(87)90181-X.

Tanovich, D.M. (2006). *The colour of justice: Policing race in Canada*. Toronto, ON: Irwin Law.

Tator, C., & Henry, F. (2006). *Racial profiling in Canada: Challenging the myth of "a few bad apples."* Toronto, ON: University of Toronto Press.

Tax, S. (1958). The Fox project. *Human Organization, 17*(1), 17–19. doi: http://dx.doi.org/10.17730/humo.17.1.b1gtr52or323687t.

Thomas, W.A. (1974). *Scientists in the legal system: Tolerated meddlers or essential contributors?* Ann Arbor, MI.: Science Publishers.

Tierney, P. (2000). *Darkness in El Dorado: How scientists and journalists devastated the Amazon.* New York, NY: W.W. Norton.

Tribute dinner tonight honours Emoke Szathmary. *Winnipeg Free Press* (3 November 2009).

Tsing, A. (2005). Anthropologists as public intellectuals. *Anthropology News*, 46(1), 10. doi: http://dx.doi.org/10.1525/an.2005.46.1.10.2.

Tully, J. (2008). *Public philosophy in a new key: Democracy and civic freedom.* Cambridge, UK: Cambridge University Press.

Turner, E. (1989). From shamans to healers: The survival of an Inupiaq Eskimo skill. *Anthropologica*, 31(1), 3–24. doi: http://dx.doi.org/10.2307/25605526.

University of Guelph Public Issues Anthropology (PIA) MA Graduate Program. Department of Sociology and Anthropology. Retrieved from http://www.uoguelph.ca/socioanthro/masters-program-public-issues-anthropology.

van de Port, M. (2006). Visualizing the sacred: Video technology, "televisual" style, and the religious imagination in Bahian candomble. *American Ethnologist*, 33(3), 444–461. doi: http://dx.doi.org/10.1525/ae.2006.33.3.444.

Vanderhaeghe, G. (2005). Introduction. In T. Findley, *The wars* (p. xiv). Toronto, ON: Penguin.

Vine, D. (2011). "Public anthropology" in its second decade: Robert Borofsky's center for a public anthropology. *American Anthropologist*, 113(2), 336–339. doi: http://dx.doi.org/10.1111/j.1548-1433.2011.01334.x.

Visweswaran, K. (1998). Race and the culture of anthropology. *American Anthropologist*, 100(1), 70–83. doi: http://dx.doi.org/10.1525/aa.1998.100.1.70.

Voyageur, C., & Calliou, B. (2011). Aboriginal economic development and the struggle for self-government. In M.J. Cannon & L. Sunseri (Eds.), *Racism, colonialism, and indigeneity in Canada* (pp. 203–212). Oxford, UK: Oxford University Press.

Wadden, M. (2001). *Nitassinan: The Innu struggle to reclaim their homeland.* Vancouver, BC: Douglas and McIntyre.

Wakin, E. (1992). *Anthropology goes to war: Professional ethics and counterinsurgency in Thailand.* Madison, WI: University of Wisconsin Center for Southeast Asian Studies.

Waldram, J.B. (1997). *The way of the pipe: Aboriginal spirituality and symbolic healing in Canadian prisons.* Peterborough, ON: Broadview Press.

Waldram, J.B., Herring, D.A., & Young, T.K. (1995). *Aboriginal health in Canada: Historical, cultural, and epidemiological perspectives.* Toronto, ON: University of Toronto Press.

Waldram, J.B., & O'Neil, J.D. (Eds.) (1989). Special issue: Native health research in Canada. *Native Studies Review*, 5(1), 1–213.

Walter, M.D. (2008). The jurisprudence of reconciliation: Aboriginal rights in Canada. In W. Kymlicka & B. Bashir (Eds.), *The politics of reconciliation in multicultural societies* (pp. 165–191). Oxford, UK: Oxford University Press.

Warren, C.A. (1988). *Gender issues in field research. Qualitative research methods* (Vol. 9). Newbury Park, CA: Sage Publications.

Warren, K.B. (2006). Perils and promises of engaged anthropology: Historical transactions and ethnographic dilemmas. In V. Sandford & A. Angel-Anjani (Eds.), *Engaged observer: Anthropology, advocacy, and activism* (pp. 213–227). New Brunswick, NJ: Rutgers University Press.

Wax, R.H. (1971). *Doing fieldwork: Warnings and advice.* Chicago, IL: University of Chicago Press.

Wayman, E.R. (2009). Engaging anthropology: From anthropologist to advisor. *Current Anthropology, 50*(1), 3. doi: http://dx.doi.org/10.1086/595621.

Weaver, T. (1985). Anthropology as a policy science. *Human Organization, 82,* 95–103, 197–205.

Wedel, J.R., Shore, C., Feldman, G., & Lathrop, S. (2005). Toward an anthropology of public policy. *Annals of the American Academy of Political and Social Science, 600*(1), 30–51. doi: http://dx.doi.org/10.1177/0002716205276734.

Werbner, P. (2010). Notes from a small place: Anthropological blues in the face of global terror. *Current Anthropology, 51*(2), 193–221. doi: http://dx.doi.org/10.1086/651041.

White, L. (1949). *The science of culture: A study of man and civilization.* New York, NY: Grove Press.

Whitfield, S.J. (2010). Franz Boas: The anthropologist as public intellectual. *Society, 47*(5), 430–438. doi: http://dx.doi.org/10.1007/s12115-010-9355-x.

Whittaker, E. (1992). Culture: The reification under siege. *Studies in Symbolic Interaction, 13,* 107–117.

Whittaker, E. (1994). Decolonizing knowledge: Towards a feminist ethic and methodology. In J.S. Grewal & H. Johnson (Eds.), *The India-Canada relationship* (pp. 347–365). New Delhi, India: Sage Publications.

Wilcox, M. (2010). Marketing conquest and the vanishing Indian: An Indigenous response to Jared Diamond's "Guns, Germs, and Steel" and "Collapse." *Journal of Social Archaeology, 10*(1), 92–117. doi: http://dx.doi.org/10.1177/1469605309354399.

Wilkes, R. (2004). A systematic approach to studying Indigenous politics: Band-level mobilization in Canada, 1981–2000. *Social Science Journal, 41*(3), 447–458. doi: http://dx.doi.org/10.1016/j.soscij.2004.04.007.

Williams, T., & Murray, K. (2007). Comment on: Police-government relations in the context of state-Aboriginal relations. In M.E. Beare & T. Murray (Eds.), *Police and government relations: Who's calling the shots?* (pp. 172–176). Toronto, ON: University of Toronto Press.

Wilson, E.O. (1978). *Sociobiology: The new synthesis.* Cambridge, MA: Harvard University Press.

Wilson, R.A. (2000). Reconciliation and revenge in post–Apartheid South Africa. *Current Anthropology, 41*(1), 75–98.

Wilson, T. M., & Donnan, H. (2006). *The anthropology of Ireland.* New York, NY: Berg.

Young, D., Ingram, G., & Swartz, L. (1988). The persistence of traditional medicine in the modern world. *Cultural Survival Quarterly, 12*(1), 38–41.

Young, D., Ingram, G., & Swartz, L. (1990). *Cry of the eagle: Encounters with a Cree healer.* Toronto, ON: University of Toronto Press.

Young, K.T. (1988). *Health care and culture change: The Indian experience in the central subarctic.* Toronto, ON: University of Toronto Press.

Young, K.T., Szathmary, E.J.E., Evers, S., & Wheatley, B. (1990). Geographical distribution of diabetes among the native population of Canada: A national survey. *Social Science & Medicine, 31*(2), 129–139. doi: http://dx.doi.org/10.1016/0277-9536(90)90054-V.

Zorn, E. (2013). *Digital ethnography: Anthropology, narrative, and the new media.* Austin, TX: University of Texas Press.

INDEX

on Human Relations Area Files, 175
on power, 20, 27, 45, 94, 95
on race, 72, 73–74, 75
on racism, 83
on redirection of anthropology, 27
on salvage anthropology, 18
on Spencer, 92
Basch, L.G.
 Transforming Academia, 61
Bashir, B., 155
Bateson, Gregory, 12
Beals, Ralph, 174
Beeman, William, 166–67
Belshaw, Cyril, 22, 61
 Sorcerer's Apprentice, 61
Benedict, Ruth, 22–23, 83, 111
 *The Chrysanthemum and the
 Sword*, 22–23
 Patterns of Culture, 23, 111
Bergmann's Rule, 97
Berkhofer, Robert
 The White Man's Indian, 145–46
Better, Shirley, 78–79
bias, male, 26–27
biological anthropology, 87
biological determinism, 73, 92. *See also*
 race
biologization of difference, 82
bio-piracy, 123
Blaut, James, 105
Boas, Franz
 applied anthropology and, 3
 on environment and culture, 98, 101
 historical particularism of, 101
 popularity of, 30
 race and, 67–68, 70–72, 73, 81, 201
 social issues and, 202
Bolaria, B.S., 77–78
Bolshevik Revolution, 159
Borofsky, Robert, 50–51, 53–54
Boston Marathon bombing, 165
bottom-up creativity, 197–98
Brace, C.L., 74

Bridge Paper ("Analysis of a Social Situation
 in Modern Zululand"; Gluckman),
 160–61
Brown, Michael, 67
Bureau of American Ethnology, 28
Burgess, J., 197

Cahill, David, 105
Callahan, Sidney, 54–55
Calliou, B., 146
Campbell, E., 42
Canada
 conflicts over Aboriginal rights in, 146–47
 forensic anthropology in, 134–35, 136–37
 Grassy Narrows and White Dog
 mercury pollution, 113–15, 127
 Indian Residential Schools Truth and
 Reconciliation Commission, 153–54
 institutional racism in, 77–78
 medical anthropology in, 109
 NATO Goose Bay military base case
 study, 180–82
 UN Declaration on the Rights of
 Indigenous Peoples and, 150–51
 war graves and lost soldiers of, 135–36
Canadian Association of Physical
 Anthropology, 135
cancer, in developing world, 118
capitalism, *see* global capitalism
Carmichael, Stokely, 76
Castellano, Marlene, 24, 25
Chagnon, Napoleon, 20, 194, 195–96
Chambers, Erve, 62–63
Checker, M., 65
Chesler, M.A., 78
Choctaw Nation, 14
Chrisman, N., 43
Christie, Gordon, 149, 151
Chrysanthemum and the Sword (Benedict),
 22–23
citizen-scholars, 171
civilization, 94
Claeys, G., 92

Clegg, Laura, 135
Clement, J.G., 138
client-oriented research, 5
Clinton, C.A., 16
Cold War era, 174
collaborative anthropology, 8–9, 26, 57–58,
    60, 202
Collapse (Diamond), 103
colonialism
    anthropology and, 18, 202
    experience of and resistance to, 146–47
    internal, 148
    Malinowski on, 10
    neo-, 152
    reinvention from, 144
    violence and, 143–44
    See also resistance
color of suspicion, 84–85
colour, people of, 84–85, 147–48
Coming of Age in Samoa (Mead), 10
community consultation, 19
confidentiality, 183
conflict, 159, 162–63. *See also* resistance
conflicts of interest, 40–41, 64–65, 159
Congram, Derek, 136, 138
consulting roles, 4
convictions, false, 136
Coōn, Carlton
    The Origins of Races, 76
Corntassel, Jeff, 143
counterinsurgency
    approach to, 165, 182–83
    anthropological knowledge and,
        174–75, 201
    anti-terrorism laws and academic
        freedom, 178–80
    Human Terrain System (HTS),
        176–77
    School of the Americas (SOA), 174
    See also global terror; military intelligence
Cove, John, *see* Gitksan First Nation case
    study
Cravens, Hamilton, 68

Race and Science, 69
Cree First Nations, *see* James Bay Cree;
    Red Cloud (Russell Willier)
criminal anthropology, 133
Cross-Cultural Survey, 175
Crowfoot, J., 78
Cultivating Development (Mosse), 205
cultural anthropology, 96–97, 182–83, 202
cultural comparisons, 62, 75, 96
cultural determinism, 101, 201
cultural ecology, 95, 99–100, 100–101
cultural materialism, 100, 101, 159, 189
cultural racism, 46
cultural relativism
    AAA Declaration of Human Rights
        and, 40
    Benedict on, 23
    as ethical basis, 201
    Farmer on, 121–22
    human rights and, 183
    public anthropology and, 45, 61, 183
    structural inequalities and, 121–22
    Tierney on, 195
    traditional medicine and, 108
cultural representation, 145
culture
    biology and, 73–74
    Boas and, 73
    changing views on, 46
    environment and, 92–93, 97–100
    as learned, 86
    media and, 189, 196, 197
    as multi-stranded, 198
    othering and, 46
    personalities and, 108
    politics of, 189
    power and, 44–45
    public, 189
Culture and Commitment (Mead), 10, 11–12,
    205
Culture and Experience (Hallowell), 111
culture area concept, 98–99
culture bound syndromes, 109

culture concept, 37

Culture Meets Power (Barrett), 20, 32, 94

cultures at a distance, 23

Current Anthropology (journal), 4, 50, 86–87

Custom and Conflict in Africa
(Gluckman), 159

Daniels, J., 199

Darkness in El Dorado (Tierney), 20, 194–96

deception, avoidance of, 19

decolonization, 143–44. *See also* colonialism

decolonizing framework of action, 153

"Decolonizing Resistance" (Sharma and
Wright), 147

De Genova, Nicholas, 168, 172

Dewbury, A., 82

diabetes, 109, 112–13, 127

dialogical approach, 26

Diamond, Jared
Collapse, 103
See also *Guns, Germs, and Steel*
(Diamond)

Dobzhansky, Theodosius, 75

Doretti, M., 138

Dorsey, George, 132

Dozier, Damon, 86

Dua, E., 147

dual-evolution theory, 74–75

Dwight, Thomas, 132

"Editorial Work as Public Anthropology"
(Johnston), 9

education
institutional racism and, 78–79
race in anthropology textbooks, 80–81, 88
teach-in movement, 167
training anthropology students, 42–43

Egypt
Internet youth in, 191–92

Eisenlohr, P., 188, 189, 196, 197

Elsass, P., 15, 52

employees, anthropologists as, 16

"Engagement and Detachment" (Firth), 9

engaging anthropology, 9–10, 12–13

environment, and culture
introduction to, 92–93, 97
assessment of approaches to, 100–101
Boas and, 98
cultural ecology, 99–100
cultural materialism, 100
culture area concept, 98–99
environmental determinism, 97
Guns, Germs, and Steel (Diamond)
and, 103
habitat concept, 100
possibilism, 98

environmental determinism, 92–93, 97, 105

Ervin, Alexander, 3, 14, 16, 52

ethics
AAA statement on, 20–22, 24, 41,
203, 204
Aboriginal research ethics initiatives,
24–26
of anthropologists in military
intelligence, 177–78
avocational truth and, 17
compliance to codes of, 22
confidentiality, 183
conflicts of interest, 40–41, 64–65, 159
cultural relativism and, 201
dissemination of research results, 19,
21–22
of engagement in local issues, 47–48
ethical neutrality, 202, 204–5
impacts on studied group, 22, 53
law and, 21
obligation to avoid harm, 24
online anthropology and, 184
of research, 18–19
See also advocacy roles; power

ethnic polarities, 13

ethnographic research
anti-terrorism laws and, 178–80
contemporary collaborative, 18, 19, 26,
58–59
male bias in, 26–27

genetic resources, 123

geographical determinism, 97–98, 101.
    See also environmental determinism

Ghost Dance Religion study, 3, 202

Gibel Azoulay, K., 82

Gill, L., 173–74

Gillborn, D., 76, 78

Gilroy, Paul, 82

Gitksan First Nation case study, 14–15, 37,
    59–60

global capitalism, 122, 127, 128

Global Task Force on Expanding Access
    to Cancer Care and Control in
    Developing Countries, 119

global terror
    approach to, 34, 165, 182–83
    anthropologists as experts and, 170–71
    anthropologists in public sphere against,
        167–68
    researching, 168
    See also counterinsurgency; terror

global village, 35, 185, 189–90, 198–99

Glover, K.S., 84

Gluckman, Max, 160–62
    "Analysis of a Social Situation in
        Modern Zululand" (Bridge
        Paper), 160–61
    Custom and Conflict in Africa, 159
    Order and Rebellion in Tribal Africa, 159

Goldstein, Daniel, 171

Gonzalez, Norma, 43

Goodey, J., 83

Gorodzeisky, A., 83

Grassy Narrows mercury pollution, 113–15,
    127

Gravlee, C.C., 82, 83

Green, J., 197

Guatemala, 138

Guatemalan Forensic Anthropology
    Foundation (FAFG), 138

Gumbhir, J., 84

Guns, Germs, and Steel (Diamond)
    introduction to, 33–34, 106

anthropology and, 96, 97

argumentation of, 102, 103

assumptions underlying, 93

critiques of, 91, 92, 93, 102, 103–4, 104–5

environmental determinism and, 92–93

popularity of, 90

racial determinism and, 104–5

on social inequality, 94–95

support for, 103

thesis of, 90–91, 101–2

Gustav, J., 82

Gutenberg Galaxy (McLuhan), 189

habitat concept, 100

Hage, G., 179

Haiti, and AIDS, case study, 34, 107,
    119–21, 127

Hallowell, Irving
    Culture and Experience, 111

Harada, Masazumi, 114, 115

Harper, Stephen, 153–54

Harris, Marvin
    on Boas and environment, 101
    cultural materialism of, 95, 100, 159, 189
    on environmental determinism, 97
    on Forde's habitat concept, 100
    on Mead and Benedict, 23
    on objectivity in social sciences, 14
    on public engagement, 15, 50
    on race and culture, 72, 81

Hastrup, K., 15, 52

Hatch, John
    Race and Reconciliation, 156

health care, 121, 127–28

Helleiner, Jane, 83

Henriksen, Georg, 17, 180

Henry, Frances
    Racial Profiling, 84

Heyman, J., 167

Hinshaw, R.E., 61

hired hand, anthropologist as, 16

historical materialism, 95

historical momentum, 79

historical particularism, 101
holistic perspective, 17, 53
Hollywood, 196
Hooton, Ernest, 133
Horse, the Wheel, and Language
    (Anthony), 93
Howell, S., 42
HRAF (Human Relations Area Files), 96,
    175–76
HTS (Human Terrain System), 34, 172,
    176–77, 177–78
HTT (Human Terrain Teams), 176–77
Huber, Mary, 80
Hughes, D., 84
human ecology, 97. *See also* environment,
    and culture
Human Relations Area Files (HRAF), 96,
    175–76
human rights
    AAA declaration on, 39–40
    anthropologists' engagement with, 37–39
    conflicts of interest and, 40–41
    cultural relativism and, 183
    cultural tolerance and, 40
    ethnographic research and, 173–74
    forensic anthropology and, 137–38,
        139, 140
    in transnational organizations, 205
    See also food security
Human Rights Watch, 138–39
humans, physical traits of, 85
human societies, 91–92, 96–97, 103–4
Human Terrain System (HTS), 34, 172,
    176–77, 177–78
Human Terrain Teams (HTT), 176–77
Hunting Humans (Leyton), 135
Hymes, Dell
    Reinventing Anthropology, 57

inclusiveness, 31–32
India
    Kolli Hills case study, 124–26, 128
Indian Act, 78, 143

Indian Removal Act, 145
Indian Residential Schools Truth and
    Reconciliation Commission (TRC),
    153–54
Indigenous peoples, *see* Aboriginal
    peoples
informed consent, 19
Innu, 180–82
institutional racism
    introduction to, 76–77
    in Canada, 77–78
    in education, 78–79
    First Nations and, 78
    racial profiling and, 84–85
    understanding roots of, 79
    See also racism
insulin, 109
internal colonialism, 148
Internet, 189, 190, 199. *See also* media
Internet enemies, 190
Internet youth, 191–92
Iraq, 138–39
Iraq war, 38, 172–73
Irish mental health case study, 37, 53–56
Irish Travellers, 83
Isaac, B., 82

James Bay Cree, 5–6, 15
Jenness, Diamond, 110–11
Jensen, Arthur, 75
Johnson, Chalmers, 38, 172–73
Johnston, Barbara, 6, 39, 173
    "Editorial Work as Public
        Anthropology," 9

Kallen, E., 82, 84
Kardiner, Abraham, 108
Katzenberg, Anne, 136
Keesing, Roger, 46
Kennedy, John F., 186
Kirsch, S., 6, 8
kleptocracies, 95
knowledge, as power, 45

Kolli Hills, India, case study, 124–26, 128
Kroeber, Alfred, 98–99, 101
Krogman, W.M., 133
Kumalo, Duma, 157
Kunnah, G.T., 14, 22
Kymlicka, W., 155

LaForme, Harry, 154
land claims, 26, 149, 152. *See also* Gitksan
      First Nation case study
Lang, Graeme, 102
LaRocque, Emma, 144
Lassiter, Luke, 32, 42, 57, 60
law, and ethics, 21
Law, I., 78
Lawrence, Bonita, 146, 147
Lazenby, Richard, 136–37
legal anthropology, 158
legal investigations, 129–30, 136. *See also*
      forensic anthropology
legal pluralism, 158, 163
Lentin, R., 83
Levi-Strauss, Claude, 28–29
Lewis, A., 78
Leyton, Elliot
      Hunting Humans, 135
Li, P.S., 77–78
liberation therapy, 193
Little, Michael, 87
local issues and people, *see* Aboriginal
      peoples; advocacy roles; ethics
Lolita (talk show), 193
Lowrey, Kathleen, 104
Luetgert, Adolph, 132–33
Lutz, Catherine, 173

male bias, 26–27
Malinowski, Bronislaw
      advocacy role and, 13
      on anthropology as public service, 9–10,
            201, 202–3
      applied anthropology and, 3
      legal pluralism and, 158

popularity of, 30
practical anthropology and, 3–4, 36, 48
A Scientific Theory of Culture, 10
on war and Nazism, 168, 169–70, 201
market economies, 128, 148–49
Marshall Islanders, 6
Martin, Trayvon, 67, 89
Marx, E., 49
Marx, Karl, 31, 95, 96
Maskovsky, J., 8
Mazzarella, W., 197
McFarlane, Graham, 55
McGill University
      Programme in the Anthropology of
            Development (PAD), 5
McLuhan, Marshall, 185, 186, 187, 189
      The Gutenberg Galaxy, 189
      Understanding Media, 186, 187
Mead, Margaret, 10–12, 30, 201, 202, 205
      Coming of Age in Samoa, 10
      Culture and Commitment, 10, 11–12, 205
media
      approach to, 35, 184–85, 198–99
      anthropology of, 196, 198
      culture and, 189, 196, 197
      impacts of media technologies, 188
      Internet, 189, 190, 199
      Internet enemies, 190
      Internet youth, 191–92
      medium of and public events, 186–87
      religious practices and, 197
      Russian talk shows, 192–93
      understanding medium, 187, 188–89
      Yanomamo case study, 193–96
      YouTube, 197–98
media anthropology, 196, 198
mediator role, 6–7, 49
medical anthropology
      approach to, 34, 107, 128
      acculturation studies and, 127
      AIDS in Haiti case study, 34, 107,
            119–21, 127
      in Canada, 109

"Perils and Promises of Engaged
    Anthropology" (Warren), 12–13
Peterson, J.H., 6, 14
Phillips, D., 78
physical anthropology, 74, 133
Pickton, Robert William, 135, 136–37
Poison Stronger than Love (Shkilnyk), 113
police, 149–50
policy concept, 62–63. *See also* public policy
political context, of anthropology, 41–42
political economy, 95
politics of culture, 189
polyvocal approach, 26
possibilism, 98
postmodernist anthropology, 26
poverty, 121
Powdermaker, Hortense, 196
power
    culture, 44–45
    differential use of, 94–95
    in fieldwork, 20–21
    food security and, 124
    health-related problems and, 121–22
    knowledge as, 45
    racism and, 83–84
    of words, 146
power elites, 63–64, 204
practical anthropology, 3–4, 36, 48, 203
practising anthropology, 36
Preston, Richard, 15
Price, David, 7, 172, 175, 179
Proactive (newsletter), 52
Programme in the Anthropology of
    Development (PAD), McGill
    University, 5
Project Camelot, 174
protest anthropology, 8
psoriasis, 116–17
psychological anthropology, 111
public, uses of term, 141
public anthropology
    approach to, 1–2, 33, 36–37, 207
    advantages of, 141, 201–2

debate over, 49–50
development of, 13–14, 36, 201, 202–3
guidelines needed for, 50
literature on, 50
objections to, 51–52
political context of, 41–42
post-9/11, 173
scope of, 1, 43–44, 65–66
social criticism and, 37–39
understanding "public" in, 44, 45
See also advocacy roles; anthropology;
    ethics; ethnographic research;
    future, of anthropology
publication, of results, 19, 21–22
public culture, 189
public intellectuals, 37–39
public policy, 37, 60–61, 62, 63
Pue, W.W., 149
Purcell, Trevor, 43, 44, 49–50

race
    approach to, 33, 69, 88–89
    AAA statement on, 85–86, 87
    anthropology and, 72–73, 80–81, 82–83
    biological anthropology and, 87
    Current Anthropology and, 87
    dual-evolution theory and, 74–75
    engaging public about, 89
    Montagu on, 74
    news stories about, 67, 68, 87–88, 89
    public anthropology and, 67–68
    "Race: Are We So Different?" (AAA),
        86, 87
    science and, 68–69
    as social construct, 85
    socio-biology and, 75–76
    synonyms for, 87
    See also biological determinism; racial
        determinism; racism; social
        Darwinism
Race and Reconciliation (Hatch), 156
Race and Science (Farber and Cravens), 69
"Race: Are We So Different?" (AAA), 86, 87

Schensul, S.L., 16

Scheper-Hughes, Nancy, 7, 27, 37, 54, 55. *See also* Irish mental health case study

School of the Americas (SOA), 174

Science (journal), 75

scientific racism, 75, 76

Scientific Theory of Culture (Malinowski), 10

Scobie, W., 198

security, anthropology of, 171

Semyonov, M., 83

Shahine, S.H., 192

shaking tent ceremony, 116

Shanklin, Eugenia, 72, 80–81, 82, 88

Sharma, N.
   "Decolonizing Resistance," 147

Sharpeville Six, 157

Shattered Image (Cove), 59. *See also* Gitksan First Nation case study

Shkilnyk, M.
   A Poison Stronger than Love, 113

Shore, C., 61

Sinclair, Murray, 154

Singer, Merrill, 51

Singh, Simron Jit, 43

single social system approach, 161–62

Sjoberg, G., 48

Skinner, M.F., 137

Smedley, A., 82

Smedley, B., 82

Smith, Charles, 136

Smithsonian Institution, 133

Snow, C.C., 130, 131, 132, 133, 138

Snowdon, Edward, 190

SOA (School of the Americas), 174

SOA Watch, 174

social anthropology, 26, 194, 202

social change, 94, 96

social criticism, 38–39

social Darwinism, 33, 73, 91–92. *See also* race

social equality, 123

social responsibility, 9, 48–49, 206

Society of Applied Anthropology in Canada (SAAC), 6, 52

socio-biology, 75–76

Sorcerer's Apprentice (Belshaw), 61

SORO (US Special Operations Research Office), 174

South Africa
   Gluckman on, 160–62
   post-apartheid case study, 156–57, 158

specific evolution, 96

Spencer, Herbert, 91–92

Spencer, J., 179–80

Stacey, Judith, 27

Statement on Ethics (AAA), 20–22, 24, 41, 203, 204

Stepan, N., 82

Sterenberg, J., 138

Steward, Julian, 99–100, 189

Stewart, T.D., 130

Strahl, Chuck, 151

structural violence, 121, 127

structures of domination, 148

studying up, 7–8, 63–64, 204

Susser, Ida, 38–39, 42

Sweet, E., 82

systemic racism, 77. *See also* institutional racism

Szathmary, Emoke, 109, 112–13

Talking to the Enemy (Atran), 179

talk shows, Russian, 192–93

Tator, Carol
   Racial Profiling, 84

Tax, Sol, 4, 13, 86

TCPS (*Tri-Council Policy Statement*), 25–26

teaching, *see* education

teach-in movement, 167

technological determinism, 189

terminology, in anthropology, 2

terror
   as new reality, 32
   war on, 165, 167
   See also global terror

Tierney, Patrick
   Darkness in El Dorado, 20, 194–96

Wilkes, R., 147
Williams, T., 153
Willier, Russell (Red Cloud), 115–17
Wilson, Richard, 162
Wolf, Eric, 167
World Bank, 123, 205
World Ethnographic Atlas, 96
World War I, 135–36

World War II, 12, 22–23, 135–36
Wright, C.
  "Decolonizing Resistance," 147

Yanomamo case study, 20, 193–96
YouTube, 197–98

Zimmerman, George, 67, 89

Lightning Source UK Ltd.
Milton Keynes UK
UKOW03f0146060117
291450UK00002B/356/P